Great Women Collectors

Great Women Collectors

Charlotte Gere and Marina Vaizey

PHILIP WILSON PUBLISHERS

in association with

HARRY N. ABRAMS, INC., PUBLISHERS

First published in 1999 by
Philip Wilson Publishers Limited
143–149 Great Portland Street,
London WIN 5FB
ISBN 0 85667 503 2

Distributed in North America in 1999 by
Harry N. Abrams, Incorporated, New York

Library of Congress Cataloging-in-Publication Data

Gere, Charlotte.
Great women collectors / Charlotte Gere and Marina Vaizey.
p.   cm.
Includes bibliographical references.
ISBN 0-8109-6393-0 (Abrams)
1. Women art collectors. 2. Art—Collectors and collecting.
3. Art objects—Collectors and collecting. 4. Art—Private
collections.   I. Vaizey, Marina. II. Title.
N5200.G47   1999
709'.2'2–dc21   99-27678

Designed by Peter Ling
Edited by Moira Johnston
Printed and bound in Italy by
Editoriale Lloyd s.r.l., Trieste

HARRY N. ABRAMS, INC.
100 FIFTH AVENUE
NEW YORK, N.Y. 10011
www.abramsbooks.com

FRONTISPIECE
Marble group of *The Three Graces*, 1813,
by Antonio Canova (1757-1822).
The Hermitage Museum, St Petersburg.
Commissioned by the Empress Josephine in 1813 for
Malmaison, it was inherited in the following year by
her son Eugene de Beauharnais. It was taken to St
Petersburg by her grandson and eventually bought by
the last Russian Emperor, Nicholas II, for the
Hermitage. Another version of this group was made
for the Duke of Bedford and housed in a special
pavilion at Woburn Abbey; it is now jointly owned by
the Victoria & Albert Museum, London, and the
National Galleries of Scotland, Edinburgh.

Contents

Catherine II in a kokoshnik (Russian headdress), by William Dickinson after Vergilius Eriksen; mezzotint, published 1773. The Trustees of the British Museum, London.

Photographic Acknowledgements

AKG 192, 193
Anthony D'Offay Gallery 199
Abby Aldrich Rockefeller Folk Centre 170
Baltimore Museum of Art,Cone Collection 27, 149, 152, 153
Beinecke Rare Book and Manuscript Library 175
Bridgeman Art Library 17, 18, 23, 47, 75, 125
Camera Press 107, 148, 165
Christie's Images 22, 85, 90
Hermitage Museum 37, 39
Hillwood Museum 24, 117
Hulton-Getty Picture Collection 93, 102
Menil Collection 30, 187, 189
Metropolitan Museum of Art 26, 137, 138
Musée du Château, Malmaison 73
Musée du Louvre 21, 69
Museum of Fine Arts, Houston 183
Museum of Modern Art 171, 172
National Gallery of Modern Art, Edinburgh 198
National Museum of Wales 142, 143, 144
National Portrait Gallery 79, 83, 101, 111
National Trust, Waddesdon Manor 97, 98
Peggy Guggenheim Collection, Venice, The 32, 195
Solomon R. Guggenheim Foundation, The
Royal Collection, The 19, 59, 60, 63
Scottish National Museum of Modern Art 200
Shelburne Museum 25, 136
Sotheby's 65
State Russian Museum 20
Thomas Williams Fine Art, London 53
Photograph Christie's, London
Trustees of the British Museum, The 8, 35, 80, 81, 95
UPI/Corbis Bettman 28, 159, 161, 162
Wallace Collection 49, 71
Whitney Museum of American Art 29, 178, 179

Acknowledgements

Our bibliography indicates something of the range of museums, galleries, art historians, biographers and other scholars to whom we are indebted, with the caveat that mistakes are our responsibility. We owe a great debt to John Culme, formerly of Sotheby's, for his inspiration and guidance in the early planning of this book and for his knowledge on the subject of collecting in general and of Helena Rubinstein's eccentric collecting career in particular. Under the editorship of the late Denys Sutton, *Apollo* was the vehicle for many reassessments of women's role in the history of collecting. Any student of the ins-and-outs of collecting and collections, notably the contribution of women in the eighteenth and nineteenth centuries, must be indebted to the pioneering articles in *Apollo* by Barbara Scott. Marcia Pointon's ideas and writings have been equally inspiring and discussions with her endlessly stimulating. Our thanks also to the following: Moyra Ashford and Professor Stansky for their help at various crucial moments; Geoffrey Munn and Kenneth Snowman of Wartski's, London for patiently unearthing Fabergé information; Joanne Hedley, Wallace Collection, London for sharing ideas on women collectors, specifically Madame de Pompadour; George Zombakis and Alice Ross at the Museum of Fine Art, Houston; Richard Calvocoressi and Alice O'Connor at the Scottish National Gallery of Modern Art, National Galleries of Scotland; Cathy Grosfils at the Abby Aldrich Rockefeller Folk Art Center; Anne Odom; Allison Parsons at the Hillwood Museum; Petica Watson and Charlotte Lorimer at Bridgeman Art Library; Charles Merullo at Hulton Getty, and Sue Fletcher at The Royal Collection.

Introduction

*C*ollecting is the practice of acquiring knowledge and objects. It involves natural instinct, a good memory and a quick eye, the study of articles made, who made them, when, why and for whom. Everybody collects in some sense, but where should we draw the fine line between the collector and the accumulator, between following a largely rational desire and an obsession? And why does he almost invariably follow his fancy, rather than she hers? Are women collectors not only fewer, but different in their interests, methods, hopes and successes?

Art – its commission, collection and display – has always been an integral part of the complex of wealth, status and power. Thus, art in the West, once largely the preserve of church and state, of the rulers and leaders of both, became in the nineteenth century more an occupation for the individual and its collection grew fragmented in order to express many more and different desires. Interest in 'antiques' developed and, in the case of women, turned them from consumers into collectors. Collecting must, in our view, significantly alter the repute of the objects collected, not only by adding to knowledge and expanding appreciation, but perhaps even more by conferring status: the collector can make the unfashionable or ignored more central to the culture of the day.

As art has been collected by the rich – both individuals and institutions – so more and more art has entered the secular public domain. Existing museums and galleries have increased their public spaces, the number of special exhibitions they hold and the educational programmes pursued. New museums and galleries have proliferated; and as the subject of art history has expanded dramatically, so collecting has become an established topic for study. Pioneer academics have examined the history of taste, the economics of collecting, the art of patronage, the meaning of connoisseurship and the background to museum acquisitions.

Of all the great patrons, collectors and connoisseurs, most have been men, most dealers have been men, most museums have had male directors, and most artists throughout Western history have been men. Why have there been, historically, so few great women artists? Since

World War II, as women have become more independent, with greater power and economic force, closer attention has been focused on women's past achievements. The traditional reason for the historical lack of acknowledged women artists – the requirements of motherhood – is now being questioned by research, particularly into the late Mediaeval period and the early Renaissance. It is suggested that women may have provided a much more significant political, economic and social force than hitherto imagined, but until recently their roles have been little understood and examined.

The activities of women patrons in the Renaissance have been found to produce significantly different patterns from the methods used in male patronage. Women, other than royal collectors, often waited until their families had reached independence, or even until widowhood, to set about collecting seriously. Otherwise, collecting could be a by-product of homemaking in the form of furnishing and decorating. These impulses, so distinct from men's collecting instincts, produced the types of collection that, broadly speaking, could be categorized as feminine. These differences were recognized, were often disparaged, and led to 'women's' areas of interest – such as porcelain collecting, embroidery, dress and fans, as well as the botanizing of Queen Charlotte and the gardening mania of Miss Alice Rothschild of Waddesdon – being allotted a lesser place in the hierarchies of art collecting.

The Duchess of Portland's enormous collection of shells and natural curiosities overshadowed her ownership of Rembrandt etchings and Holbein miniatures and, of course, the Portland Vase, now in the British Museum. Queen Charlotte was a bibliophile and a knowledgeable botanist, but she is seen as the lesser partner in King George III's remarkable collecting activities. Her successor, Queen Mary, understood the significance of Queen Charlotte's lost treasures and, during her own collecting career, set herself to recover as many of them as possible. As well as being drawn to Fabergé, Princess Marie Louise was the creator of the Queen's Dolls House, and Lady Charlotte Schreiber may have preferred porcelain and fans, but her collections remain important landmarks of scholarly collecting and cataloguing.

Even so, in the nineteenth century there were compilations and anthologies of essays and entries on art by women. Two surveys were written by women: Mrs Elizabeth Fries Ellet's *Women Artists in all Ages and Countries* was published in New York in 1859; Mrs Clara Erskine Clement's *Women in the Fine Arts from the 7th century BC to the 20th century*, was published in Boston in 1904. And a well-known English writer, Walter Shaw Sparrow, wrote *Women Painters of the World* (1905). The number of important women art historians in the nineteenth-century is significant; Lady Morgan, Ellis Cornelia Knight, Anna Jameson and Julia Cartwright, to name only a few, made a real impact on this traditional male preserve.

The work of creative women in the Pre-Raphaelite and Arts and Crafts movements in Britain has long been recognized (with much, of course, among the applied arts, being regarded, perhaps disparagingly, as women's work). In the late nineteenth century there were several prominent Impressionists, notably Berthe Morisot, Manet's sister-in-law, and the American Mary Cassatt, an unmarried woman of independent means and a catalyst for many collectors. In the twentieth century, women have been increasingly prominent, particularly in the flurry of artistic experimentation at the beginning of the century, as equal partners in the Russian avant-garde, such as Natalia Goncharova, and, like Katherine Dreier, in the Surrealist movement.

But it requires more economic power than that possessed by an artist to be a collector. It is men who have had a near monopoly of what we might call predatory collecting, the collecting in times of war and political dominance – from Napoleon to Hitler and Goering. Other aggressive collectors used political as well as economic power. The most notable examples include generations of princely families in Italy – the Gonzaga, the Medici, the Borghese, among others – and the great Popes who so often came from these same families; and the Habsburgs, the Fuggers and Louis XIV. The woman nearest to the pattern of satisfying a voracious appetite for the pleasures of acquisition manifested by so many male rulers is Catherine the Great. Indeed, she described herself as a glutton. Collection after collection, made by men of the leading families and politicians of Europe, fell to the power of her imperial purse. She was that exception to prove the rule, a female ruler successful in a man's world, and she collected omnivorously on a regal scale. It was she who purchased Sir Robert Walpole's magnificent collection in 1779 when his heirs were left with insoluble debt after his ambitious building of Houghton Hall in Norfolk.

Economics followed politics: Charles I acquired the great collections of Mantua; in turn the greatest royal collections made in England were dispersed as he – and his fellow connoisseurs and collectors, the Earl of Arundel and the Duke of Buckingham – fell from grace and from power. British collectors profited more than a century later in the chaos that attended the French Revolution. In the late nineteenth and throughout the twentieth centuries art from Europe crossed the Atlantic, following the great fortunes being made in America.

Almost without exception, the significant women in this typically overwhelmingly masculine field have been rich – some very rich – and they belonged to the upper classes. They have had money; and they have had time. The wealth has in the main been familial, dependent on personal relationships and blood ties, the money of a father, a husband, a lover. Royal mistresses collected to demonstrate the strength of their position, though Mme de Pompadour had a pressing agenda in distracting the King, who was too easily bored. The most valuable pictures in the collection of Napoleon's first wife, Josephine, were plundered in Bonaparte's wars. These women did not have to work for their living; their hours have been in the main (except for the exceptions that prove the rule – the working ruler) taken up by the niceties of life, the arrangements of pleasure and delight. They have not had to concern themselves with the acquisition of wealth. That has only come in recent times, in the twentieth century, as women have become more financially independent. The women who hugely increased their family fortunes when they inherited from their husbands – *vide* Lady Charlotte Schreiber and Mrs Potter Palmer, to name only two – must have felt particularly justified in indulging their collecting passions. In the case of the Stein family, the promoters of the Parisian avant-garde early in the twentieth century, it was the elder brother Michael who nurtured the family wealth, and who kept his eye on his siblings, Gertrude and Leo.

Women have so rarely been independent, a rarity that is reflected in the numbers of women known in Western history to have been significant collectors. However, there has been a sea change in the visible reasons for collecting, which have mirrored changes in Western society. In the twentieth century some women have used their own earned wealth to collect. Helena Rubinstein and Coco Chanel made large personal fortunes in the cosmetics and fashion industries and used their money to collect, for purely self-indulgent reasons, anything that attracted their wayward artistic fancy. Also in the same century we meet some women whose wealth was comparatively modest, although of course still substantially greater than most; even Peggy Guggenheim's money was tied up in small family trusts.

It has been fascinating to see how often the growing number of women without strong familial obligations to descendants have seen their mission as leaving their collections almost intact – if they could afford to do so – for the public interest. They have believed in the power and importance of art in its own right, and in particular this has been an attribute of the collections made of contemporary or modern art. Gertrude Vanderbilt Whitney founded the Whitney Museum of American Art in New York in 1920, twelve years before she died; and Ima Hogg gave her Bayou Bend to the Museum of Fine Arts in Houston in 1957. It has been observed that museums and galleries have become the secular cathedrals for a secular age. Many of the women collectors we have described have come from religiously observant families, but they have seen their collecting activities in a proselytizing light, wishing to share their interest, with missionary zeal, to persuade others to adopt something almost tantamount to faith and to convey their own absorption. As well as building, with her husband, their own museum, Dominique de Menil opened a non-denominational chapel in Houston to house a series of paintings by Mark Rothko.

The field of women collectors provides a microcosm of changes in the patterns of collecting. The last two centuries have seen an almost unimaginable expansion of the public display of art in all its manifestations. The first institutions that function in some way as public state museums on a massive scale date from this period: the British Museum (1759) and the Louvre (1792), for example. In the late nineteenth century and in the twentieth, collections made by women with their names attached have either entered public institutions as some kind of entity – the Katherine Dreier Collection at the Yale University Art Gallery and the Keiller Collection in the Scottish National Gallery of Modern Art for example – or become the core of museums or museums in their own right, as in the Isabella Stewart Gardner Museum in Boston and the Peggy Guggenheim Collection in Venice. Indeed, it is probably in America in the twentieth century that the most active and prominent women collectors have flourished, reflecting not only the economic power of the United States but the growing social status and independence of women.

There are, over the centuries, two categories of women who have been influential, as catalysts or activists, in the collecting of the visual arts and in material culture, in such a way that their reputations, histories and lives are intertwined with such collecting activities. Some in the twentieth century have been professionally affiliated with the collecting activities of millionaires, or even billionaires. These include Belle da Costa Greene, the librarian for J. P. Morgan, who was inextricably responsible for the glories of the J. Pierpont Morgan Library in New York, another example being Baroness Hilla Rebay's association with Solomon Guggenheim and the Museum of Non Objective Art.

Others have been partners whose roles are difficult to differentiate from those of their spouses: for example, John and Josephine Bowes, the illegitimate aristocrat and his artist wife, created the Bowes Museum in the North of England, and, in a neat parallel, Edouard André and Nélie Jacquemart, a Parisian banker and his artist wife, were responsible for the Jacquemart-André Museum in Paris's Faubourg St Honoré. Mr and Mrs John D. Rockefeller III collected American art together, and the most important and beautiful works of their pioneering collection form an intact group in the Fine Arts Museums of San Francisco. Although an initial impulse towards Impressionism came from Mrs H. O. Havemeyer (Louisine), the Havemeyers collected much of what has been called the 'splendid legacy' together.

In some cases the tastes of partners diverged: John D. Rockefeller Jr was not particularly sympathetic towards the contemporary tastes of Abby Aldrich Rockefeller, and it was she who was one of the co-founders of the Museum of Modern Art, New York, as well as making an immense collection of American folk art that bears her name. Moreover, she helped open the eyes of her daughter-in-law, Blanchette Hooker Rockefeller, to modern art, to which her husband, John D. Rockefeller III was not attracted.

In other cases, the husband subsidized the interests of the wife. 'Big Alma', Mrs Adolph Spreckels of California, wife of the West Coast sugar king, collected in part out of conviction, in part out of philanthropy, and in part just for the fun of it, with her husband's bemused support. He was to pay for his wife's convictions by financing the building of the California Palace of the Legion of Honour, which houses much of the French art, in particular the sculptures of Rodin, bought by Alma Spreckels. In contrast, Marjorie Merriweather Post was an heiress and she had the money, but her husbands supplied the inspiration for her collecting, first of the French eighteenth century and then of Russian works of art.

Finally, what kind of pattern, if any, can be discerned among the handful of women collectors whose activities have been documented, by themselves and by others?

Sometimes their roles as collectors, particularly the royal mistresses and royal consorts, were complementary to the central relationships of their lives. Second, almost all had mentors and advisers, artists or dealers sympathetic and understanding of their goals, which is not so very different from the patterns of many men collectors. Louisine Havemeyer looked up to and admired Mary Cassatt's perspicacity. And in some cases, notably in the twentieth century, the relationships were personal, with perhaps a significant emotional or intimate content. Certainly Marcel Duchamp was adored, even if platonically, by the women collectors he advised.

And third, particularly in modern times, the independent-minded woman endowed her collecting with a proselytizing zeal, attempting to convert an audience to the significance of the art that was being collected, both spiritually and educationally. In this women do seem to be different from their male counterparts. The male collector may be a philanthropist, seeking the public betterment, as well as perhaps paying tribute to his own discernment and making a gesture towards his own commemoration. It is fascinating and instructive to see how many of the women who collected in the later periods were involved in good works and charity in other ways, even feminism; the Davies sisters supported welfare for girls and women, medical studies and, through the academic institutions of Wales, various intellectual pursuits. Women seem also often to have as part of their attitudes a sense of nurturing. They seem drawn to the contemporary, to disinterestedly fostering the careers of those in whom they are interested; they are involved, emotionally as well as intellectually. Many collectors, like the Cone sisters of Baltimore, travelled widely, and looking at art and providing suitable safe-keeping for beautiful and interesting objects gave a framework and structure to their lives. How some well-known women collectors operated in this area, some of the choices they made in their lives and in what they collected form the substance of the pages that follow.

Charles Cameron (1745–1812), fireplace and stucco decoration in the Green Dining Room, Catherine Palace at Tsarskoye Selo, St Petersburg, 1780s.

Portrait of Madame de Pompadour by François Boucher (1703–70); oil on canvas, 1756.
Alte Pinakothek, Munich.

Queen Charlotte with her two elder sons, George, Prince of Wales and Frederick, later Duke of York by Allan Ramsay (1713–84); the musical instrument, book and sewing basket are emblematic of her interests; oil on canvas, *c.*1765.
The Royal Collection by Gracious Permission of Her Majesty The Queen.

View in the gardens at Pavlovsk in the early nineteenth century by Mikhail Ivanovich Lebedev (1811–37). State Russian Museum, St Petersburg.

The Empress Josephine at Malmaison by Pierre-Paul Prud'hon (1758–1823); oil on canvas, 1805.
Musée du Louvre, Paris. This was regarded as one of the truest likenesses of the Empress.

A portrait of Lady Dorothy Nevill (née Walpole, daughter of the 3rd Earl of Orford) by The Hon. Henry Richard Graves (fl.1846–81), seen in her boudoir, wearing a pink and gold embroidered eighteenth-century dress; oil on panel, 1855 (exhibited at the Royal Academy, 1856).

Portrait of Isabella Stewart Gardner by
John Singer Sargent (1856–1925); oil on
canvas, 1887–8. Isabella Stewart Gardner
Museum, Boston.
Mrs Gardner is standing before a dramatically patterned length of antique textile
from her collection.

Marjorie Merriweather Post at Tregaron, photographed for *Vogue* in 1945 among her treasures.
Hillwood Museum, Washington DC.
The Imperial 'Catherine the Great' Egg by Fabergé can be seen in the showcase.

Louisine Havemeyer and her daughter Electra by Mary Cassatt (1844–1926); pastel, 1895.
Shelburne Museum, Vermont.

Portrait of Gertrude Stein by Pablo Picasso (1881–1973); oil on canvas, 1906.
Metropolitan Museum of Art, New York, bequest of Gertrude Stein, 1946.
This most celebrated image of Picasso's early patron features in many
of the photographs of Gertrude Stein in her Paris apartment.

A room in the Etta Cone apartment, Marlborough Apartments, Baltimore.
Cone Collection, Baltimore Museum of Art.

Helena Rubinstein's drawing room, showing the eclectic mix of thirties furniture upholstered in brilliantly coloured silks with American Victoriana and African sculpture.

Portrait of Gertrude Vanderbilt Whitney by Robert Henri (1865–1929); oil on canvas, 1916.
Whitney Museum of American Art, New York.

Portrait of Dominique (Dominique de Menil) by Max Ernst (1891–1976); oil on canvas, 1934.
Menil Collection, Houston, Texas.

Miss Peggy Guggenheim seated on a sofa with her two dogs, a painting by Fernand Léger behind her, photographed in her New York apartment in about 1970.

Circumcision by Jackson Pollock (1912–56); oil on canvas, 1946.
The Peggy Guggenheim Collection, Venice: the Soloman R. Guggenheim Foundation, New York

CHAPTER I

Catherine the Great
(1729-96)

In broad outline, a fairytale plot will become familiar throughout much of this book. It repeats again and again. An obscure princess is plucked from the intricate cousinage spread throughout northern Europe, makes a great dynastic leap by marrying an unknown bridegroom and rises to unimagined heights of wealth and power. Modestly reared in small, remote courts, nevertheless each princess is aware of her royal destiny; the stories are so strikingly similar as to beg the question whether this kind of upbringing produced a predisposition to collect.

In a sense to describe Catherine as a woman collector – albeit one of the greatest the world has ever known – is somehow to miss the point. True, she was a woman and a voracious collector, but she was also the absolute ruler of the vast lands comprising 'all the Russias', a ruthless autocrat, and in command of seemingly unlimited resources. Her agents scoured Europe for Old Masters and works of art, and she commissioned on a grand scale. She laid the foundations of the great Russian imperial collections of antiquities and works of art in the Hermitage in St Petersburg, which remain among the wonders of the world in spite of careless and unthinking dispersals by her successors. She elevated her fashionable passion for patronage and collecting into a single-handed bid to establish one of the leading centres of world culture, fit to rival Paris and London. From her position at the very pinnacle of collecting in her time she surveyed the web of patronage and purchasing in Europe, and many of the players in this story show up here, among them her daughter-in-law Marie Feodorovna of course, Mme de Pompadour, Mme du Barry and Queen Charlotte and, peripherally, the Duchess of Portland, whom British diplomat and antiquary Sir William Hamilton teased with his stories of Catherine's willingness to buy the 'Portland Vase'.

Catherine II, Empress of all the Russias – this was the title she held during her reign, her accolade of 'the Great' having only come into use after her death – was the daughter of a minor German prince, Christian August of Anhalt-Zerbst. He was a low-paid general in the employ of King Frederick William of Prussia, who sent him to command the garrison at Stettin, a remote

Baltic port. It was here that Sophie Auguste Fredericke was born and christened into the Lutheran church, of which her father was a devout adherent. She had royal blood through her mother, Johanna of Holstein-Gottorp, but neither parent had any money and her childhood circumstances were straightened. She always remembered with gratitude her sound education from a beloved French governess, and she became proficient in handwriting and drawing, but not in music, for which she had no aptitude. She was considered plain as a girl, and it is interesting to follow the transformation that led in middle age to her being able to take her pick of handsome young lovers in their twenties. Sophie remained hardy throughout her life. She survived illnesses that would have killed someone less robust, she could spend hours in the saddle like a soldier – she adapted man's uniform for this purpose – and her regime included an early-morning constitutional with her dogs, followed by ten-mile walks.

Her father was a quiet man, interested in books while his wife was sociable and extravagant. Sophie learnt discretion through hard experience; she and her mother made many visits to the ducal court at Brunswick without servants or lavish clothing. In spite of her upbringing in an unsophisticated outpost, she learnt the ways of a wealthy and cultivated court. When she was thirteen her father succeeded as ruler of the small sovereign principality of Anhalt-Zerbst, a considerable improvement in the family's social circumstances, but little to their financial position.

Early in 1744 Sophie and her mother were summoned to Russia by the Empress Elizabeth (1709–62), who wished to vet the young princess as a wife for her nephew and designated heir, Peter, Duke of Holstein, who was also Catherine's first cousin. In spite of both her parents' dislike of submitting their daughter on approval, and of Prince Christian's unease at Russia's recent dark history and the unscrupulous methods by which the Empress and her predecessors held on to their power, mother and daughter embarked on the terrifying journey into the unknown. Sophie's prospective bridegroom was just sixteen, but he seemed much younger, and his strange, disordered personality emerged more clearly as he matured. They were married after nearly two years of preparation, during which time Sophie learned Russian and was persuaded, after anguished heart-searching, to abandon her Lutheran faith for the Orthodox Church. On her conversion she took the name of Catherine Alexeyevna. The source for early life is her own *Memoirs*; there have also been numerous biographies.

From the start Catherine's marriage was troubled; she was forced into dismal seclusion, excluded by the Empress and repudiated by Peter. In 1754, after two miscarriages, a son was born, and she had fulfilled her primary duty. The child, who was widely rumoured to have been fathered by Catherine's lover, was immediately removed by the Empress and brought up under her supervision. Catherine was left without occupation or status at court and she retired to Oranienbaum, the summer palace built by one of Peter the Great's favourites and handed over to Peter and Catherine by Elizabeth. As in her girlhood, she again learned hard lessons, this time of duplicity, scheming and spying to save herself. During these frustrating years she did not waste her time and read widely – she discovered the letters of Mme de Sevigné (1626–96) and Voltaire's works – and added English to her fluent French as well as cutting her teeth as a patron by furnishing and decorating her apartments.

Catherine II of Russia Walking in the Park at Tsarskoye Selo with her Greyhound,
engraving by N. I. Utkin, 1827. Trustees of the British Museum, London.

That Catherine's collecting was as successful as it was, given the hazards of bulk-buying and arms-length commissioning, was a tribute to the excellence of her advisors. At this time one of the most cultivated men of his time, Dimitri, Prince Golitsyn, was Russian Ambassador to France, and he was on terms of friendship with Voltaire and the encyclopaedist Denis Diderot (1713–84); one of Catherine's earliest acquisitions was Diderot's famous library. She acquired Voltaire's 7,000-volume library, along with almost all his papers and her letters to him, after his death in 1778.

French was the language of court and aristocracy in Russia at this date and Russians were familiar with Diderot's reports of the paintings at the Paris Salons. Evidence of the Russian love affair with French culture abounds in the architecture and interior decoration of the St Petersburg palaces and mansions that sprang up along the River Neva and the Fontanka and Moika canals in the eighteenth century. French eighteenth-century painting and decorative art is outstandingly represented in the imperial collections. However, the crowning achievement of the Empress Elizabeth's reign had been the Winter Palace, a masterpiece of Baroque architecture whose architect, Rastrelli, was an Italian, as were many of the foreign architects employed in Russia. This vast undertaking was not completed until shortly after her death, and the first people to use it were her successors, Catherine and her husband, Peter III.

After lingering in poor health for some years Elizabeth died in 1762 and Peter, who had failed to win the trust or affection of the Russian people, succeeded as Emperor. Learning of his plan to divorce and banish her, Catherine mounted a successful coup and deposed Peter only six months after his accession. He was imprisoned in a small outlying palace and shortly afterwards Catherine heard that he was dead; although she had not ordered his murder and presented his death as occurring from natural causes, the means by which she achieved the throne cast a shadow over her reign. Far away in England, Horace Walpole's many correspondents quickly learned from his spirited letters of the developments in Russia, and he did not scruple to brand her a murderer.

Walpole (1717–97), for many years a Member of Parliament, was the fourth son of Sir Robert Walpole, 1st Earl of Orford, long-serving prime minister and owner of the celebrated picture collection at Houghton in Norfolk. Horace was a passionate collector of curiosities and *objets de virtu* (particularly valued for their antiquity or craftsmanship), which he installed in his Gothick-style castle, Strawberry Hill at Twickenham near London, but above all he was one of the greatest English letter-writers. Walpole collected news as eagerly as antiquities; his voracious appetite for gossip and scandal ensured a legacy of vigorously expressed views, which will be heard often in the following pages, his comments on fellow collectors being particularly pertinent. Walpole loathed Catherine long before he had any reason to, but the sale of the Houghton pictures to the Russian Empress in 1779 by his nephew, who had succeeded as the 3rd Earl of Orford, gave him real grounds for his antipathy.

Although at her accession Catherine had more pressing concerns than art collecting, her first priority being to improve Russia's financial position through trade and manufactures, she was also anxious to raise Russia's cultural standing in Europe. This was the aim that she stuck to,

Three items from the 944-piece 'Frog' service, Wedgwood & Bentley; 'Queen's Ware (creamware) painted in enamel with English arcadian views, 1773–4. Commissioned by Catherine the Great for the Chesme Palace (known as La Grenouillière from its location on a frog marsh) and now in the Hermitage Museum, St Petersburg.

rather than to promote Old Russian traditions, as her successors were to do later. She did not care for the ancient capital, Moscow, and her energies were concentrated on the projects already established by Peter the Great and the Empress Elizabeth in and around St Petersburg, Russia's 'window on the West'. The development of Russian manufactures was to be towards standards set in the West, at the Sèvres porcelain factory and the Gobelins tapestry works, for example. The success of this policy was to be amply demonstrated at Pavlovsk (see Chapter III), the palace built by Catherine for her son and daughter-in-law, where the products of France and Russia are mingled together. One Russian asset that she utilized lavishly, the indigenous hardstones from the Urals, line rooms in her palaces with malachite and coloured marbles. In spite of a century of relentless Westernization, Russian life remained obstinately unaltered, with lingering reminders of its Asiatic origins sufficiently exotic to excite the interest of travellers and to inspire many accounts, in which the sights and sounds of eighteenth-century St Petersburg are conjured up with startling immediacy.

The Hermitage collections in St Petersburg were inaugurated in 1764 with the purchase of a collection of 225 Old Master paintings from a Berlin picture dealer, Johann Gotzkowski. In 1755 he had been commissioned by Frederick the Great to find Italian, Dutch and Flemish pictures to match the modern French masters already in his collection, but the outbreak of the Seven Years War and its disastrous financial consequences left Frederick reluctant to complete the deal, and in desperation Gotzkowski approached Catherine. At a single stroke she came into possession of some very fine works, including three Rembrandts and a Frans Hals. Meanwhile Prince Golitsyn was acting as her advisor and mediator in acquiring contemporary works in Paris. Through his friendship with Diderot he steered her towards Greuze, Chardin, Louis-Michel van Loo and Joseph-Marie Vien. Diderot recommended one of Greuze's greatest works, *The Paralytic*, the centrepiece in what was to develop into an entire gallery devoted to his work. The Chardin, a still-life with the attributes of the Arts surrounding a statue of Mercury, was intended for the St Petersburg Academy of Arts, founded in 1757 by Elizabeth. The Academy building, designed by the French architect J. B. Vallin de la Mothe (1729–1801) in the classical style, was put in hand soon after Catherine's accession as part of her cultural strategy. Yuri Veldten, who was to embank the Neva with great granite ramparts, was named director, and he was also called upon to design the first stage of Catherine's picture gallery, the 'Little Hermitage' alongside the Winter Palace. Vallin de la Mothe was installed as the first professor of architecture at the Academy. He was responsible some ten years later for the 'Old Hermitage'. The 'Raphael Gallery' and the beautiful little Hermitage theatre were designed by the Italian architect Giacomo Quarenghi (1744–1817). It was used to stage plays written by Catherine.

In about 1766 Catherine acquired François Boucher's *Rest on the Flight into Egypt* from the posthumous sale of Louis XV's most notorious official mistress, Mme de Pompadour. It was painted for her private chapel at Versailles. Golitsyn also acquired in 1768, against stiff competition, three pictures from the collection of Louis XV's secretary, Louis Jean Gaignat, including an important Bartolomeo Murillo, *Rest on the Flight into Egypt*. In 1769 the purchase of the whole of Count Heinrich von Brühl's important collection of some 600 Flemish, Dutch and French paintings, including masterpieces by Rembrandt, Rubens, Poussin and Watteau, elevated the imperial holdings to a new level. Among the works were ten views of Dresden and its environs by the Venetian Bernardo Bellotto, painted for von Brühl in gratitude for his part in securing for Bellotto the patronage of his employer, the Elector Augustus II of Saxony (Augustus III of Poland). Catherine was so taken with them that she tried to persuade Bellotto to come to St Petersburg, but he went to work for the next King of Poland, Catherine's former lover Stanislas Poniatowski (1732–98), in Warsaw. Ironically, his views of Warsaw eventually came to the Hermitage with the rest of Poniatowski's collection but were returned to Poland under the terms of the 1921 Russo-Polish Peace Treaty.

Along with the Brühl pictures came, almost by default, a group of 1,076 Old Master drawings. The same had happened a year earlier with the purchase through Golitsyn's agency of the Coblenzl Collection formed by Johann-Philipp, Count Coblenzl, in Brussels; acquired principally for the pictures, including an important allegorical work by Rubens, it also brought very fine Italian, French, German and Flemish Old Master drawings among the somewhat uneven collection of 4,000, many with ambitious but mistaken attributions. More Old Master drawings came with the Crozat Collection; in 1772 Catherine came in possession of the greater part of one of the most important European collections formed in the eighteenth century, that of the French banker, Pierre Crozat. Crozat had died in 1740 and the purchase was made from his heir, Baron Crozat de Thiers, who had added to the collection on his own account. The sale caused consternation in France and the Marquis de Marigny, Mme de Pompadour's brother, tried to stop it, but was unable to raise the money. Some 500 of the finest paintings came to Russia, by

The Infant Hercules Strangling the Serpents by James Walker after Sir Joshua Reynolds (1723–92) mezzotint, published 1792. The Trustees of the British Museum. Reynolds's painting was commissioned by Catherine the Great in 1785 and it arrived in Russia in 1789. It is now in the Hermitage Museum in St Petersburg.

Lucas van Leyden, Rembrandt, Van Dyck, Rubens, Poussin, Raphael, Giorgione and Veronese. One of the Poussins, the beautiful so-called *Birth of Venus* (the subject, once believed to be *The Triumph of Neptune and Amphrite* is still in dispute); it was sold by the Soviets in 1932 and is now in Philadelphia. About a dozen more of the most important paintings were bought by Andrew Mellon from the Soviet Government in 1937; they are in the National Gallery in Washington. The Van Dyck portrait of Charles I from the collection, which is now in the Louvre, was claimed by Mme du Barry, the last of Louis XV's official mistresses, on the rather dubious grounds that she was a descendant of the royal Stuart line.

In 1779 Catherine secured the collection of paintings from Houghton that had belonged to Sir Robert Walpole. Many of the artists represented in the Crozat Collection appear again among the Walpole pictures, and Catherine's Italian holdings were significantly augmented. One of the features of Walpole's paintings was the importance of the former owners. With this purchase Catherine acquired works with French royal provenance, as well as from earlier collectors and the British aristocracy; for her its most significant former owner was Britain's great

Prime Minister. The sale caused outrage – it had even been proposed that the collection should be bought by the British Parliament as the basis of a National Gallery – just as the Crozat affair had a few years before in France, and with the expenditure of £43,000 Catherine was thought to have secured a bargain. Although Walpole was sorrowful at the departure of the pictures, on the point of the money he was not in agreement. He wrote to an old friend, the Countess of Upper Ossory on 1 February 1779: 'The pictures at Houghton, I hear, and I fear, are sold; what can I say? I do not like even to think on it. It is the most signal mortification to my idolatry for my father's memory, that it could receive.' In July he wrote to the Rev. William Cole in a cooler frame of mind: 'Partial as I am to the pictures at Houghton, I confess I think them much overvalued. My father's whole collection, of which alone he had preserved the prices, cost but forty thousand pounds; and after his death there were three sales of pictures . . .' Perhaps he was also guiltily conscious of purchases, unwisely urged by him on his father, that had turned out disappointingly.

The Van Dyck portraits of members of the Wharton family from Houghton established the British School on a high note in the Hermitage collection. Catherine commissioned works herself from Sir Joshua Reynolds and Joseph Wright of Derby, as well as patronizing other British artists, who made the journey to St Petersburg. She received as a present a painting by Angelica Kauffman, an artist then much admired in Russia. One of the three works by Wright is a version of his dramatic fire-lit *Iron Forge*, which Horace Walpole had noticed at the Society of Artists in London in 1773. 'Very good', he jotted in a note in the margin of his catalogue. Reynolds painted an historical subject, *The Infant Hercules strangling the Serpent*, intended as a flattering reference to the might of Russia. Richard Brompton painted Catherine's portrait and a double portrait of her grandsons. Brompton travelled to Russia in about 1780 after Catherine secured his release from prison for debt, and he spent the rest of his life there. By the time of her death Catherine's collection numbered 3,926 paintings.

Catherine's admiration for British culture extended to the decorative arts, probably as much for their evidence of a successful manufacturing economy as for their qualities of taste and refinement for which the French still excelled above all. She had come into possession of magnificent silver services, jewellery, gold boxes and watches commissioned by Elizabeth and to these she added mechanical musical novelty clocks by the admired London craftsman, James Cox (fl. 1757–91). Her most flattering patronage of British manufactures concerned the Wedgwood factory, whose international reputation was largely due to the patronage of Queen Charlotte. The famous 'Frog' service, so-called as it was destined for La Grenouillère (nickname of the Chesme Palace from its position on a frog-marsh), was ordered through the Russian consul in London in 1773 (page 37). Chesme, built in 1774 in the Turkish style to celebrate victory in the Russo-Turkish War, was a staging post between the Winter Palace and the palace at Tsarskoye Selo, and the service was the most important of its furnishings. Each of the 944 pieces with its emblem of a frog in a shield is decorated with vignettes of idyllic English landscapes, castles, abbeys, palaces and parks. None among the total of 1,222 views was repeated, and it caused Josiah Wedgwood and his partner, Thomas Bentley (c.1730–80), an enormous effort to commission them from artists or to gather from other sources such as topographical prints. It has great historical importance as a

Sèvres Porcelain Manufactory, ice pails from the 800-piece 'Blue Cameo' service, made for Catherine II.
The 60-setting dessert-service was commissioned in 1776 and delivered in 1779. The 90,000 livres paid in
1792 to clear the remaining debt on this massive commission all but saved the factory from collapse in the
troubled years of the French Revolution.

record of a long-lost English Arcadia, but at the time it was also a reference work for all
that Catherine admired of the English style of landscape and gardening. The service of
cream-coloured Queensware painted in sepia enamel was delivered in 1774, after having been
exhibited at Portland House in London where it was seen by Queen Charlotte herself.

Catherine was an admirer of English gem-engraving, then enjoying a revival under the
auspices of the Society of Arts and the newly established Royal Academy. She more or less pre-
empted the life work of the Brown brothers William (1748–1825) and Charles (1749–95), with 200
of their cameos in her collection. She also ordered a full set of the 20,000 casts of cameos and
intaglios from the leading European gem cabinets issued by James Tassie (1735–99), and these
were housed in magnificent inlaid cabinets ordered from London. Complementing the gem
collection, Wedgwood issued a number of black basalt and jasperware portraits of Catherine
based on medals and on a cameo cut by her daughter-in-law, Grand Duchess Marie Feodorovna.

Catherine had been buying up whole collections of engraved gems, including the French
royal collection of Louis, Duc d'Orléans, sold by Philippe-Egalité in 1787 and the Dresden
collection of Jean-Baptiste Casanova, painter and director of the Dresden academy, in 1792. The
post-classical Western European cameos and intaglios span the whole spectrum from antiquity

to work commissioned from gem-engravers of her own time, and the collection is one of the most extensive in the world. One of the finest surviving cameo portraits of Queen Elizabeth I, which had belonged to Crozat, came with the Orléans Collection, as did the profile head of Charles I and a rare cameo of Cupid as a gardener by Mme de Pompadour's master gem-engraver, Jacques Guay.

Like every collector of any stature in the eighteenth century Catherine loved porcelain. Before the development of the porcelain factories in Europe, immensely costly oriental porcelain was prized by collectors almost above gold, as a symbol of wealth, prestige and power, and Catherine had fine Chinese pieces – 'prodigious fine Chinese Jarrs' according to Baroness Dimsdale, a visitor in 1781, in the Chinese room at Tsarskoye Selo. When the European porcelain industry was established, rulers exchanged their country's wares as diplomatic gifts. The Elector of Saxony, instigator of the first true porcelain in the West, presented the lovely Rococo 'St Andrew Service' to the Empress Elizabeth in 1745. Meissen figures by Johann Kändler, the most celebrated modeller of his day, decorated the Meissen room in one of the pavilions at the imperial palace of Oranienbaum. French porcelain, Sèvres above all, was in the ascendant in the 1770s and 1780s, and the great service commissioned from the factory by Catherine dates from this period. The neo-classical 'Blue Cameo Service', of dinner, dessert, tea and coffee services for 60 people, was made in 1778–79. A reflection of what she termed her 'cameo fever', Catherine had imitation 'cameos' in wheel-cut, hard-paste porcelain set into the borders of the pieces. The brilliant turquoise blue colour that gives the service its name was a secret known only to the painters at Sèvres. The commission was put in the hands of a favourite, Grigory Potemkin (1739-91) and the intermediary in France was the Russian Ambassador, Prince Bariatinsky, who was soon to play host to Catherine's son and daughter-in-law on their European tour in 1782. It was one of the great achievements of the factory and the most expensive commission of the time. Catherine's lavish patronage of the factory casts an interesting light on the warm reception of her son Paul by Louis XVI and Marie Antoinette, by no means a foregone conclusion given her unconcealed dislike of the King's grandfather, Louis XV.

In the terrible fire that devastated the Winter Palace in 1837 about 160 pieces from the service were looted and found their way by a roundabout route to London. With considerable restraint the Marquis of Hertford acquired just six items from the dealer John Webb in Bond Street; these are now in the Wallace Collection and the other pieces that Webb had returned to Russia, probably through Lord Hertford's intervention, are back in the Hermitage.

Apart from Denis Diderot, Prince Golitsyn's other advisor was the sculptor, Etienne-Maurice Falconet (1716–91), favourite of Mme de Pompadour. Falconet undertook one of the great sculptural commissions of the age, the monumental bronze statue of Peter the Great on horseback, erected by Catherine on a great granite boulder beside the Hermitage. When Falconet arrived in Russia he had with him the unfinished figure of *Winter* begun for Mme de Pompadour a year before her death. He finished it in St Petersburg and it is now in the Hermitage with one of the many versions of his *L'Amour menaçant,* the first of which had also belonged to Mme de Pompadour. It is curious, given her passion for engraved gems, which are sculpture in miniature, that monumental sculpture features far less in Catherine's collecting than paintings – her one marble by Michelangelo, the unfinished *Crouching Boy* bought with the Lyde Brown Collection, an otherwise rather mixed bag of antique busts, was destined for the Grotto at Tsarskoye Selo. The seated full-length figure of her hero Voltaire, commissioned from Houdon (1741–1828), also lived in the Grotto.

Tsarskoye Selo (Tsar's village), the lovely palace and gardens a short distance from St Petersburg, was another legacy from the Empress Elizabeth, and it was here that Catherine indulged her mania for building, altering the existing Baroque interiors in a way that she had not contemplated in the Winter Palace or at Peterhof, Peter the Great's palace overlooking the Gulf of Finland. Catherine's favourite architect, the Scottish Charles Cameron (c.1743–1811), is much in evidence at Tsarskoye Selo. He was given a suite of eight rooms to construct using indigenous materials; coloured woods for floors and furniture – the prized Karelian birch with its distinctive markings and satin-like finish established the character of the finest Russian furniture – silks, glass and porcelain from the imperial factories and furniture and fittings from the Imperial Iron Foundry and the steelworks at Tula. In the 'Lyons' drawing-room French silk hangings provided a backdrop for Russian products, a table with an inlaid hardstone top from the Peterhof Stonecutting Works and white and gold porcelain from the imperial factory. The Green Dining Room, with its striking stucco reliefs, is one of Cameron's finest achievements (see page 17).

At Tsarskoye Selo Catherine gratified a taste, already tentatively indulged at Oranienbaum, for English-style gardens, and it was here that her gardener John Busch (d.1795) designed a park filled with pavilions, follies and even a whole Chinese 'village'. The 'Paladian Bridge' at the far end of the lake was copied from the bridge at Wilton House in Wiltshire. In common with other collectors of her time Catherine was very interested in horticulture and botany – it is a thread that runs particularly through the story of women's collecting – and she owned the nine volumes of Lord Bute's lavishly illustrated *Botanical Tables* of 1784, which he had dedicated to Queen Charlotte, one of the most important botanical patrons of the time. Catherine had an eager successor in her daughter-in-law, and the Pavlovsk gardens continue developments begun at Tsarskoye Selo. Palaces were built for her lovers, the Marble Palace on the Neva for Grigory Orlov (1734–83), to whom with his brothers she owed her throne, and the exquisite neo-classical Tauride Palace in the Smolny district for Grigory Potemkin. Potemkin was a noted art patron, commissioning history paintings from Joshua Reynolds alongside Catherine and buying from Wright of Derby, as she did. Catherine lavished presents on him, among them James Cox's masterpiece, the mechanical 'Peacock' clock, now in the Hermitage. The Marble Palace housed proof of Catherine's affection of an even greater value, the French silver 'Orlov Service' by Jacques Nicolas Roëttiers (b.1736), of more than 2,500 pieces, some of which is now in the Hermitage, but there are pieces elsewhere including the Metropolitan Museum in New York. Stanislas Poniatowsky occupied the Marble Palace after he lost the Polish throne; after his death it lay in ruins until being refitted in the mid-nineteenth century to house one of the grand dukes.

In 1776 Catherine's heir, the Grand Duke Paul, married a princess of Württemburg and Catherine presented them with an estate that was to become the lovely palace and park of Pavlovsk (see Chapter III). Her hold on the progress of the palace remained strong for a number of years, as she oversaw the work of Cameron and gave detailed advice about the garden, but eventually her daughter-in-law, Maria Feodorovna, succeeded in stamping it with her own personality.

In later life Catherine was inspired to write the *Memoirs* of her early years, detailing the wrongs she endured in her disastrous arranged marriage. She must have hoped that reading them would bring some understanding of her actions to her son Paul. She was still working immensely hard, sometimes foregoing a rest during the day in order to work for twelve hours at a stretch. In 1796, aged 67, Catherine suffered a stroke, and after lingering for hours longer than seemed possible through the great strength of her constitution, she died amidst weeping family and courtiers. In spite of the cold a huge crowd attended her funeral; ruthless autocrat as she was, she had made herself beloved by her people and had brought immeasurable benefits to Russia.

CHAPTER II

Royal Mistresses

Madame de Pompadour (1721–64)
Madame du Barry (1769–93)

The collections amassed by the mistresses of the King of France were made possible by their publicly acknowledged position, which conferred almost unlimited spending power. Collecting and furnishing elegant apartments were suitable diversions in the circumscribed existence of the royal favourite, who had to be always on the watch and prepared for the unannounced arrivals of the king. Mme de Pompadour was intelligent and cultivated, and she had a considerable influence on French eighteenth-century taste. She secured the financial security of the Sèvres porcelain factory and thus promoted one of the glories of French decorative art. Mme du Barry's power lay in her sexual attraction for the ageing king; her tastes mark the change from rococo to neo-classical. In spite of wide differences in temperament and intellectual power, their collections show significant overlaps, largely through deliberate emulation on the part of Mme du Barry, who was encouraged to consolidate her position by claiming the privileges of her predecessor.

Madame de Pompadour

> *Not a man alive but would have had her for his mistress if he could. Tall, though not too tall; beautiful figure; round face with regular features; wonderful complexion, hands and arms; eyes not so very big, but the brightest, wittiest and most sparkling I ever saw. Everything about her was rounded, including all her gestures.*

> (Description of Mme de Pompadour by Comte Dufort de Cheverny, 1731–1802)

Jeanne-Antoinette Poisson was born in Paris in 1721; her father was steward to the Pâris brothers, court bankers and army contractors and immensely powerful in the workings of the economy of France. Her mother was a beauty, and on this account – and because detractors of

45

the future Mme de Pompadour wished to endow her with all the conventional attributes of a royal paramour – it was suggested that the child was illegitimate, Pâris-Duvernoy being one of the favoured candidates as her father. When scandal overtook the Pâris brothers it brought down the Poisson family too, and as M. Poisson fled to safety over the German frontier, Mme Poisson was obliged to accept the protection of M. Le Normant de Tournehem, a *fermier général* (or tax-collector). Tournehem, an old friend of the Pâris brothers, took on the welfare of the whole family and saw to the education of the children.

Jeanne-Antoinette's careful instruction in polite accomplishments was supplemented by a year in a convent. She emerged from this with a range of talents: she could act, dance and sing; her elocution was perfected under the dramatist Crébillon (1707–77); she could play the clavichord, paint, draw, etch and engrave gem-stones and she was well-versed in botany and horticulture. Her handwriting was clear and legible. Most importantly she was very amusing, and she prepared herself to converse interestingly by assiduous reading and by committing plays and poetry to memory. It was from the Tournehem circle that both Jeanne-Antoinette and her brother Abel imbibed their excellent taste and their sure touch as patrons in the future. Jeanne-Antoinette was thoroughly instructed in the art of housekeeping, at which she excelled. One episode enlivened this conventional preparation for a good marriage. A fortune-teller predicted that the nine-year-old girl would one day reign over the heart of a king, foreshadowing the similar incident in the Empress Josephine's childhood.

Now the difficulty arose of establishing her in a suitable way – she had been obsessed by thoughts of the King ever since the visit to the fortune-teller – and the reputation and origins of her family stood in the way of a good marriage. At this point Tournehem moved in, and, to put it bluntly, sold her to his nephew, M. Le Normant d'Etoiles; they were married in 1741. Her career as a hostess and *maitresse de maison* commenced with the Château d'Etoiles, where a theatre was built to display her talents as an actress and dancer and where she started to furnish and equip her house and her person with the exquisite taste developed in her youth. She attracted clever men to her entertainments, among them Voltaire and her former instructor Crébillon. Gradually she insinuated herself into the highest circles and moved inexorably towards her goal, Versailles and the King himself. This is not the place to enumerate the stratagems that she employed first to attract the King's notice and then to become his mistress. By 1745 their liaison was common knowledge, in September she occupied an apartment at Versailles as *maitresse en titre*, and at the end of the year the King contrived the presentation to the Queen of the newly enobled Marquise de Pompadour.

Mme de Pompadour was more or less obliged to emulate the *dépenses nobiliaire* – the expenditure that resulted from maintaining social status – of the circle into which she was reluctantly admitted when it became apparent that the King had every intention of establishing her at court. She was much more than just a new mistress for the King, for in many ways that was her least important function and one whose physical side she abandoned long before the title that went with it. She was interested in affairs of state and meddled to some effect; and she welcomed opportunities for patronage and encouragement of the decorative arts as likely to give Louis XV

Madame de Pompadour by François
Boucher, (detail). Alte Pinakothek, Munich.

new interests and divert his attention from dallying at the infamous Parc aux cerfs. She was
probably the first woman in France since Marie de Médicis to take a leading role as a patron
of the arts.

Mme de Pompadour was in a position of considerable power through another channel,
the office of the Bâtiments du Roi, controlled successively by her uncle-in-law and then her
brother over a period of nearly 30 years. Le Normand de Tournehem was appointed in 1745 and
by 1746 her brother, the future Marquis de Marigny, was already director designate. He was to
occupy the post from 1751 until 1773, nearly a decade after her own death. Brother and sister are
shown together in 1754 in a portrait by Alexandre Roslin (1718–93) now in the Konstmuseum,
Göteborg, she holding a tray of *objets de virtu* and he the architectural model of a building.
Marigny's official commissions for great public works in Paris and for the royal manufactories
interweave with the more intimate patronage of his sister. While he was ordering cartoons for the
Gobelins tapestry works from François Boucher, Carle van Loo (1705–65) and others, Mme de
Pompadour was arranging for the same artists to design tapestries for her exclusive use. Marigny
was responsible for the important commission to Joseph Vernet (1714–89) to depict the *Ports of
France*, and it was he who bought Vernet seascapes in Rome for Mme de Pompadour.

It was in no spirit of reluctance that she embarked on her career of extravagant expenditure. She knew how to approach the King, and he allowed her almost unlimited spending money. She was a natural collector, with a particular penchant for acquiring houses. The number is bewildering and the turnover was often rapid, but some she loved and embellished above the others. The first was Crécy, near Dreux, a great improvement on the quarters that had so recently housed her predecessor, Mme de Châteauroux. The King was highly diverted by planning improvements to Crécy and Mme de Pompadour, always in terror of the King's boredom, saw that this was a perfect way to amuse him. Other properties followed, giving the King endless scope for his natural talents as a patron of the arts. Mme de Pompadour was a talented impresario, deftly negotiating with artists and craftsmen, whom she treated perfectly by giving them encouragement and inspiration and by paying promptly. Most of her properties already existed and were enlarged and redesigned for her, but Bellevue, on the River Seine between Sèvres and Meudon, was entirely her own creation. Her Parisian house acquired in 1753, the hôtel de Pompadour in the Faubourg St Honoré (*ancien* hôtel d'Evreux), is now the Palais de l'Elysée. The most distinguished architect in her employ was Ange-Jacques Gabriel (1698–1782), who was responsible for the hôtel des Réservoirs at Versailles and for additions and alterations to the Château de Ménars near Tours.

Sadly little remains in terms of the physical legacy of her patronage and decorating activities, but her influence was long lived and brought France to the forefront of the luxury trade. She was in no sense a 'collector' of paintings, buying only contemporary works, and, initially at least, following the King's example in commissioning from Jean-Baptiste Oudry (1686–1755), Boucher and Jean-Baptiste Huet (1745–1811). Many of the items sold after her death were unframed, and with rounded or irregular shapes were clearly intended as overdoor and inset panels in her many properties. By the mid-1760s this would have been greatly to their detriment, as being typical of the now unfashionable rococo.

Her name is linked above all with François Boucher's; they somehow epitomize each other. She lives and breathes in his wonderful and varied full-length portraits; at the same time intimate – they show her with books, music, sewing implements in her own highly personal settings – and grand, they represent the ultimate in conspicuous consumption in matters of dress and decor. He was an experienced decorative painter and adorned many of her rooms; she bought the large pair of pictures showing the *Rising* and *Setting of the Sun,* now in the Wallace Collection in London, from the 1753 Salon, as designs for tapestry for her château at Bellevue. The *Toilette de Vénus*, now in the Metropolitan Museum, New York, was for the bathroom there. His *Arts and Sciences* (Frick Collection, New York) was for Crécy. One of his rare religious paintings, a *Nativity*, was commissioned for the chapel at Bellevue.

Boucher's decorative subjects were ideally suited to tapestry design, and the flavour of Mme de Pompadour's taste spread widely through this medium. An artist whom she also admired was Carle van Loo, and it is said that the decorative overdoor panel for the Turkish *salon* at Bellevue of her in costume as a sultana was the best likeness of any of her portraits (Musée des Arts Décoratifs, Paris). François Drouais' late portrait (National Gallery, London), dating from

One vase from a garniture of three vases with elephant-head handles, made for Madame de Pompadour, 1750s from the Sèvres Porcelain Manufactory. The Wallace Collection, London. Madame de Pompadour secured a Royal monopoly for the Sèvres factory, ensuring its profitability and effectively destroying the competition.

the last year of her life, shows her looking middleaged and in low spirits. She sits bravely at her tambour frame of polished green lacquer for embroidery with, at her side, a wonderful mid-eighteenth-century worktable by Jean-François Oeben mounted in chased ormulu. She was only 43 but, plagued all her life by ill health, the immense emotional and physical effort of her relationship with the King had taken a visible toll. It must have been a good likeness, because it was Marigny's favourite, and after he inherited it he would take it with him from Paris to Ménars – which he also inherited – on his annual visits.

Mme de Pompadour was a leading influence on developments in sculpture in the middle years of the century and a good friend to sculptors, commissioning from Sigismund Adam, Jean-Baptiste Lemoyne, Guillaume Coustou the Younger, Christophe-Gabriel Allegrain and his brother-in-law Jean-Baptiste Pigalle. Pigalle's 1755 group of *Love and Friendship* was an allegory, alluding to her now platonic relationship with the King. The subtle, classical head of a child by Jacques Saly, duplicated in different media, is commonly identified as Alexandrine, the short-lived daughter from her marriage to De l'Etoiles. Figures of girls butter-churning and making cheese, designed by François Boucher for her dairy at Crécy were particularly attractive. Etienne-Maurice Falconet was to find lasting fame through the patronage of Catherine the Great, but commissions from Mme de Pompadour included works for Bellevue and the Crécy dairy. She purchased the childish figure of *Cupid* seated on a cloud with roses at his feet (1757, Musée du Louvre, Paris), one of the most famous – and much-copied – eighteenth-century sculptures. Her preference for Falconet's elegant figures and the new material, *biscuit de Sèvres,* (unglazed white porcelain) set a fashion for statuettes as ornaments.

Mme de Pompadour was both patron and pupil of the gem-engraver Jacques Guay, whose portrait of the King, encircled in emeralds and diamonds, she wore on a bracelet (now in the Cabinet de Médailles, Paris). She studied drawing, gem-engraving and etching with him, and under the supervision of Charles-Nicolas Cochin II (1715–90) she produced a suite of prints after Guay on her own press at Versailles. Also at Versailles was her table 'à tour' for gem-engraving.

In the decorative arts Mme de Pompadour had a preference for porcelain and her collection would have furnished a fine museum. She owned historic examples, Chinese wares as well as the newly developed European porcelains, and she was an important supporter of the industry in France. Her great achievement was the Sèvres factory. She was an early buyer of Meissen, and in order to promote French ventures, lent her support to the Vincennes porcelain factory, which she had moved to Sèvres, near her château of Bellevue in 1756. Jean-Jacques Bachelier (1724–1805), whom Marigny had appointed to train artists for craft industries, was retained as the flower painter on porcelain at Vincennes, and he became the principal painter at the newly established royal manufactory at Sèvres. Mme de Pompadour saw the development of the Sèvres factory as another useful ploy to divert the King, and many of the shareholders were her friends. One of the most extensive early commissions, a service of tableware painted with flowers on a white ground, was made for her. Many more followed, including the complex *pots pourris fontaines* decorated with chinoiserie figures, of which one is in the Getty Museum in California. The *vases à têtes d'éléphants* in the Walters Art Gallery, Baltimore, also decorated with chinoiserie figures, are thought to have been bought by her in 1762. The brilliant pink colour, known as *rose pompadour,* was introduced in 1758. Her inventory provides tantalizing evidence of the extent of her collection. Though little is directly attributable to it, much can – and has – been deduced about the factory production and her taste from studying it.

Mme de Pompadour employed Louis XV's flower painter Madeleine Basseporte to paint flowers for her. Her gardening activities have become the stuff of legend; it was said that to achieve absolute perfection she had the flowers renewed each day in the gardens at her charming little Hermitage at Versailles. The garden was designed for scent, with myrtle, tuberoses, jasmine and gardenias; the formal design was carried out with orange and lemon trees in spite of the fact that the hermitage was meant to be a rustic retreat. Her midwinter garden at Bellevue consisted of spring and summer flowers all made of Vincennes porcelain.

The Marquis d'Argenson reported that the King had ordered from the Vincennes factory 'des fleurs de porcelaine peintes au naturel avec leurs vases pour plus de cent mille livres, pour toutes ses maison de compagne et spécialement pour le château de Bellevue de la Marquise de Pompadour. On ne parle que de cela dans Paris, et véritablement ce luxe scandalise beaucoup.' The Marquis hated Mme de Pompadour so much that his diary became nothing less than an attempt to destroy her in the eyes of posterity.

The inventory taken after her death gives an idea of the sheer quantity of Mme de Pompadour's possessions. The inventory was ordered by Marigny, who was her heir, and took more than a year to compile. Marigny had taken charge of her diamonds and jewellery and her engraved gems. The collections of gold boxes, étuis (small cases), watches, precious sewing implements – including seven *outils à tambour* (sets of embroidery tools), one of solid gold – and other valuable *objets d'art* were taken with the jewellery. Some items, paid for out of the State coffers and deemed not to be her property, were not included, but this factor hardly diminished the value and huge extent of her possessions. She never threw anything away, even things which were no longer useful or pleasing to her. All the collections were sold by Marigny, starting at the end of 1764 with the vast *batterie de cuisine* from the hôtel de Pompadour, and continuing over the next eight months.

As well as the paintings, sculpture and masterpieces of craftsmanship the lists include quantities of wine, horses, saddlery, kitchen equipment, servants' furniture, an enormous collection of textiles and embroideries, upholstery, packets of *papiers des Indes* (Chinese and Japanese painted papers) for screens and shutters, and French wallpaper imitating *papiers des Indes* for wall-coverings. These seem to have come from her favourite supplier, the celebrated *marchand-mercier*, or dealer in furniture and works of art, Lazare Duvaux. Duvaux's *Livre-journal* was published in 1873, and provides fascinating glimpses of the furnishings of Mme de Pompadour's properties. She was responsible for lifting the embargo on the importation of Indian cloth and the manufacture in France of *Indiennes*, which had been imposed in 1686. She also used wallpaper in her private rooms, hitherto unknown for the decoration of a royal residence, and the fashion spread rapidly.

Deeply immersed in the 1860s in their study of Louis XV's mistresses, the Goncourt brothers were disgusted to find no trace of Mme de Pompadour among the portraits in the newly established gallery of French history at Versailles and none of her fabled collection of Sèvres porcelain at the museum attached to the porcelain manufactory. On the other hand, scandalous anecdotes of extravagance still circulated nearly a century after her death, and Edmond de Goncourt reported hearing of the generous pension paid to one of her *ébenistes* (cabinet-makers) simply for providing a *chaise percé* or close stool; the *ébeniste* in question was Migéon, a favourite of hers, and in their study of her the Goncourts doubted the truth of the tale. The fact remained that the expenses of la Marquise remained a synonym for unthinking lavishness. In comparison with her famous successor, she would seem highly constructive, and motivated largely by public interest. Her influence on the French luxury trade stored up a legacy of pre-eminence that was to endure for nearly two centuries.

Madame du Barry

Madame du Barré's residence, Lusienne, is on the hill just above this machine [at Marly]; she has built a pavilion on the brow of the declivity for commanding the prospect, fitted up and decorated with much elegance. There is a table formed of Seve [Sèvres] porcelain, exquisitely done. I forget how many thousands of louis d'ors it cost. The French, to whom I spoke of Lusienne, exclaimed against mistresses and extravagance with more violence than reason in my opinion. Who, in common sense, would deny a king the amusement of a mistress provided he did not make a business of his plaything.

(Arthur Young, *Travels in France and Italy*, London (Everyman edition), 1915, p.83)

Old resentments die hard; in 1787, when Arthur Young wrote the piece quoted above, Louis XV had been dead for thirteen years and Mme du Barry herself was living in discreet retirement. Young was an English tourist and diligent diarist, and his reflections on Mme du Barry underline the extent to which she was, by design, a mirror-image – albeit distorted – of her illustrious predecessor. The great difference between the two of them, however, was of crucial importance; Mme du Barry's hold over the King was physical, he was violently attracted to her sexually, and her deficiencies in culture and intelligence beside Mme de Pompadour faded into insignificance as a result. She was not interested in politics or trying to influence events, and in this, too, she differed from Mme de Pompadour.

Marie-Jeanne Bécu was the illegitimate daughter of a dressmaker, born in Vaucouleurs on the Meuse in 1743. When she was eight her mother took her to Paris and through her protector, a wealthy financier, managed to secure her a convent education before finding her a place in the establishment of the fashionable milliner, Labille. She was very beautiful and quickly caught the eye of the dissolute Comte Jean du Barry, who had the reputation of being little more than a common pimp. He was, in fact, a man of family and education and a collector with a taste for Dutch seventeenth-century painting, but was a debauched character. He installed Marie-Jeanne in his house in 1763, where she presided over the entertainment of the actors and writers who met there and was groomed for the future role that du Barry had planned for her. It was he who stage-managed her introduction to Louis XV at Versailles. In 1768 she was traded in marriage to du Barry's brother, from whom she secured the title necessary to her acceptance at court, for she had by this time achieved her position as the King's mistress. Her convent education had given her a love of reading and several polite accomplishments, including a talent for drawing, but she was not popular with the King's friends, and in order to create a little social circle for her he had to lay out considerable sums in paying debts and pensions to more needy members of the nobility.

In 1769, only five years after he had completed the last portrait of the Marquise de Pomadour, Drouais was exhibiting portraits of the newly established favourite, depicting the Comtesse as *Flora* and disguised as a young man in a silk riding dress. The gossip about her was so exciting that it was impossible to reach the exhibits through a crowd of curious spectators, as

Study for a sculpture of
Madame du Barry as Hebe by
Augustin Pajou (1730–1809);
red chalk drawing, about
1770–74. The sculpture was
never executed though Pajou
made a bust of the Comtesse
in 1770.

Horace Walpole discovered. He wrote from Paris to John Chute: 'I have not yet seen Madame du
Barri, nor can get to see her picture at the *Exposition* at the Louvre, the crowds are so enormous
that go thither for that purpose. As royal curiosities are the least part of my *virtu,* I wait with
patience.' Like many of his contemporaries, Walpole took her to be a former prostitute. In 1770,
despite accepting the hospitality of her Paris house in the Rue de l'Orangerie, the Duchess of
Northumberland painted a very disobliging picture of Mme du Barry:

I own I had expected her to be much handsomer. She had nothing on her head, but 7
fine Diamond Pins, a negligée of Chintz wth very little gold. She is rather of a tall,
middle size, full breasted, and is pretty but not to be call'd handsome, very like the print
but not so well, & has a strong Look of her former profession. Her Complexion is fair &
clear & her skin very smooth but her bloom is entirely gone off . . .

(James Greig (ed.), *The Diaries of a Duchess*, London, 1926, pp.116–17)

More detail follows: her eyes have a 'wanton look', her voice is loud and, greatest condemnation of all, 'her Language is very rough & indelicate when she is angry'. The Duchess was witness to Mme du Barry's foul-mouthed impatience with her servants, but noted the handsome uniforms that they wore. The household was notoriously disorderly; Henry Swinburne, another English traveller in 1787 described the house as 'dirty but magnificent', but her servants stayed with their kind and easygoing mistress for years.

Madame du Barry occupied a suite of rooms in the Petits Appartements at Versailles, and these she had renovated by Ange-Jacques Gabriel. She designed some of the furniture herself. The King gave her the château at Louveciennes, but she went there rarely before his death and her consequent disgrace and banishment. Her most significant architectural contribution was the Pavillon Du Barry at Louveciennes, a single-storey suite of reception rooms built in 1771 for the entertainment of the King. The architect was Claude-Nicolas Ledoux (1736–1806), distinguished exponent of the neo-classical style. The interior was a jewel-box of contemporary French interior decoration and craftsmanship, with sculpture, *boiseries* (carved wood panelling), and exquisite fireplaces, mirrors, sconces, girandoles (candelabra), chandeliers, locks, hinges and bolts, all of the finest quality and latest fashion. Jean-Michel Moreau le Jeune (1741–1813) made a watercolour (Musée du Louvre) of the most glittering entertainment to take place there, the banquet for Louis XV in 1771, in which the luxury and elegance of the interior can be appreciated. It is possible to pick out the magnificent *surtout de table* (table centre) and the gilt-bronze capitals and bases to the pilasters, which, like the window catches and door-handles, were all made by Pierre Gouthière (1732–1812/14).

Mme du Barry indulged the taste for Dutch seventeenth-century paintings absorbed through Jean du Barry, acquiring works from the Choiseul sale by masters like David Teniers (the Younger) and Adriaen van Ostade. Her most distinguished painting – the portrait by Van Dyck of Charles I – was bought, it was said, in order to remind the King of the fate that awaited a monarch who surrendered authority to Parliament. It had belonged to the banker Pierre Crozat, and had been withdrawn from his collection before it was sold to Catherine the Great; it was bought for du Barry from his heir, Baron du Thiers. Mme du Barry later sold it to Louis XVI. She employed an agent to buy paintings and copies of antique statuary for her in Italy, but her real love was for luxurious trifles and for decorative art to enrich her rooms.

Mme du Barry admired some of the artists patronized by her predecessor, among them Greuze and François-Hubert Drouais, who painted her portrait many times, and Carle van Loo, whose best-known subject, *Le Concert du Grand Sultan* (Wallace Collection, London) was reproduced on a Sèvres porcelain plaque and set into the top of a *guéridon* or candlestand by Martin Carlin (d.1785), which is now in the Musée du Louvre. It later belonged to the Empress Josephine. She bought a *Venus* by the sculptor Christophe-Gabriel Allegrain (completed 1767) for Louveciennes. In other ways her taste was more for obvious panache and for novelty.

Her whole claim to be a patron of the arts is called in question by a disastrous lapse of judgement. She commissioned four panels charting *The Progress of Love* from Jean-Honoré Fragonard to decorate the *salon en cul-de-four*, one of the principle reception rooms at the Pavillon de Louveciennes, but when they were finished rejected them in favour of modish, neo-classical subjects – much inferior in every respect – from Joseph-Marie Vien. The irony is that the replacement commission was in the name of artistic progress, to be in keeping with the avant-garde character of Ledoux's architecture. Fragonard's unquestioned masterpieces – for those are what she was sacrificing to her notions of the fashionable – are now in the Frick Collection in New York. Two of the insipidly pretty panels in the antique manner by Vien, *Two Young Greeks swearing Friendship not Love* and *Two Greek Girls finding Love Asleep,* were shown in the Salon of 1773. However, she certainly admired Fragonard; he painted the overdoors in the Grand Salon of the Pavillon, which she bought from Drouais for a high price. Two of them, representing *Night* and *Day*, were commissioned by Mme de Pompadour for Bellevue.

Jean-Jacques Caffiéri made a sparkling portrait bust of her, garlanded with roses (Hermitage, St Petersburg), which has a somewhat meretricious air, but Augustin Pajou (1730–1809), who portrayed her a number of times, used classical restraint. The Goncourt brothers preferred the Caffiéri portrait, finding Pajou heavy and dull. Pajou worked for her on embellishing the Pavillon de Louveciennes. J. B. Pigalle made a bust of her in 1771, which was reproduced in *biscuit de Sèvres,* and she ordered seven of these in 1773 for distribution to her admirers and members of her entourage to whom she owed gratitude.

Mme du Barry's patronage of the Sèvres factory never equalled Mme de Pompadour's, but she is credited with an important innovation in popularizing the use of Sèvres porcelain plaques for the decoration of furniture. Her favoured supplier, the *marchand-mercier* Simon-Philippe Poirier, was, in the 1760s, the biggest buyer of these plaques from the factory, and Arthur Young, on his visit to Louveciennes, commented on Mme du Barry's liking for this style of furniture. A complete table service with her initials in monogram and flower garlands was delivered in 1771. Her accounts with the factory reveal many other items, usually the most difficult to make, and a note excuses the high cost of flower vases on the grounds that a number had been destroyed in the kiln before success was achieved.

Apart from Gouthière's wonderful gilt-bronze work at the Pavillon de Louveciennes, she had plate and precious metalwork by the Germain brothers and Roëttiers, gilded chairs by Louis Delanois (1731–92) and tapestries from the Gobelins factory. She played an important part in establishing the taste for neo-classical and Etruscan styles in furniture and interior fittings.

The Goncourt brothers trawled through her papers to discover evidence of what they called 'the Luxury of a Woman of Pleasure', and had no difficulty in finding 'a frenzy of expenditure'. With their study of the Marquise de Pompadour, the book was part of a trilogy exploring the lives and characteristics of the mistresses of Louis XV, and some exaggeration of wanton behaviour is to be expected. She was a slave to fashion, buying jewels and clothes with reckless abandon. Her accounts with all the various suppliers, such as dressmakers, tailors, milliners, silk mercers, lace merchants, embroiderers and makers of silk flowers, were for enormous sums. But one observer noticed that, after the death of the King and her retirement from court, she wore dresses that she had owned for fifteen years and more.

The jewellery was certainly regarded as an investment against the inevitable future without the King's protection, but the pieces were constantly being altered to conform with the latest mode. One of her stiffened bodices was so encrusted with diamonds that it was given to a jeweller to dispose of when she was in need of funds. The story of the theft of her jewellery from Louveciennes in 1791 has been told in detail, in *The Du Barry Inheritance* by Marion Ward, a book that is also revealing about her life and character, and this is not the place to go over that episode again, involving as it does betrayals and disloyalty among people she trusted. The business of her jewellery cast a shadow over Mme du Barry's last years. She might have survived the Revolution if she had acted differently. The desire to recover her property clouded her judgement and she made a journey to England that left her position undefended at home in 1792; when she returned in 1793 she found that accusations had been brought against her that no amount of protestation could stave off. She was arrested and tried as an enemy of the Revolution and an intending emigré; she was found guilty and guillotined in December 1793.

CHAPTER III

Royal Consorts

Queen Charlotte (1744–1819)
Empress Marie Feodorovna (1759–1828)
Empress Josephine (1763–1814)

*A*lthough neither reigning monarch nor privileged royal mistress, the royal consort was unusual in that she had control of her own finances. Queen Charlotte and Empress Marie Feodorovna were serious-minded German princesses who were both married at the age of seventeen, and there could hardly be a greater contrast in attitude than between these two and the Empress Josephine, who was more like a royal mistress. Temperamentally indolent and frivolous, Josephine had an impulsive attitude to patronage and acquisition, whereas the British Queen and the Russian Empress were brought up to occupy positions of responsibility, and this is reflected in their collecting. Josephine was not born to her destiny, and the predictions of a fortune-teller in her birthplace on Martinique can hardly be considered adequate preparation. Queen Charlotte was often in dire financial straits, and for the same reasons as Josephine – household expenditure, her wardrobe, endless charitable disbursements and her unfailing generosity to her friends – but there was always an undercurrent of duty and philanthropy present in her patronage.

Both Queen Charlotte and the Empress Marie Feodorovna took a highly informed and technically expert view of contemporary art and craft and little was bought on impulse. Queen Charlotte's circle included women collectors – through her friend Mrs Delany she had reports of the progress of the Duchess of Portland's collection – artists, musicians and writers. Many of Marie Feodorovna's tastes were formed in childhood, but her Grand Tour of Europe with her husband opened her eyes to contemporary art and sculpture, Old Masters and the decorative arts. Josephine was the involuntary recipient of masses of Napoleonic plunder – and this effectively defined her collecting – but her own taste was distinctive and influential. The collections of Queen Charlotte and the Empress Josephine survive only in an incomplete state, achieved by their successors' assidious efforts and recovery, so the relative intactness of Pavlovsk is all the more significant. Despite fundamental differences in background, the similarities in taste and intellectual interests of these three women are striking.

Queen Charlotte

The King is well-acquainted with business, and with the characters of the principal manufacturing merchants, and artists, and seems to have the success of our manufacturers much at heart, and to understand the importance of them. The Queen has more sensibility, true politeness, engaging affability and sweetness of temper than any great lady I ever had the honour of speaking to.

(Thomas Bentley in a letter to his partner, Josiah Wedgwood, 1770)

On 8 September 1761 a seventeen-year-old German princess who spoke no English arrived in London. That evening she was married to King George III of Great Britain, a man she had never met. Sophia Charlotte of Mecklenburg-Strelitz had been chosen from a list of candidates of suitable age, status and, most importantly, correct religious faith. She was reputedly charming and with a good heart, able to play the harpsichord and to sing, but she was shy and no beauty.

She was born in the remote Baltic princely domain of Mirow-Strelitz and people wondered if her modest upbringing fitted her for a powerful, cosmopolitan court, but she was to prove her mettle many times over. Her life and her family of fifteen children, two of whom died in childhood, brought unimaginable trials; faced with a husband who was diagnosed as insane, with the opposition of her eldest son – and shamed by the extravagant and dissolute behaviour that masked his qualities – the death in childbirth of the heir presumptive, Princess Charlotte, her namesake and only legitimate grandchild, and the misconstruction of her motives by the British populace, she responded with unshaken dignity and discretion. She had individuality in taste and a sharp intellect; she was also gay and good-humoured with those who knew her.

Being only seventeen years old when she married, the Queen's first essays in patronage were heavily dependent on her husband's influence and on earlier royal taste, but as a Queen-Consort she was free to choose how she should spend her household money. She was not extravagant or self-indulgent, but so hopeless with money and so unable to comprehend budgeting that she was the despair of her advisers. Her collecting was intimately bound up with her successive residences; these were Buckingham Palace, then known as The Queen's House, the White House at Kew (long since demolished), Windsor Castle and Frogmore, situated on the edge of the Great Park at Windsor.

Buckingham House at the end of The Mall was bought as a dower house for the Queen in 1762. The King immediately engaged Sir William Chambers (1723–96), who had been his architectural tutor, to transform it into a comfortable modern residence. The Queen had already begun to employ her husband's talented cabinet-maker William Vile (c.1700–67) with an order for an elegant secretaire or writing desk. Now she commissioned a 'very handsome Jewel Cabinet made of many different kinds of fine Woods in a Mohogany frame very richly Carved . . . lined with black velvet' for her wedding jewels; it was decorated with panels of marquetry and engraved ivory and it cost £138 10s. A little flood of useful articles by Vile followed – bookcases, work-boxes, a music and painting desk, stands for birdcages and 'two Mohogany Houses for a Turkey

Queen Charlotte (detail)
by Allan Ramsay.
The Royal Collection,
by Gracious Permission of
Her Majesty The Queen.

Monkey'. He also accomplished the transfer of the black and gold lacquer panels that had adorned the Duke of Buckingham's Japan room – one of the finest examples in England of japanned chinoiserie – to the adjoining Breakfast Room; for this and for 'making a quantity of new Japan' he charged £572 12s. Horace Walpole, in his *Journal of Visits to Country Houses*, noticed the collection of 'moderne jars of Chinese porcelaine' displayed there in about 1783.

At her coronation Queen Charlotte was laden with pearls and diamonds. These jewels, enriched by gifts and seven great diamonds from the Nawab of Arcot, were a far from negligible item in her collections, but they were either sold after her death or lost to a claim by the Hanoverian Crown in the 1850s. J. Watkins, whose biographical account of the Queen was published in 1819, remembered that she 'did not affect splendour in her apparel . . . She seldom wore jewels except on public ceremonies; and . . . so far from devoting hours to her dress, she

Queen Charlotte's Jewel
Cabinet, by William Vile,
mahogany, 1762.
Royal Collection, Buckingham
Palace, By Gracious
Permission of
Her Majesty The Queen.
Sold after Queen Charlotte's
death, the Jewel Cabinet was
returned to Buckingham
Palace by Queen Mary, who
was remarkably successful at
recovering Queen Charlotte's
dispersed possessions.

studied neatness and simplicity.' At seventeen, when she became Queen, it was only her eyes that
were dazzled, not her mind, and the delusion speedily vanished, but the jewels remained dynastic and ceremonial in their implications. The magnificent gifts that followed the births of
her children adorned her person on the grand occasions of the court. The Queen's collecting
was overshadowed by her husband's and her identity as a collector was lost when her personal
possessions were sold after her death at 'Mr Christie's Great Room, Pall Mall' under a veil of strict
anonymity. The catalogues reveal a treasure-trove of books, prints, drawings, furniture, *objects
d'art*, jewels and decorative trifles. Beginning on 7 May 1819 the sales continued for 35 days.

At the Queen's house the King's rooms remained plain and workmanlike, true to his character, while the Queen's were carpeted, a luxury of which he disapproved. The Queen's Breakfast
Room (i.e. the 'Japan' room) and the Blue Velvet Room, showing the magnificent, patterned
carpets, are illustrated by W. H. Pyne in his *History of the Royal Residences* (vol. II, *Buckingham-*

house, 1819). Enormous quantities of rich fabrics were consumed for hangings and wall-coverings, up to 500 yards per room, all British made. Mrs Lybbe Powys, indefatigable house visitor and commentator, who had gained access in 1767, saw 'The most capital pictures, the finest Dresden and other china, cabinets of more minute curiosities'. Like the King, Queen Charlotte favoured Allan Ramsay – painter of the royal coronation portraits – and Johann Zoffany, both of whom made portraits of the Mecklenburg-Strelitz family for her. She gave the King one of Zoffany's finest works, *The Tribuna of the Uffizi*, a monument to Florentine art. Otherwise her name is associated with Thomas Gainsborough, who portrayed her so attractively and reputedly taught her drawing. She bought Gainsborough's portrait of his dear friend, the musician Carl Friedrich Abel (1723–87), who performed at court on the viola da gamba; the portrait is now in the Huntington Art Gallery, San Marino. There were few paintings or drawings of importance in her sales, apart from two flower-pieces by Jan van Huysum and ten of Gainsborough's drawings.

Zoffany's charming 1765 portrait shows the Queen by her toilet table with her two eldest sons. Through the door to the right can be glimpsed densely hung paintings and one of the flower bouquets, which the Queen loved to 'dispose in the prettiest manner', on the console table. A silver-gilt toilet set, also noticed by Mrs Lybbe Powys, is clearly visible; the most important pieces, including the looking-glass and the candlesticks, were bought at the auction of the Queen's possessions by Earl Grosvenor. It is impossible to imagine that Mrs Lybbe Powys did not notice the lace flounce draping the looking-glass. Queen Charlotte's collection of lace was enormously valuable; it was probably the most costly item in the Queen's wardrobe, worth as much as or more than the precious jewellery.

The Queen favoured Dresden and Chelsea porcelain, and the 'Mecklenburg' service, ordered in 1763 for Duke Adolphus Frederick, is among the masterpieces of the Chelsea factory. It was returned to Buckingham Palace in 1948 and is now displayed in the Bow Room. The Queen's two Chelsea porcelain clocks and a pair of vases in the Rococo taste of about 1760 are in the palace, bought at her sale by the Prince Regent. She had porcelains from Sèvres, Berlin, Vienna, Angoulême and Fürstenberg. Josiah Wedgwood named his newly developed creamware 'Queen's ware' in 1763, and it enjoyed a great success. Fine examples were made for the Queen, and some survive at Buckingham Palace in a collection greatly enlarged by Queen Mary. She also liked Worcester and Derby porcelains and imitation 'Old Japan' from the Coalbrookdale factory.

Queen Charlotte was a celebrated collector of ivories, which featured at the auction as 'Rare and Costly Ivory, Sopha, Chairs, Cabinets, &c'. Made in Madras, the English-style carved furniture veneered with ivory was bought by George III in the sale of contents at West Thorpe House, near Marlow, and given to the Queen in 1781. The Prince Regent bought the suite for the Brighton Pavilion and it is now back in Buckingham Palace. Four ivory chairs with leopards' head arms are still at Frogmore.

Meanwhile the Queen had enormously improved the comfort and cleanliness of Windsor Castle. Mrs Lybbe Powys had been shocked when dining there in 1766: 'The furniture is old and dirty . . . and the whole kept so very un-neat that it hurts one to see almost the only place in England worthy to be styled our King's Palace so totally neglected.' Things had changed by 1788, and she saw 'four or five apartments newly furnished', following the King's decision to live there. Queen Charlotte had been sorry to return from the Queen's House to the cold and often gloomy castle and Mrs Delany, writing in 1778, was struck by the contrast with her private rooms across the Great Court: 'The entrance into the first room was eblouissante after coming out of the sombre apartment in Windsor, all furnished with beautiful Indian paper, chairs covered with different embroidery in ye liveliest colors, glasses, tables, sconces, in the best taste, the whole calculated to give the greatest cheerfulness to the place, and it had its effect.'

Writing from Windsor in 1787 Mrs Delany described the evening occupations of the royal family. She was often invited to join the Queen, princesses and ladies-in-waiting in the drawing room at Queen's Lodge, '*everyone* is employed with their pencil, needle, or knotting'. The Queen was a connoisseur of needlework, showing avid interest in the work of friends who excelled in this art. For 50 years Queen Charlotte contributed £500 a year to an establishment set up to train girls from good but impoverished families in embroidery, as a genteel means of earning their living.

The Queen shared the King's passion for book-collecting, and her library grew to number about 5,000 books. There were large sections on theology and history, arts and sciences, biography and novels and romances. She added to her library until the end of her life, with the newly published novels of 'Mrs Austin' (*sic*) bought as they appeared. One stipulation in the selection of books to be sold was that no items of personal association should be included, but the catalogues of the sales are redolent of her personality. Her botanical publications were exceptional; her scientific botanical knowledge had inspired Lord Bute's dedication to her of his splendidly illustrated *Botanical Tables* of 1784, the great work in nine volumes of which only twelve copies were printed at a cost, it was rumoured, of £10,000. The Queen's presentation copy was sold for a mere £111 6s in the Christie's auction of 1815.

The royal commitment to botany, and the considerable funds expended, were crucially important to maintaining Britain at the forefront of botanical science. At Kew, where she was surrounded by gardens developed by Caroline of Ansbach and the Dowager Princess of Wales, Queen Charlotte was able to pursue her interest in botany. It was a period of huge horticultural expansion, and she set out to draw herself or have drawn by the princesses every one of the plants in the gardens. By this date the gardens contained many thousands of plants, but barely a trace remains of this botanizing. The Viennese Franz Bauer (1758–1840), a Kew draughtsman, was the Queen's teacher. It was he who published the exotic new introduction, *Strelitzia reginae* or Bird of Paradise flower, named in her honour. The Queen's Bauer drawings were sold with the botanical books.

Frogmore was a little 'paradise' where Queen Charlotte and her daughters could spend their days in artistic and scientific pursuits. The house and grounds in Windsor Park were bought for her by the King in 1792. Most indicative of the Queen's serious intellectual pursuits, the Library was a severe, almost masculine room furnished with desks and presses for prints and drawings and decorated with 'library busts' of literary worthies in bronzed plaster. The newly introduced 'Davenport' desk shows her still active patronage of the cabinet-making trade. In about 1810 she bought a novelty in the form of a 'Globe' sewing table made by Morgan &

The Library, Frogmore, from *'Pyne's Royal Residences'*, 1817–20; William Henry
Pyne (1769–1843), publisher, and Charles Wild (1781–1835), illustrator.
The Royal Collection, by Gracious Permission of Her Majesty The Queen.

Saunders, an astonishingly original piece fifteen years ahead of the similar Austrian Biedermeier
designs. A printing press at Frogmore was used to print tracts and pamphlets and the works of
Ellis Cornelia Knight, a writer and historian, who was in the Queen's service from 1805 to 1808.
Queen Charlotte died at Kew on 17 November 1818, after a long and distressing illness. By the end
of the year her executors had taken the hard decision to sell her possessions at auction to benefit
the unmarried royal daughters, and early in the new year her carriages and horses went under the
hammer at Tattersall's. The Christie's sales realized more than £59,000, far more than could have
been raised by selling piecemeal, as the princesses gratefully acknowledged. The last, on 26 August
1819, was the most intimately domestic and the saddest, with Frogmore implicit in every line of
the catalogue. Unascribed paintings on velvet, on silk, on glass, needlework pictures and

landscapes in seaweed, with patent lamps of every description, hint at royal artistic activities. It has the desolation of a house clearance, services of porcelain incomplete and the Tunbridge Ware implements for work – i.e. embroidery, knotting, spinning, canvas work – as well as the printing press and its accessories jumbled together in lots fetching hardly more than shillings.

Empress Maria Feodorovna

In 1776, fifteen years after Queen Charlotte's storm-tossed journey to England, a seventeen-year-old German princess, Sophia-Augusta-Dorothea of Württemberg, travelled across the pitiless Russian countryside to marry Paul, son and heir of Catherine II, Empress of all the Russias. At least she had met her husband, if only briefly, and knew that she loved him. She had ten children and outlived five of them; her husband and two of her sons became Emperor. She was loyal and faithful to her difficult, unfaithful and unhappy husband. Paul I succeeded Catherine the Great in 1796; he was suspected of madness and was brutally murdered only five years later; his wife survived him for 27 years.

Catherine was well pleased with her daughter-in-law and described her as having 'the figure of a nymph and a complexion of lilies and roses'. Paul discovered that she was serious minded and reserved, well educated in history and literature and bilingual in French and German – her library eventually numbered 5,000 volumes – that she was musical, able to embroider beautifully, and understood the principles of gardening and the natural sciences, notably botany. She was eager to learn Russian and to meet his demanding standards in her own conduct and that of her household. This included the utmost discretion in her financial dealings. Artistic talents, developed with almost professional dedication, were to emerge later. She mastered cameo-carving, ivory-turning, medal-engraving and botanical illustration. Her talent impressed Catherine, one of the most important gem-collectors in any age. The Wedgwood factory in England reproduced her cameo portraits of Catherine II and Paul I as jasperware medallions.

Maria Feodorovna's formidable mother-in-law celebrated the birth in 1777 of a grandson, the future Alexander I, by instantly removing the child into her own control and giving the young parents an estate on the outskirts of St Petersburg, which came to be known as Pavlovsk. Paul's interest in Pavlovsk effectively ceased when in 1784 Catherine gave him the fortress-like palace of Gatchina, where he could more freely indulge his military obsessions, but it remained the tranquil centre of his turbulent life. For his wife Pavlovsk was an occupation of fascinating interest and creative fulfilment, her exclusive domain, and Paul gave it to her in 1788. Marie Feodorovna made a life's work out of the construction and furnishing of the exquisite palace and its dependencies, and the landscaping of the English-style park. It was a country retreat and even after being enlarged into an imperial residence in 1792 it never lost its look of being a country house or *dacha*. The first architect to work there was Catherine's favourite, Charles Cameron. The first stone was laid on 6 June 1782, and work was completed in 1794.

Miniature portrait of the Empress Marie Feodorovna, wife of Catherine the Great's son and heir, Paul II of Russia, *c.*1797; attributed to Giovanni-Batista Lampi.

Acquiring the paintings, sculpture, furniture and decorative pieces that eventually filled the palace started during a European Grand Tour in 1781. The collections made on these travels conform, broadly speaking, to the prevailing Rule of Taste, with appreciation of Classical art as a recurring theme, and, as far as the Old Master paintings were concerned, a bias towards the seventeenth century. Many modern artists were commissioned, and purchases were made from the leading craftsmen and manufacturers.

The Emperor and Empress adopted the pseudonyms of Comte and Comtesse du Nord, and their progress can be followed in reports by the periodical *Nouvelles de St Petersburg*. This thin veil of anonymity did not inhibit their hosts from laying on lavish fêtes and receptions at every stage, and they travelled through Europe in a triumphal progress. In addition to attending glittering receptions, operas, regattas in Venice and al fresco supper parties, time was spent in diligent sightseeing. They visited botanical gardens and collections of scientific interest, and in Naples they climbed Vesuvius with Sir William Hamilton. In Rome they were received by Pope Pius VI, who presented them with a model of Trajan's Column incorporating an ingenious mechanism that allowed a stone to fall through the centre and then climb back up to the top. He also gave them a superb example of mosaic-work, a view of the Colosseum by Aguatti, which hangs in the palace today.

In Rome they bought seventeenth-century Italian masters, history paintings from Angelica Kauffman, landscapes from Carl-Phillip Hackert and Louis Ducros, and commissioned portraits from Pompeo Batoni, favourite of the English Grand Tourists. An album by Volpato (1733–1803) of coloured engravings after Raphael was to serve an important decorative purpose. As they progressed they bought at every opportunity, and the French paintings at Pavlovsk are still dominated by the 1782 commissions and purchases, for example, the large views of the antiquities of Rome by Hubert Robert and works by Greuze and Claude-Joseph Vernet.

At the Académie Française in Paris in 1782 the couple were shown ivories turned by Peter the Great in 1717. They revealed themselves to be so formidably well informed that the literary critic La Harpe, who was present, remarked on the contrast with the superficiality of French interest in art and craftsmanship. Chevallier du Coudray wrote: 'M. the comte and Mme. the comtesse du Nord have surprised everyone with their extensive knowledge of arts and trades. In our factories they enter into the tiniest detail with the workers . . .' Here are echoes of Josiah Wedgwood's partner, Thomas Bentley, describing George III and Queen Charlotte in 1770.

Meanwhile, Louis XVI and Marie Antoinette conducted their guests round their factories, showering them with lavish gifts. Marie Antoinette gave them an exquisite Sèvres toilet set of sculptural and jewelled hard-paste porcelain, still in the State Bedroom at Pavlovsk; she pointed out that the set bore Marie Feodorovna's arms (like all the gifts, it was really a diplomatic present from the King). At the Savonnerie factory they were given twelve panels after Oudry's designs from the *Fables de la Fontaine*, six carpets and covers for an extensive set of seat furniture. Intensive shopping provided the finest French gilt-bronzes, clocks, lamps, candelabra, sconces and fireplace furniture. Furniture was ordered from some of the most important Parisian makers, Henri Jacob, Martin Carlin and Adam Weisweiller.

Pavlovsk, under Marie Feodorovna's direction, managed to retain a feminine freshness and delicacy. White and gold for the decoration admirably set off the fine pictures, tapestries and gilt-bronze light-fittings. Her own apartments were hung with some of the most ravishing flowered silks ever made. Consistency throughout was due to an exceptional degree of readiness on her part to do whatever was needed to ensure progress was made in all aspects of the work. Purchasing and palace proceeded together, and devices to show works of art to advantage were incorporated into the design, such as the use of curved walls in the Tapestry Room and in Marie Feodorovna's Library to intensify the effect of the crimson-rose background of the Gobelins tapestries. The fireplace in the Tapestry Room is purely ornamental, its large overmantel mirror reflecting the tapestry opposite and apparently altering the shape and dimensions of the room. Four of Hubert Robert's Roman views were set into the panelled walls of the small ballroom, and the Savonnerie tapestry fables were inset around Paul's Library. Here, low bookcases at dado-height made a continuous pedestal all round the room for the display of antique sculpture. The Volpato prints after Raphael's Vatican decorations acquired in Rome were set into the walls of the New Study in Paul's private apartments.

The Grand Tour purchases inspired Russian design and craftsmanship. Marie Feodorovna combined Russian, German, French and English work and somehow managed to preserve a harmonious effect. In her Dressing Room a toilet service with sculptural biscuit figures and *grisaille* plaques on an apple-green ground, made by the St Petersburg Imperial Porcelain Factory (1800–03), bid fair to rival the Sèvres set that inspired it. Weisweiller's fine desk with gilt-bronze caryatids at the corners was inset with a large Wedgwood jasperware plaque designed by the sculptor John Flaxman in 1778, and another large Wedgwood plaque was let into an earlier mahogany-and-ormolu Russian console table. Brilliantly coloured and crisply detailed Beauvais tapestries were used to cover chairs designed by Andrée Voronikhin. Voronikhin emerged as a master-designer, particularly after a disastrous fire in 1803, when the Empress's library of books and engravings was destroyed along with many of the rooms. He restored the interior to its former appearance, turning out furniture, porcelain, magnificent stone fireplaces for Marie Feodorovna's bedroom, and vases of hardstone and amber – a prized Russian specialty, made at Yekaterinburg and Peterhof – for the Grecian Hall and the Lantern Room, his masterpiece. The St Petersburg Imperial Glass House provided chandeliers and tables combining jewel-like coloured glass and intricate cut designs.

In the Dining Room four views of the Pavlovsk park painted in 1800 by A. Martynov, the first Russian artist whose work entered the Hermitage collection, mimicked Hubert Robert's views of Rome. The following year Marie Feodorovna's idealistic eldest son, Alexander, succeeded as Emperor and the push to establish Russian art began in earnest. The 1,000-piece Guryevsky service, decorated with views of the palace and park and costumed peasants in country pursuits, from the Imperial Porcelain Factory, was ordered for the Empress by Alexander in 1807. Her State Bedroom and dressing room already provided a showcase in the palace. She described these rooms herself in 1795:

> *The ceiling [of the dressing room] is vaulted, painted with a cradle of roses; the walls*
> *are divided into panels painted with views of Pavlovsk in borders of roses . . . the*
> *furniture is covered with beautiful white toile, with rose borders, made at Mulhouse;*
> *the chaise-longue and chairs varnished white.*

She had a dressing table and stool of Tula steel by the master iron-forger Semion Samarin, purchased at great cost and given to her by Catherine. For the State Bedroom there was a wall covering of white *pékin* painted with different *trophées champêtres* after the designs of Willem van Leen, celebrated flower painter . . . the great bed, armchairs, chaise-longue, carved and gilded in

Paris [by the French furniture-maker Henri Jacob], covered in white *pékin* painted in tempera [by Mettenleiter] like the wall covering.

Much of the palace furniture was executed in native woods by David Roëntgen's pupil Heinrich Gambs, who became the leading St Petersburg cabinetmaker. Gambs was a protegé of Marie Feodorovna, and her artistic productions in a variety of media – miniatures on parchment and opaline glass as well as engraved gems and imitation cameos in papier mâché – were incorporated into his furniture for the palace. Desks for Paul and his wife, designed by Brenna in the manner of Roëntgen and made by Ott and Gambs, were ornamented with ivory columns and cameos made by her. As a present for her husband she made an open Ionic temple of ivory and amber with his portrait in cameo in the centre.

With Paul's accession as Emperor an upper storey was added to the curving wings of the palace for picture galleries. After his death Marie Feodorovna continued buying pictures, and the masterpiece of the collection is probably Bronzino's *Madonna and Child with St John the Baptist*. She bought a *Mary Magdalene* by Carlo Dolci, works by Alessandro Turchi (1578–1648), Annibale Caracci and Dutch landscapes by Roelandt Savery (1576?–1639), de Moucheron, and Karel Dujardin (1622–78). Modern Flemish landscapes by Simon Denis complemented the Hackerts that were acquired in 1782. Nicholas I, her third son, gave her paintings by Guido Reni the year before her death.

Marie had been educated to take a keen interest in gardening. The natural history section of her library numbered nearly 2,000 volumes, including guides to the botanic gardens at Kew, Chantilly, Malmaison, Berlin and Weimar. She assembled lists of the rare flora of Pavlovsk and albums of botanical drawings. The many features in the park, such as the simply furnished 'hermitage', the Swiss chalet, the aviary, the dairy and the 'Rose Pavilion', recall the Grand Duchess's upbringing at Etupes, her father's summer residence, where she learned her gardening and botanizing skills. Plants came from all over the world; oaks from Finland, bulbs from Holland, rare plants from England, some her own choice and some as gifts. Members of the Russian nobility gave her fruit trees for her orchard and hothouses. In 1795 she was building a new conservatory and wanted to try plants from South Africa, the Cape and the South Seas. Through Sir Joseph Banks, George III sent 126 plants from Kew. She would spend an hour a day in the hothouse learning the names of the plants and drawing them as they came into flower. Always fanatically prudent in all her expenditure, she often managed to obtain plants and trees for nothing.

Pavlovsk was twice completely destroyed, by the 1803 fire and by the Germans during World War II. It narrowly escaped devastation in the early years of the Revolution, and the 1930s saw terrible abuse and neglect of the building and contents. The palace is exceptionally well documented, notably by a large body of correspondence in the palace archive. Marie Feodorovna made what amounted to an inventory of the decoration and furnishings of the private apartment in a long letter to her mother in 1795. Architects' drawings by Cameron and others survive from all stages of the building, along with a large number of contemporary views of the park and its pavilions, all of which enabled the remarkable restoration to be undertaken. Pavlovsk re-opened in 1976.

Empress Josephine (detail) by Pierre-Paul Prud'hon. Musée du Louvre, Paris.

Empress Josephine

'Malmaison, c'est Joséphine'; even if this wasn't strictly true – the contrast with her modest rose-strewn house in Paris was too marked and to a large extent the grandiose works of art and furnishings were wished upon her – it was stamped with her personality. In the spring of 1799, with Napoleon absent on his victorious Egyptian campaign, she accomplished her previously frustrated ambition to buy Malmaison. It had been an attractive property in the eighteenth century, surrounded by a garden in the fashionable Anglo-Chinese taste. Although deeply in debt, she embarked on the refurbishment of the badly neglected house and estate as a setting for her fast-growing collections of paintings, sculptures, antiquities, curiosities, rare *objets d'art* and jewels.

She established her famous gardens and her menagerie of animals and rare birds. She retreated to Malmaison after the divorce from Napoleon in 1809, surrounded by the accumulations of a life of unimagined grandeur.

In the autumn of 1799 Bonaparte accomplished the overthrow of the outworn Directory and made himself master of France. Both he and his wife had travelled a very long way from their origins. His wife was born Marie-Joseph-Rose Tascher de la Pagerie on a sugar plantation in the French colony of Martinique, and was known as Rose until she met Napoleon, who called her by the name Josephine. They married in 1796. With Napoleon's elevation to First Consul, Josephine's attractive, but now inappropriate, Parisian home was exchanged for the Tuileries palace, where she was haunted by the ghostly presence of Marie Antoinette and always felt unhappy.

Malmaison was to be different, where something approaching a private life could be enjoyed. Laure Junot, Duchess d'Abrantés, has left a detailed description of life at Malmaison in her gossipy and indiscreet *Mémoires*. Napoleon came to love Malmaison and personally directed the creation of a suitably regal residence. Furiously impatient of any delay he harried the architects Percier and Fontaine to finish each successive scheme in no more than ten days, and as Fontaine's diary reveals, it was done.

Josephine was rare – even unique – among the queens of France in being free to make a collection without any of the pressures of royal etiquette. She was charming and generous, not brilliantly intelligent, but artistic and with a highly developed aesthetic sense. She was hopelessly inconsistent, being both compulsively unfaithful and insanely jealous of her husband's *affaire*s. She suffered from terrible headaches and cried copiously at the slightest provocation, but she was utterly fascinating. She was wildly extravagant, buying clothes and jewels with abandon, and her debts were so phenomenal that they had to be concealed from her husband. An inventory of her wardrobe taken in 1809 gives staggering totals: for example, 673 dresses of velvet or satin and 202 summer dresses, 980 pairs of gloves, 252 hats and 60 cashmere shawls; 520 pairs of shoes were bought in that year alone.

Josephine's collecting instincts did not extend to orderly arrangement, and many who saw the rooms at Malmaison were horrified by the jumble and incongruity of the juxtapositions. The extensive library was curiously impersonal, a litany of the great classics in plays, poetry, travels and history, illuminated by Josephine's interest in art, music and botany, but bindings with her arms or cypher are very rare. The Belvedere at the château and a small property on the estate at Bois-Préau contained an old-fashioned cabinet of curiosities; Egyptian mummies were jumbled together with ostrich eggs, Chinese costume, African ritual objects and stuffed birds. The gardens were full of statuary from the gardens of the old royal palaces. Marble bas-reliefs showing the pleasures and duties of the countryside came from Marie-Antoinette's dairy at Rambouillet.

The most valuable of Josephine's pictures were spoils from Bonaparte's campaigns, fall-out from the cavalcade of pictures arriving in Paris. Egyptian antiquities were a by-product of archeological activities conducted in the wake of Napoleon's victorious armies. Gifts came from the City of Milan, from the Pope and from the Kingdom of the Two Sicilies. After the battle of Jena in 1806 a collection of Dutch and Flemish seventeenth-century masterpieces, crated and

The Sleep of Venus and Cupid, oil on canvas, 1806 by Marie-Françoise-Constance Mayer-Lamartinière (1775–1821). Wallace Collection, London. Bought from the artist by the Empress Josephine for Malmaison. Constance Mayer was Prud'hon's pupil and companion until her suicide in 1821, and this painting may be a collaboration with him. Prud'hon was one of Josephine's most admired artists.

secreted in vaults by the Landgrave of Hesse-Cassel, was shipped to France and presented to Josephine for Malmaison.

The Grande Galerie at Malmaison was built in 1809 to house Old Masters and Classical antiquities. There were works by Leonardo da Vinci, Raphael, Andrea del Sarto, Carlo Dolci, Rembrandt, Rubens, Claude and the foremost Dutch seventeenth-century artists and no less than sixteen paintings by Paulus Potter and five by David Teniers the Younger. About forty of the most important paintings were bought in 1814 by the Russian Emperor Alexander I, for the Hermitage in St Petersburg. These included a Leonardo, a Raphael, a Rubens and a Carlo Dolci, and most of the Hesse-Cassel pictures, among them Rembrandt's *Descent from the Cross*, the four ravishingly romantic *Hours of the Day* by Claude, a wonderful Ter Borch, all the Potters and three of the pictures by Teniers. Although inevitably a number of them have new attributions – for example the Leonardo is now called Luini and the Titian has been demoted to his son – they are impressive by any standards and bear comparison with masterpieces from the Walpole and Crozat collections bought by Catherine the Great. The finest of the remaining Italian pictures were taken to Munich by Josephine's son, Eugène de Beauharnais.

The choice of contemporary works reflects Josephine's own taste. She was an important patron of the sculptor Antonio Canova. She told the Marquise de la Tour du Pin that Canova had presented her with his *Danseuse* and *Hebe*, and she eventually owned three more major pieces, his group of *Cupid and Psyche* exhibited at the Paris Salon in 1808, a figure of *Paris*, also shown in 1808, and the premier version of *The Three Graces,* completed only shortly before her death. All are now in the Hermitage; the *Cupid and Psyche, Danseuse* and *Hebe* were bought in 1814 and the *Paris* in 1816 by Alexander I; the *Graces* was inherited by Eugène and bought from his heirs by Nicholas II.

Napoleon's addiction to the blind poet Ossian (a creation of the Scottish poet Macpherson) inspired Girodet's romantic Salon painting of 1802, *Apothéose des Héros français morts pour la Patrie pendant la guerre de la Liberté,* showing the dead heroes received into paradise by Ossian, and its Ossianic pendant by François Gérard. They were commissioned for Malmaison and set the seal of literary Romanticism on Josephine's taste. Alexandre Lenoir, the antiquarian who was her curator as well as director of Napoleon's Musée des Monuments Français, stimulated her interest in the Middle Ages, and she owned many paintings in the so-called *style troubadour*. She had no less than seven by one of the foremost troubadour painters, Fleury-François Richard (1777–1852). Richard was named 'Painter to Her Majesty' in 1808.

Josephine admired the contemporary neo-classical landscapists such as Bidauld, Chauvin, Thiénon, Du Perreux, Demarne, Turpin de Crissé and Nicolas Taunay. Two works, Taunay's *Josephine while travelling receives the News of a Victory,* and Lecomte's *Josephine at Lake Garda,* brought welcome realism and modesty into the flagrantly romantic propagandist record of Napoleonic military triumphs presented by Baron Gros – incidentally, another of Josephine's protégés. Lancelot Théodore Turpin de Crissé (1781–1859) was made Chamberlain to Josephine in 1809, and it was rumoured that he was her lover, largely on the strength of a charming sketchbook, preserved at Malmaison, recording expeditions that they enjoyed together.

The flower painters included Madame Vallayer-Coster, Gerard van Spaendonck and both his celebrated followers, Jan-Frans van Dael and Pierre-Joseph Redouté (1759–1841). Josephine owned van Dael's masterpiece, *The Tomb of Julie* (returned to Malmaison in 1874) and its pair, *The Offering to Flora* (now lost), as well as four more of his works, and a stunning collection of botanical and natural history paintings on vellum, among them Redouté's illustrations to *Les Liliacée,* (issued in eight volumes, 1802–16*)* and several other of his publications. Opinions differ as to how much Josephine paid for the *Liliacées* watercolours, but it was a very large sum. Only fourteen of the sixteen folios are listed in her inventory, since two were not completed until after her death; nonetheless the valuation was absurdly low at 5,500 frs It was disputed by the heirs and raised to 20,000 frs. The *Liliacée* watercolours were inherited by Eugène and went to the family seat of the Dukes of Leuchtenberg in Bavaria. They descended in the family until 1935, when they were sold. They surfaced in 1985 and were sold again at Sotheby's in New York.

The Empress Josephine at Malmaison by Baron François Gerard (1770–1837).
Musée du Château, Malmaison.

Redouté was recruited to record Josephine's most personal creation, the celebrated flower garden and collection of plants at Malmaison. The watercolours were originally conceived as decoration for her bedroom. They were published in two volumes (1803–5) with text by the horticulturalist Ventenat. Josephine collected seeds avidly, from her family in Martinique, from the Jardin des Plantes in Paris and from friends all over the world. Notwithstanding war and an embargo on trade with the British, rare plants continued to arrive from the Royal Botanic Gardens at Kew and from English nurserymen. During her time 184 new species flowered in the gardens and hothouses. Redouté's watercolours for the *Liliacées* and *Les Roses* were produced at a high point in botanical illustration and are acknowledged to be among the loveliest of all time. Redouté's last project for Josephine was *the Déscription des plantes rares à Malmaison* (1812–17), including the plants at her dismal property at Navarre, to which she was banished by Napoleon when he remarried.

One of Josephine's finest and most cherished possessions was the silver-gilt combined tea, coffee and toilet service by Marie-Joseph Gabriel Genu, Martin-Guillaume Biennais and Jean-Baptiste-Claude Odiot. The individual pieces are supremely elegant neo-classical forms crisply ornamented with engraving and chasing. Josephine's jewel cabinet was the combined product of some of the greatest talents of the period, made to a design inspired by the painter and designer Pierre-Paul Prud'hon, and by the metal-workers Jacob-Desmalter and Thomire (Musée du Louvre). The gilt-bronze 'Victory' candelabrum designed for Malmaison by Thomire is a signature piece of the Empire style. Josephine's magnificent diamonds came from the leading Parisian jeweller, Nitot. The porcelain manufactory of Honoré Dagoty was named manufacturer to the Empress. The maker of Josephine's harp – 'Cousieau père et fils of Paris' – on which, it is said, she always played the same tune, was also styled 'maker to the Empress'. The silks at Malmaison were ordered from the Lyons firm of Camille Pernon, the first to utilize the technical innovations of Joseph-Marie Jacquard (1752–1834). Pernon was succeeded in 1808 by his nephews, Grand frères, who perfected the art of printing in colours on silk velvet. Even after Napoleon and Josephine's divorce in 1809 the furious rate of commissioning and acquiring hardly faltered.

The widespread impact of Napoleonic taste is the more remarkable given the brevity of his reign from 1799 to 1815. Art can serve political ends and Napoleon was in a tearing hurry to stamp the seal of legitimacy on his regime. At Compiègne and St-Cloud some of Josephine's furniture is still *in situ*; for example, the Yellow Drawing Room in her private apartments at Fontainebleau, where panels of Gros-de-Naples silk embroidered in purple form a background to furniture by Jacob-Desmalter. Rooms in the Empire style survive intact in the hôtel de Beauharnais, now the German Embassy, in Paris. These superb interiors were carried out in 1803, very much under Josephine's influence, for her son Eugène. Many of the artists involved in other imperial projects worked on this house, and it is apparent how Josephine's delicacy could overcome the heavy masculinity of Empire taste.

By 1812 the seeds of disaster were already sown when Napoleon took an exhausted and disaffected nation into a doomed campaign in Russia. Defeat and fall were only two years away. Josephine saw his first exile, and wished that she was still his wife and could share his lonely fate. She did not live to see the second and more frightful banishment to St Helena. In 1814 she attracted renewed attention from the Allies, who gathered in Paris to discuss the terms of peace. Tsar Alexander I visited to assure her of her safety under the new regime and was with her very shortly before she died on 29 May 1814.

Josephine's personal possessions were recorded in an inventory taken after her death and

Hemerocalis fulva by Pierre-Joseph Rédouté (1759–1840), plate from 'Les Liliacées'; water-colour on vellum, 1802–16. Rédouté made some of his finest botanical drawings for the Empress Josephine, who was his most prominent patron.

then dispersed like Queen Charlotte's. The 'house sale' at Malmaison took place in March 1819, just two months before Christie's sold the Queen's collections. The house was inherited by her son, but he never lived there. His widow sold Malmaison in 1829, and it fell into terrible neglect and disrepair, but like the 'little paradise' at Frogmore, it has been restored and many of its contents recovered and it is now open to the public.

The inventory pictures in minutest detail the equipment of an imperial lifestyle, down to the most private items of wardrobe, toilet, linen cupboard, kitchen, cellar and garden shed. With 2,916 entries, it comprises many thousands of items. The breadth of the collections is breathtaking, with paintings by the greatest masters of the Renaissance and about 100 contemporary works rubbing up against modern sculpture, Greek vases, wall-paintings from Pompeii, bronzes from Herculaneum and gold jewellery from Etruria. The value of Josephine's property at the time of her death far exceeded her much vaunted debts, which were, in effect unpaid bills from the last years of her life.

CHAPTER IV

The Duchess of Portland
(1714-85)
and her Circle

The catalogue of the Duchess of Portland's collection is come out. The auction begins on the 24th. Out of the thirty-eight days there are but eight that exhibit anything but shells, ores, fossils, birds' eggs, and natural history. And in the eight days there are hundreds of old-fashioned snuff-boxes that were her mother's, who wore three different every week; and they probably will sell for little more than the weight of the gold. I once asked the Duchess to let me see them; and after two drawersful, I begged to see no more; they were so ugly. Madame de Luxembourg has as many, but much finer and [more] beautiful. The Hamilton vase is in the last day's sale. It will not, I conclude, produce half of what it cost the Duchess unless it is sent for to the Houghton collection in the north.

(Letter from Horace Walpole written in 1786)

There is a great community of interests among English eighteenth-century women collectors, especially the Duchess of Portland, Lady Betty Germain and Mrs Mary Delany. A peculiar bond was shared by the Duchess and Lady Betty Germain (1680–1769), who both owned important material from Thomas Howard, Earl of Arundel (1586–1646), the first great British collector in the modern meaning of the term. China collecting was a strong link, along with a passion – it was no less – for natural sciences. Bevis Hillier noted in his fascinating analysis of china collecting the frequency with which connoisseurs of old china also collected shells, and to this he might have added fossils and geological specimens. Another uniting factor was a serious and well-informed interest in botany, horticulture and zoology, this last being expressed in the collections of exotic animals and birds that were to be found as an adjunct to many great estates. Aristocratic patronage of botany and plant-hunting was often combined with the study and collecting of antiquities and natural curiosities. Botany was viewed as an appropriate pursuit for women, and it was left to them to promote its study and application in horticulture.

The royal commitment to botany, and the considerable funds expended, were crucially important to maintaining Britain at the forefront of botanical science. Inevitably with the passage of years, the botanizing and plant-collecting women who made important gardens appear less significant now than they did in their own time. They are just a sub-plot in the story of British gardening, not to be compared, for example, with the creators of great masterpieces like Stourhead and Stowe, but the women themselves were serious in their scientific interests. Descriptions, lists and beautiful drawings recording the finest rarities are all we have left of many, if not most, of the collectors' gardens, but these cumulatively constitute a sort of 'paper museum' from which some notion of their character can be understood.

The Duchess of Portland's collecting transcended the boundaries of gender. An auction lasting for 38 days (it began on 24 April 1786) bespeaks an enormous accumulation. The 'Portland Museum' of curiosities was among the largest in Europe, but ownership of the Barberini-Hamilton-Portland Vase (now in the British Museum) makes the Duchess's collection remarkable irrespective of her sex or her myriad collecting passions. She bought the vase only twelve months before her death, but her acquisition of it is enshrined in the name that it has borne ever since, and it stands as a landmark in the possession by women of great works of art.

Walpole remarked of her: 'A simple woman, but perfectly sober and intoxicated only by *empty* vases', but for all his cool appraisal of her collection he was pleased enough with his purchases from the sale, among them 'Queen Bertha's Comb' (now, like the Portland Vase, in the British Museum) and a fine antique head of Zeus Sarapis from the Barberini Collection. He paid over £170 for the little head, but when it came up for sale in 1842 it fetched less than half that sum.

The Duchess of Portland was born Lady Margaret Harley, heiress of the Cavendish, Holles and Harley families and brought up amid a brilliant circle of writers, scholars and artists. Her father, Sir Edward Harley, 2nd Earl of Oxford, was a generous host and the painter Sir James Thornhill (1675–1734) remembered the mixture of splendour and informality that characterized the household. Edward Harley expended huge sums in adding to the library of rarities amassed by his father, Robert, 1st Earl of Oxford, and built up what was almost certainly the largest private library ever assembled in this country, the bulk of which was sold by his widow in 1753. His daughter married the 2nd Duke of Portland in 1734. She brought Welbeck Abbey into the Bentinck family and a large collection of pictures and relics, bought in 1720 by her father from the collection of Thomas Howard, 2nd Earl of Arundel.

Walpole said that the Duchess 'inherited the Passion of her Family for Collecting. At first her Taste was chiefly confined to Shells, Japan & Old China, particularly of blue & white with a brown Edge, of which last she formed a large Closet at Bulstrode; but contenting herself with one specimen of every pattern She could get, it was a collection of odd pieces'. He was sceptical of the celebrated 'Raphael' of *The Holy Family* at Bulstrode Park in Buckinghamshire (bought in 1758 for over £700), believing it to be a copy, but envious, nonetheless, of her fortune which allowed her to collect without counting the cost. He admired the historic relics, which included more

Margaret Cavendish Harley, 2nd Duchess of Portland in coronation robes by Thomas Hudson (1701–79). The portrait is a pair to one by Hudson of the 2nd Duke in coronation costume. Both paintings belonged to the Portland family.

than a dozen Holbein miniatures, cameo portraits in jewelled pendants of Queen Elizabeth I and Mary Queen of Scots, as well as Charles Ist's single pearl earring and the chalice from which he received Communion on the morning of his execution.

Seeing the Duchess through the eyes of Queen Charlotte and of her friend and companion Mrs Mary Delany (née Granville, 1700–88), we are presented with a beguiling figure, the clever member of the Blue Stocking Circle who formed a great collection of antiquities and curiosities. Her 'fine old china' was shown to the King and Queen on their visit to Bulstrode on 12 August 1778 and Mrs Delany remembered that 'they all went in a train thro' the great apart-

The Portland Vase, Alexandrian glass cameo vase, Roman, 1st century BC. The Trustees of the British Museum, London.

ment to the Duchess of Portland's china closet, and with wondering and enquiring eyes admired all her magnificent curiosities.' The Duchess of Northumberland, visiting Bulstrode in 1760, was impressed with the paintings, notably the Snyders and the famous Raphael, and intrigued with the Duchess's Dressing Room 'where there are a thousand curiositys'. This seems to have been not unusual; the Dressing Room next to the State Bedroom at Norfolk House in London was put to the same use. The Duchess of Northumberland would have been even more amazed at the sight of the 'Portland Museum' in the house in Westminster. It was then common practice for collectors to keep their most remarkable possessions in London where fellow enthusiasts and foreign visitors could easily see them.

The Duchess of Portland was fascinated by geology and collected fossils with passion; she gardened and botanized, tended her exotic birds and made shell frames and grottoes. In addition to shellwork she turned in wood and ivory – she had a 'turning room' in her London house – she was an accomplished needlewoman and she designed feather work; she made a herbarium and collected unusual species from the animal and vegetable kingdoms. Walpole was forced to beg a rare red spider for her from Admiral Boscawen (whose wife, Frances, was a member of the Blue Stocking Circle).

The 'Portland Museum'.
Frontispiece from the sale
catalogue of the Duchess of
Portland's collection, 1776.
The Trustees of the British
Museum, London. The
Portland Vase takes a prom-
inent place among a vast array
of shells and natural curiosities.

The Duchess was intimate from girlhood with Mrs Elizabeth Montagu, most famous of
the Blue Stockings, and their letters provide fascinating sidelights on collecting. Elizabeth
Robinson, as she was before her marriage, promises shells from her brother's naval voyages to add
to the Duchess's collection, both as rarities and for grotto-making. She sends descriptions of
gardens visited and in August 1747, mindful of the Duchess's great interest in shellwork, a
carefully detailed account of Lady Fane's grotto at Basildon:

> *The first room is fitted up entirely with shells, the sides and ceiling in beautiful mosaic,*
> *a rich cornice of flowers in baskets and cornucopias, and the little yellow sea snail is so*
> *disposed in shades as to resemble knots of ribbon which seem to tye up some of the*
> *bunches of flowers. There is a bed for the Hermit, which is composed of rich shells, and*
> *so shaded that the curtain seems folded and flowing.*

81

The Duchess writes back of her visits to Sir Hans Sloane (1660-1753), whose cabinet of curiosities was the founding collection of the British Museum, and of exchanging items with him. Both the Duchess and Mrs Montagu were attended by the physician and antiquary Dr Richard Mead, and the Duchess thought his collection superior to Sloane's, admiring in particular an Egyptian mummy with a gilded face. When Dr Mead died in 1754 his collection was put up for sale, and Walpole set his heart on buying the miniatures, even while fearing that it would ruin him. With some relief, mixed with chagrin, he learned that the whole collection had gone to Frederick, Prince of Wales. The miniatures were inherited by George III, and were displayed in Queen Charlotte's apartments at Buckingham House, where they were seen by Mrs Lybbe Powys.

After the death of the Duke in 1762 the Duchess lived mainly at Bulstrode, and Mrs Delany spent many months each year with her after she too was widowed in 1768. The Duchess welcomed into her house many eminent men in her various fields of interest to discuss her collection of curiosities, her cabinet of china, the menagerie of unusual birds and animals, her gardening experiments, and above all her botanizing – her circle included the botanist and explorer Sir Joseph Banks, Banks secretary, the Swedish botanist Daniel Solander and the famous nurseryman, Philip Miller. Among her protégés, her chaplain the Reverend John Lightfoot was in effect her curator; Richard Pulteney, another eminent botanist helped with her shells and Thomas Yeats, the entomologist, organized the insect collection. She employed the leading botanical artist of the day, Georg Dionysius Ehret. In 1769 Mrs Delany wrote to a niece: 'Mr Ehret is here, and she is very busy adding to her English herbal; she has been transported at the discovery of a *new* wild plant, a Helleboria.' The herbal numbered more than 150 plants, recorded in some of Ehret's finest drawings, and the whole collection occupied the best part of a day at the auction with many hundreds of drawings – sometimes as many as 25 to a lot – put up for sale. When Jean-Jacques Rousseau (1712–78) was at Wootton Hall in Derbyshire, taking refuge in England from the scandal of *Emile,* published in 1762, she corresponded with him and they made a joint plant-finding expedition to the Peak District in 1766. These personal contacts were important since much Blue Stocking botanizing was in advance of the proliferating publications in the late eighteenth century.

Walpole was also fascinated by another collector, the Duchess of Portland's friend, Lady Betty Germain, and bought from the auction held in 1770 after her death. Lady Betty was an enthusiastic china collector. Walpole's *Description* (1787) of his pseudo-castle at Strawberry Hill includes this passage on his own china cabinet, which was hung with paper imitating Dutch tiles: 'The following collection was made out of the spoils of many renowned cabinets; as Dr Mead's, Lady Elizabeth Germain's, Lord Oxford's, the Duchess of Portland's and of almost forty more of celebrity.' Lady Betty was the second wife of Sir John Germain and many years his junior. Her three children died young and in recognition of her devotion in looking after them Sir John left his wife the Drayton estate in Northamptonshire and the vast property that he had inherited from his first wife. Lady Betty remained a widow for 50 years and left both fortune and estate to Lord George Sackville, second son of the 1st Duke of Dorset. Walpole visited Drayton in 1763, and noted with envy the rooms crammed with portraits, old china and ancient furniture, all kept with

Portrait of Mary Granville, (Mrs Delany) by
John Opie (1761–1807); oil on canvas, 1780s.
National Portrait Gallery, London.
This portrait of Mrs Delany, with its fine frame
designed by Horace Walpole bearing emblems of
her accomplishments in music and art, was
painted for the Countess of Bute. Another by
Opie was commissioned by George III for
Queen Charlotte and hung in her bedroom at
Buckingham House; it is now at Windsor.

loving care. 'I rummaged it from head to foot', he confessed. 'Examined every spangled bed, and
enamelled pair of bellows . . . the garden is just as Sir John Germain brought it from Holland;
pyramidal yews, *treillages*, and square cradle walks, with windows clipped in them.' He had rummaged to good effect some three years earlier, when Lady Betty gave him a handsome present, the
chased and engraved silver-gilt clock, supposed to have been given to Anne Boleyn by Henry VIII,
now in the Royal Collection. In a somewhat roundabout fashion Walpole came into possession
of one of Lady Betty's most curious objects, the 'magic' mirror of polished black stone from the
seventeenth-century alchemist Dr John Dee (now in the British Museum).

Strangely, Walpole did not remark on the cameos and intaglios from the Arundel
Collection that had come to Germain from his first wife. Lady Betty offered the gems to the
British Museum for £10,000, but they were declined and in 1762 passed to her niece Lady Mary
Beauclerk, who married into the Marlborough family. In this way they entered the celebrated
collection of the 4th Duke of Marlborough (sold at auction in 1875). The ownership of the gems

by two women, one a recognized collector, is barely recorded as they pass from Earl to Duke. Her most famous picture, the so-called Leonardo of 'a laughing boy with a plaything in his hand', was bequeathed to Sir William Hamilton; it was bought by William Beckford of Fonthill at Hamilton's picture sale in 1801 and descended to his daughter, the Duchess of Hamilton. It is now called *Boy with a Puzzle* and attributed to Bernardo Luini (c.1481–1532).

Lady Betty is one of the very few modern collectors to be credited as a former owner in Beckford's sale catalogue. Lot 51 on the fifth day in October 1822 is 'A magnificent vase of carved ivory, with a frieze of infants carved by the celebrated Fiamingo, and superbly mounted with silver gilt. It formerly belonged to the famous Earl of Arundel, and was left by Lady B. Germaine to the late Margravine of Anspach, at whose sale it was purchased'. It is now in the British Museum.

Lady Betty's curios and fine china were sold at auction after her death in a sale lasting four days, from 7 March 1770, and comprising 'the noble collection of Pictures, Miniatures, Bronzes, Gems . . . of the Right Honorable Lady Elizabeth Germaine Lately Deceased Being the Collection of the Old Earls of Peterborough and also of the Arundelian Collection'. Again, as in the case of the Duchess of Portland, a sale catalogue has to act in part as an inventory to a lost collection. She had been a frequent guest of her friends the Duke and Duchess of Dorset at the home of the Sackvilles, Knole in Kent, and her china room and bedroom there are preserved with some of her possessions; these include a little four-poster bed lined with cream quilting and topped with ostrich plumes at each corner, a spinning-wheel and a ring box, all presided over by her portrait in a blue brocaded dress. The pot-pourri at Knole was always made to her recipe.

Mrs Delany shared the Duchess of Portland's passion for natural history – she had been a keen gardener and collector of new plants – and her great achievement, nearly 1,000 cut-paper mosaic studies of flowers, is preserved in the British Museum. The flowers were sent from the hothouses of their acquaintances and by order of the Queen from Kew. The accuracy of these 'paper mosaics' was admired by Sir Joseph Banks. Mrs Delany was a collector of china, shells and minerals and rare plants, as much as her slender resources allowed. Picture collecting was out of her reach financially, but her sensibility, acquired through the diligent copying of works that she admired, probably equalled or exceeded more fortunate connoisseurs. She was an outstanding embroideress, another accomplishment to share with Queen Charlotte. These interests were all reflected in the possessions detailed in her Will, which acts almost as an inventory of her collection. It is published as an appendix to the six volumes of Mrs Delany's *Autobiography and Correspondence,* edited by Lady Llanover.

As keen china collectors, the Duchess and Mrs Delany had heard of Wedgwood's important commission from Catherine the Great, and in June 1774 Mrs Delany described in a letter her visit to see the completed 'Frog' service: 'It consists I believe of as many pieces as there are days in the year, if not hours . . . every thing that can be wanted to serve a dinner'. She was very taken with the decoration: '. . . the drawings in purple, the borders a wreath of leaves, the middle of each piece a particular view of all the remarkable places in the King's dominions neatly executed. I suppose it will come to a princely price; it is well for the manufacturer, which I am glad of, as his ingenuity and industry deserve encouragement.'

Gold and enamel portrait box set with four miniatures by Christian Frederick Zinke (1663/4–1767) including on the cover Mrs Delany in a russet dress, inside the cover the Duchess of Portland in a blue dress and on the base Mrs Elizabeth Montagu in Tudor costume as Anne Boleyn, 1740. The sittings to Zincke for these miniatures are described in the letters of Mrs Delany and Mrs Montagu.

Mrs Delany also recounts many adventures in pursuit of shells and minerals in her letters; but more importantly she was privy to the prolonged negotiations between the Duchess and Sir William Hamilton which resulted in the purchase of the Portland Vase. They went to view the Vase at Hamilton's London hotel on New Year's Eve 1783. It had been in the Barberini family for 150 years and was already famous when Hamilton acquired it from the Scottish dealer James Byres. The price was such that he could barely afford it and he probably always meant to sell it on. The sale was first mooted at the end of 1783, arranged though Hamilton's niece Mary, who had been in the royal household until the year before and was a member of the Blue Stocking Circle. She had been a correspondent for many years of Mrs Delany and the Duchess and had been staying at Bulstrode for some months that summer.

Sir William dangled a vague threat of offering the vase to Catherine the Great in order to bring the sale off, and the business was concluded in June 1784, with Hamilton asking Mary to convey the vase 'secretly to the Duchess'. In spite of his teasing her with rival purchasers the

Duchess seems to have borne Sir William no ill-will and, according to Mary's diary, in the course of their business discussions she showed him her collections; for example 'some very rare & beautiful pieces of Japan, some Medals, &c'. In September he sent a pedestal for the vase, made by his cabinet-maker, Crighton, in Soho. The vase was installed along with the rest of the 'Portland Museum' in the Duchess's London house in the Privy Garden at Whitehall.

Mary's diary written at Bulstrode gives a vivid picture of the cultural pursuits in aristocratic intellectual circles. The days were spent telling historical anecdotes, reading the newspapers, looking over jewelled lockets and miniatures, early manuscripts, fossils, drawings of shells, birds and flowers and working at embroidery and other pastimes. Mrs Delany had a spinning-wheel and Mary sat knotting a fringe. The Duchess read letters dating from the previous century and on one occasion told a scurrilous story about Sarah, Duchess of Marlborough. Mrs Delany gave a shocking account of the doings of the famous Hell Fire Club. Mary Hamilton fed the menagerie: 'Every bird and animal in this place, of wch there are a great variety, are tame and sociable.' Never idle, she mended a firescreen that Mrs Delany had decorated many years before with coloured prints, copied manuscripts, sorted cases of shells and made paper cases for the manuscripts. In London in August (1784) we find her at Mrs Delany's 'very busy arranging some curious old China in a cabinet. This dear woman wd not trust any hands but mine to do it; I wash'd it, & she wiped it. Two days later she was there again and arranged a Glass Cabinet of fossils, Spas & Minerals for her, she gave me a few specimens. When I came home I found a Present from good Mrs. Handcock of some valuable small tea cups of Egg shell China wch she bought in Holland many years ago & knowing I was beginning a collection, she kindly sent me.'

Mrs Delany's health was of concern to Mary, but in spite of her fourteen years' seniority it was the Duchess whose life was coming to an end. She was ill only briefly and died on 17 July 1785, leaving Mrs Delany at the age of 85, bowed down with intense grief. The King offered her a home at Windsor, and there she spent the last three years of her life, no longer able to practice her art, through blindness, but still an interested observer of events in the royal circle. Her portrait in old age, painted by John Opie (1761–1807), hung in the Queen's bedroom in London.

The ubiquitous presence in these circles of the great explorer, naturalist and scientific polymath, Sir Joseph Banks – the *de facto* director of the Royal Botanic Gardens at Kew and correspondent of botanizing monarchs across Europe, whose tentacles reached into the lives of many of the *virtuosi* and their protegées – is a reminder that both his wife and his sister were collectors. Lady Banks (née Dorothea Hugesson; 1758–1828), collected Chinese porcelain. She was described by her husband as being 'a little old-china mad'. Nevertheless, in 1807 he put his mind to the classification and cataloguing of the collection at Spring Grove, the retreat at Isleworth just across the river from Kew, where Banks and his wife went to escape the pressures of London and their Soho Square house which had gradually transmuted into a centre of scientific research. Banks approached the task as if compiling a scientific paper, reading every known publication on the subject available at the time. He was a great believer in national self-sufficiency, and the porcelain display was intended for English manufacturers 'who might wish to consult it for the purpose of improving their Wares'. The manuscript catalogue survives in the papers of the Knatchbull-Hugesson family. Illustrated in watercolour with some 40 items of porcelain, it is among the most attractive documents of eighteenth-century collecting. It bears a dedication to Lady Banks:

> *This little essay founded entirely on her correct Judgement in Collecting & her excellent Taste in arranging and displaying the Old China with which she has ornamented her Dairy at Spring Grove, is offered to Lady Banks, as the pure tribute of A Husband's affection unabated during an Union of 27 Years Marriage.*

Sarah Sophia Banks (1744–1818), who shared her brother's interests and spent her life as his hostess and amanuensis, was an enterprising collector on her own account. For convenience she wore a dress with two large pockets, always stuffed with books; she owned an immense quantity of coins and tokens, along with her pioneering collection of printed ephemera, consisting of engravings, costume prints, caricatures, playbills, admission tickets, trade-cards, visiting cards, letterheads and newspaper clippings. She left her collection to Lady Banks, who immediately handed it over to the British Museum, and the tens of thousands of items were shared between the Prints and Drawings Department and the British Library.

Collecting provided a network of female friendships and a particular social milieu, which enlarged the horizons of women far beyond the concerns of fashion, domesticity and philanthropy to which they were customarily confined. It meant that they had contact on an equal footing with men prominent in Enlightenment circles, scientists, architects, artists and fellow antiquarian enthusiasts. The usual round of countryhouse visiting became a voyage of exploration rather than a social obligation. The King and Queen were indefatigable visitors to sights that interested them and many accounts survive of occasions when a household was caught unawares by their arrival. The King would insist that no ceremony should be observed and looked with informed interest at everything. Even though much of the physical legacy is lost, or at least dispersed so that the integrity of the collections is now hard to envisage, the flavour of this is conveyed with startling immediacy in letters and diaries, none more than Mrs Delany's.

CHAPTER V

The Decorative Arts

Lady Dorothy Nevill (1826–1913)
Lady Charlotte Schreiber (1812–95)
Alice de Rothschild (1847–1922)
Queen Mary (1867–1953)
Princess Marie Louise (1872–1957)

China vessels are playthings for women of all ages.

(Joseph Addison, writing in 1714)

In the eighteenth century, collections of the decorative arts were a mixture of old and new, often with the new predominating. Even then rich ladies, like Mme du Barry, were buying novelties from the Sèvres factory, in the form of cabinet cups and saucers with newly introduced ground colours and techniques, as collectors' pieces. Mme de Pompadour's inventory is a treasure trove of bibelots, right down to the toilet sets of Sèvres – thirteen water-jugs and basins for the Chateau de Ménars alone – embroidery shuttles and special tambour-hooks for embroidery frames of ivory and solid gold. Advances in all fields of manufacture, notably the ceramic industry, made patronage exciting and these women amassed great accumulations of porcelain, gold boxes, enamels, embroidery, lace, personal accessories, sewing implements and every kind of bibelot and trinket.

China collecting has a long history as a feminine interest, and in the nineteenth century ceramic collecting attracted many women enthusiasts. This activity was focused on the deliberate choice of second-hand material in European porcelains as well as oriental wares. Sir Joseph Banks remarked in 1807 that Chinese porcelain had 'fallen in total neglect' owing to the superior attractions of European porcelains, which had developed by leaps and bounds since the 1740s; he made this observation in the manuscript catalogue of his wife's collection of Chinese porcelain.

Even in the twentieth century writers like Maurice Jonas conspired to marginalize china collecting as a woman's area: 'This is a hobby that ladies should cultivate; the exquisite Chelsea and Dresden figures seem to be made especially for the delicate fingers of women to handle. Many of the fair sex have told me that if they possessed the means, china, above all other hobbies, would be their speciality.' He goes on to equate china with household preoccupations: 'Women, as a rule, have little taste for collecting books, prints or pictures, but it is a fact that they evince quite an attachment to their ordinary china services .'

This cool assessment of women's capacity for serious connoisseurship reflects the strictures of C.L. Eastlake as expressed in his hugely influential work Hints on Household Taste (1868); after disparaging women's education and credulity he continues: 'We may condemn a lady's opinion on politics – criticise her handwriting – correct her pronunciation of Latin, and disparage her favourite author with a chance of escaping displeasure. But if we venture to question her taste – in the most ordinary sense of the word – we are sure to offend. It is, however, a lamentable fact that this very quality was until recently deficient, not only among the generally ignorant, but also among the educated classes in this country.'

From 1835 ceramics were on view to the public at the Museum of Practical Geology, shown as a branch of mineral use, and initially these collections rivalled those of the newly founded Museum of Ornamental Art. This situation was to be transformed in 1885 when the South Kensington Museum (as it was then called) received the munificent gift of the Schreiber Collection from Lady Charlotte Schreiber, the outstanding collector of the period. The first book on ceramic history to be published in England, *Collections towards a History of Pottery and Porcelain*, was written in 1850 by Joseph Marryat; his sister was Fanny Palliser, herself a collector as well as the respected historian of old lace, and it was she who brought out the second edition. She wrote her own ceramic collectors' guide in 1874.

Lace is another traditional area of women's collecting. Both Queen Charlotte and the Empress Josephine had quantities of very valuable lace, as did Mesdames de Pompadour and du Barry. Mme du Barry's account with her lace merchant was enormous. Lady Charlotte Schreiber was paying high prices for lace on the Continent in the late 1860s, and a little later Baroness Edmond de Rothschild was making the choice collection now at Waddesdon Manor, Buckinghamshire. Isabella Stewart Gardner bought wonderful early Italian lace for Fenway Court in Boston. Before concentrating on ceramics Mrs Bury (Fanny) Palliser wrote a pioneering *History of Lace* in 1865; she played a leading part in the exhibition of old lace held at South Kensington in 1874, bringing the subject to the notice of collectors.

Lady Dorothy Nevill saw herself as a porcelain collector, but was unable to resist the temptation of all kinds of knick-knacks and ephemera. She probably made as great an impact, if not a greater one, in her own time as Lady Charlotte Schreiber, who focused her formidable intelligence on collecting antique porcelain, enamels, playing cards and fans. Her collections are in the Victoria & Albert Museum and the British Museum. Queen Mary concentrated on recovering the possessions of her predecessors, particularly Queen Charlotte's collections, and her fan collection was famous. Meticulously catalogued by herself, the carefully assembled items are still with the British royal family. Alice de Rothschild inherited Waddesdon Manor on the death of her brother Baron Ferdinand. She shared the Rothschild taste for the eighteenth century and her discriminating choice of precious *objets de virtu* is still at Waddesdon, now owned by the National Trust and magnificently restored by the present Lord Rothschild.

Lady Dorothy Nevill (detail) by
The Hon. Richard Henry Graves,

Lady Dorothy Nevill

*The word collection which appears at the head of this paper seems to me something of a
misnomer, for such a term is hardly applicable to the various objets d'art which I have
in the course of my life gathered together . . . I may add that in many cases I have, I
must confess, preferred the curious to the beautiful.*

(From 'My Collection' by Lady Dorothy Nevill in *Connoisseur,* 1902)

Among the enthusiasts collecting in the 1850s was Horace Walpole's kinswoman, Lady Dorothy
Nevill. By her own admission (see the quotation above) her collection was not formed method-
ically, but the fact remains that the newly founded *Connoisseur* chose to feature it in their first

year of publication (1902). On her marriage in 1847 she had immediately set about buying French eighteenth-century furniture, porcelains and pastels – the Nevills owned the *Girl with a Cat* by Jean-Baptiste Perronneau (c.1715–83), for years one of the most popular works in the National Gallery in London. One of the highlights of Lady Dorothy's porcelain collection, and the most valued by her, was a fine Sèvres 'Rose du Barry' tea service, said to have belonged to Marie Antoinette, who had been her heroine since girlhood. She bought it at Webb's in Bond Street, the successful old-established broker who had been a buyer at many of the major auctions – both the sale of Walpole's Strawberry Hill and the Stowe sale, for example – in the 1840s. In case it appears improbable that Marie Antoinette would have owned porcelain bearing the name of the hated du Barry, it should be noted that this name was not used in the factory at the time, and only became attached to the colour subsequently. Sèvres porcelain was the *ne plus ultra* of ceramic collecting, and accounted for the largest number of collectors in the lists published by Joseph Marryat in his book, and to be interested in Sèvres was the mark of a serious enthusiast. Lady Dorothy also had a fine *Sèvres garniture de cheminée*, ornaments for chimney-pieces, and a biscuit group (unglazed white porcelain). She owned a Meissen bust of Frederick the Great and delicate porcelain Neapolitan Capo di Monte cups and saucers that had belonged to Lady Bessborough, bought in 1849 at the auction of the contents of Gore House in Kensington. She had a great preference for Chelsea porcelain groups of which she had a number. Whateverthe collecting situation in 1902, nearly a century later her possessions still look highly desirable and rare. She ended her chatty piece by recommending beginners to buy a few things of good quality, advice she herself was manifestly unable to profit by. She was the living embodiment of '*bricabracomanie*', Edmond de Goncourt's brilliant coinage for his description of the Goncourt collection, *La maison d'un artiste* (1880).

With the arrival of her children Lady Dorothy came into the possession of a large country house and there began to surround herself with the fascinating clutter that she loved. She bought snuff boxes, scent bottles, sewing implements and buttons, silhouettes, wax portraits, lockets enclosing hairwork, posy rings, and any Walpole family souvenirs, especially relics of Horace Walpole's Gothick extravaganza, Strawberry Hill. And this was just the bric-à-brac; she amassed quantities of worthless junk, ephemera of all kinds, toothpicks, paste jars, menu cards, anything on which her wayward curiosity alighted. She added endless examples of her own fancy-work, silk painting, shellwork, paper filigree, armorial illumination and embroidery. There was hardly one useless Victorian skill of which she was not a master. At one time she planned to set up a silk worm industry, but this was abandoned when the grubs invaded the whole house. A more serious enterprise was her garden, in which she pioneered the herbaceous border and the wild garden before Mrs Earle and William Robinson wrote about this form of planting for an enthusiastic audience in the late nineteenth century, and installed – echoes of illustrious predecessors – a menagerie of exotic birds and beasts. She pestered Sir William Hooker at the Royal Botanic Gardens, Kew, with queries and requests for seeds and plants.

For all the apparent absurdity – even frivolity – of Lady Dorothy's enthusiasms (outlined in detail in the entertaining account of her by Guy Nevill) it would be a mistake to patronize her.

Her death in 1913 produced no less than 200 obituary notices, because she had 'known everyone' and entertained indefatigably. She was an intimate friend of Disraeli (Lord Beaconsfield) and her volumes of reminiscences have been the source of much anecdote and political comment for modern historians of the Victorian period. Her friend Mrs Jeune (Lady St Helier) wrote of her: 'Lady Dorothy's house was a sort of whispering gallery; all her friends were *dans le mouvement*, and she knew everything that was going on. Added to all this, her personal appearance and the arrangements of her house were piquant and original, and few women seemed to have had a wider and happier experience of life and people'.

Lady Charlotte Schreiber

One of the most celebrated – and best-documented – collections of decorative arts was formed in the second half of the nineteenth century by Lady Charlotte Schreiber. Lady Charlotte Bertie was the daughter of the 9th Earl of Lindsey, who died when she was only six years old. She grew up with an ailing mother and a difficult stepfather; she was too intellectual for her position in life and not beguiled by the social round that came with it. She may have found her stepfather unsympathetic, but it was he who was responsible for her lifelong habit of keeping a journal, from which it is possible to reconstruct the minutest details of her life.

Her marriage when she was just 21 had been preceded by a passionate attachment to the family tutor – a staggeringly apt premonition of the future – and a more-than-flirtation with the young Disraeli. She married the widowed ironmaster Sir John Guest MP of Dowlais near Merthyr-Tydfil, Wales, who was more than twice her age, bringing him social status far beyond his expectations; for her the marriage was to confer substantial financial rewards as well as an exciting enlargement of her horizons. She established herself as a successful London hostess, immersed herself in her husband's political concerns and attended the theatre and the usual round of London's cultural diversions. She also threw her considerable energies into her new life in Wales, particularly the social welfare of her husband's workforce. She pursued the studies in oriental languages and other literary interests of her girlhood and, having mastered the Welsh language perfectly, embarked on translating the Welsh epic tales, *The Mabinogion*, from an ancient manuscript.

In 1846, with her husband's purchase of Canford Manor, near Wimborne in Dorset, Lady Charlotte resumed her position among the landed gentry. It was a timely move, for in spite of her many activities, she was restless and on the lookout for new diversions of a cultural nature. With her husband she hunted for works of art to fill the house – Old Masters and portraits and relics from her own Bertie family – but she still had time on her hands. It was to Canford that her cousin Henry Layard (1817–94), with whom she had long been out of touch and who was now transformed into the celebrated and controversial discoverer of the lost cities of Nineveh and

Portrait of Lady Charlotte Guest (later Lady Charlotte Schreiber) by Richard Buckner (1812–83); oil on canvas, 1848. The portrait was commissioned in 1846 and completed in time to be shown at the Royal Academy in 1848, but Sir John Guest did not care for it and it had to be sent back to the artist to be repainted.

Nimrud, was invited in the spring of 1848. He was exhausted and short of funds, and at his wits' end over the publication of his discoveries. She eagerly involved herself with fund-raising and his project of publishing *Nineveh and its Remains*, two handsome volumes illustrated with his drawings. In gratitude, Layard presented her with a 'Nineveh head' in 1848; more Assyrian sculptures and reliefs began arriving in 1849, and they were installed in the cruciform porch, built specially to house them. The structure was at the same time both an antiquities museum and a sort of secular chapel; Layard was regarded by some as the man who made the Bible come true, and the religious dimension of the finds was part of their attraction for Lady Charlotte. The sculptures are now in the Metropolitan Museum in New York, including a relief which had languished unrecognized in a school tuckshop before being rescued and sold at Sotheby's.

Lady Charlotte took a practical and informed interest in her husband's ironworks. As Sir John's health declined she virtually assumed control of the company, and at his death in 1852 she was successfully running the largest iron foundry in the world. Only 24 days after her husband's death she steeled herself to receive her son Ivor's new tutor; it was Charles Schreiber, then aged 26, who was to be her second husband and the companion of her collecting career.

The couple married in 1855 and were shunned by her family and society as a whole. They lived modestly in London and moved in artistic circles. By the mid-1860s Lady Charlotte's latent interest in old china – she had owned Joseph Marryat's book on *Pottery and Porcelain* since 1853 – began to manifest itself in the forefront of her life. There were still astonishing bargains to be had, particularly in the lesser-known factories, and Lady Charlotte was capable of sustained scholarly effort. Her taste was for the English porcelains of the eighteenth century – Bow, Chelsea, Bristol, Worcester, Plymouth and so on – which were still little known and could be found unrecognized in bric-à-brac shops. She liked nothing better than to wrest a bargain from an ignorant vendor. She was both discriminating and shrewd, leaving things that were in less than perfect condition or overpriced for other more credulous collectors.

Although she called her own obsession 'China Mania' Lady Charlotte had no time for 'Chinamania', the 1870s fad for oriental blue-and-white, describing it as a 'ridiculous rage'. The connoisseurs of blue-and-white most frequently cited are mainly artists and male – Whistler and Rossetti, for example – but curiously George du Maurier's famous comic drawings for *Punch* satirizing the fashion frequently stress the female role in this branch of collecting. Lady Charlotte's enthusiasms can be followed on an almost daily basis through her *Journals*, where one after another the entries show the Schreibers pursuing what Charlotte called the '*chasse*', indulging in their daily occupation of 'ransacking the shops'. *Notes Ceramic*, two volumes covering 1869 to 1885 extracted from her journals and edited by her son Montague Guest, himself a collector of wide if obscure interests, record purchases of all manner of antiques and bibelots: lace, fans, playing cards, jewellery, old cabinets, paintings, glass, enamels, buttons, tortoiseshell boxes, miniatures and many trifles for her family.

Although the *Journal* entries are summary to a fault, they leave an indelible impression of sheer industry. The Schreibers were tremendous sightseers, never missing a museum or gallery wherever they stopped in their travels, and talking their way into any private collections that they

Fan from the Schreiber Collection. French Revolutionary
Fan, costumes of the Revolution, Schreiber Collection
of Fans. Trustees of the British Museum, London.

were told about. Lady Charlotte was also a tremendous needlewoman, and on the grand scale, making screens and even curtains. Inevitably she was involved with the Royal School of Art Needlework. An important thread running through the years is charity work, and one project in particular, the plight of the Turkish refugees from the Russo-Turkish War. She mounted exhibitions and persuaded many of the newly invented department stores to buy Turkish embroideries.

Charles Schreiber died in 1884, having being ill for nearly a year. Lady Charlotte presented her collection of English ceramics, as well as the 'Battersea' enamels and glass, to the South Kensington Museum in his memory. Her extensive holdings of Continental wares were distributed round her family or presented to friends like Sir Augustus Wollaston Franks of the British Museum, confidant of many fellow collectors. A sale in 1890 disposed of the rest. Increasingly her attention turned to fans and playing cards and games.

Lady Charlotte can fairly be regarded as among the most eminent fan collectors. The subject was ripe for revival, and 1870 saw the important *Loan Exhibition of Fans* at the South Kensington Museum, followed in 1871 by the Arundel Society publication of *Fans of All Countries*. The Schreiber fan collection is rigorously scholarly rather than decorative, most of the leaves being printed rather than painted and many of them unmounted. They reveal historical and political issues more commonly associated with printed ephemera and caricature. She started collecting playing cards very late on, in about 1880, and many of the packs came in block purchases from collectors. These were not bargains, unlike the china-hunting finds of earlier times, but she believed herself to be making an important collection. In these last years of her life, racing against threatened blindness, she made the catalogues of her collection; she chose her collaborators well, Franks for the playing cards, Lionel Cust for the fans. She is one of the only women to feature at any length in Frank Herrmann's *The English as Collectors* (1971). Although she was a near contemporary of Queen Victoria, she lived not so much as a Victorian wife and mother, but a life more akin to her Blue Stocking predecessors, the *litterateurs* and collectors of the eighteenth century.

Miss Alice de Rothschild

Alice reigns absolutely, there is nothing constitutional about this monarchy. No wonder the Queen has named her 'The All Powerful' . . .
Constance, Lady Battersea, in her journal.

(Quoted in Lucy Cohen, *Louisa de Rothschild and her Daughters*, London, 1935, p.235)

Miss Alice was the great-granddaughter of Mayer Amschel (1743–812), founder of the Rothschild banking dynasty and youngest of the seven surviving children of Baron Anselm von Rothschild of Vienna. She was brought up in an extended family circle where command of almost unlimited riches was normal, and she was imbued with both a love of works of art and an acquisitive instinct. Alice was an heiress from a very early age, and when she came into possession of one of the legendary Rothschild collections she proved herself a more than worthy custodian; intelligence combined with an astonishing memory gave Alice a natural authority. She was heir to her brother, Baron Ferdinand, the great collector and patron of the arts and builder of Waddesdon Manor. Baron Ferdinand was said to have inherited £2 million from his father in 1874, and it is surely no coincidence that the building of his great French Renaissance-style château began in that year. Waddesdon, inspired by the great châteaux of the Loire, Chambord, Anet and Blois, was designed by a French architect, Gabriel-Hippolyte Destailleur, and built between 1874 and 1889; the garden was also the work of a French designer, Elie Lainé.

Ferdinand had married in 1865 one of his English cousins, Evelina de Rothschild; she and her unborn child died following a railway accident only eighteen months later, and he never remarried. His sister Alice, barely twenty years old, moved to England to become his hostess and to oversee his household. A year after the start of building at Waddesdon, she bought the neighbouring property of Eythrope, where she built a house designed by George Devey, an architect known for his sympathy with the landscaping of the grounds of his houses. In the event, having

Alice de Rothschild, portrait print
in a gilt-metal frame.
The National Trust, Waddesdon Manor.

been warned after a bout of rheumatic fever that she should never spend the night there because of the damp situation, she always slept at Waddesdon, and she had her own bedroom and private sitting-room there. It was at Eythrope that she housed her own collections of mainly eighteenth-century pictures and works of art, and there made a garden to rival Waddesdon's, one called a 'fairy garden . . . too perfect, if that is possible' by Sir Algernon West in his *Private Diaries* (1922).

Following her illness, Miss Alice was advised that she should spend the winters in the South of France. She became very attached to Grasse, where she had a house, renamed Villa Victoria in honour of the Queen of England. Alice was a gifted landscape gardener and passion-ate botanist who had fallen in love with the Mediterranean flora. In her terrain of 135 hectares she employed 100 gardeners and each year planted 55,000 daisies, 25,000 pansies, 10,000 wallflowers, 5,000 forget-me-nots and 23,000 bulbs. In order to escape the attentions of crowds of sightseers in public places Queen Victoria loved to visit the beautiful garden, and in order to smooth her path – literally – Miss Alice had a new road constructed.

Gold snuff box with Sèvres porcelain plaques, Paris 1772-3; set with painted
porcelain plaques of Mme de Pompadour's dogs and birds.
The National Trust, Waddesdon Manor.

After Ferdinand's death in 1898, Miss Alice came into possession of Waddesdon and its
collections. She was 51 and an experienced hostess and manager, as well as a collector and
connoisseur of considerable stature who had filled three houses – her townhouse at 142 Piccadilly
as well as Eythrope and the Villa Victoria – with her purchases. Waddesdon was fully furnished,
apart from the New Smoking Room in the Bachelors' Wing, where the *objets d'art* (Renaissance
works of art and jewels) forming the Waddesdon Bequest, which on the death of Baron
Ferdinand in 1898 went to the British Museum, had been housed. She had no intention of
making great changes.

However, it was at Waddesdon that she was to make a remarkable contribution to her
collecting activities, and one that stands out as uncommon in the annals of women's collections.
She chose to replace the material that had gone to the British Museum from the Smoking Room
and the corridor leading to it with armour and small arms of the sixteenth and seventeenth
centuries. Of course her collecting was not faultless; she was buying at the end of a period when

finely decorated arms had been much in demand amongst wealthy collectors like Sir Richard Wallace (1818–90), a demand that exceeded the available supply. Even the Rothschilds were not immune to imitations, but the outstanding pieces far outweigh the doubtful objects.

The eighteenth-century guns, rifles, small-swords and hunting knives, with inlays of gold, silver and ivory and mounts of porcelain and hardstone, are elegant and in keeping with the precious *objets de virtu* that all Rothschilds collected with passion. To make up the loss of the Renaissance jewellery and works of art, she also made some purchases in this field – miniatures, majolica and sixteenth-century German silver-gilt cups and a rare Norman Sicilian ivory casket.

Miss Alice brought to Waddesdon one of its most charming paintings, the portrait of Philippe Egalité, duc d'Orléans aged two, by François Boucher. The two commodes by Jean-Henri Riesener (1734–1806), now in the Red Room, were in her sitting-room, and the Bohemian and Venetian glass that was moved into the Smoking Room was possibly transferred from Eythrope. Items among the outstanding representation from the Sèvres porcelain factory came from her collections, and she added to the rustic china in the Dairy Curio Room. The gold boxes, *étuis*, nécessaires, bodkin- and needle-holders and portrait miniatures are exceptionally important; Miss Alice added twenty-four items connected with the eighteenth-century van Blarenberghe family of miniaturists, among them eight boxes and seven rings. She loved portrait miniatures and dogs, especially pugs, and collected objects representing them. She also had a number of feminine personal accessories, such as needle-cases, sewing boxes and *étuis* made of precious materials and through her heir came another Rothschild collection, a small but very choice collection of fans, lace and eighteenth-century French buttons, the last made in the 1880s; it would be difficult now to match its quality.

Both Baron Ferdinand and Miss Alice were intensely secretive about their collecting and both instructed that all traces of provenance were to be destroyed after their deaths. Miss Alice left little inventory information beyond a few scattered comments as to provenance or purchase. Most deals were probably made privately through contacts known to their advisers; dealers would not hesitate to approach Rothschild collectors by whatever means offered. The Waddesdon collections are now fully recorded in catalogues of the pictures, the Sèvres, Meissen and Oriental porcelains, sculpture, arms and armour, furniture, clocks and gilt-bronzes, gold boxes, glass, faience (tin-glazed earthenware), enamels and fans.

With her decision to leave Waddesdon largely unchanged, Miss Alice seems to have acquiesced in the traditional female role as 'keeper of the flame'. Although she was an immensely wealthy woman and an active collector in her own right she accepted her destiny almost as a sacred trust, taking her curatorial responsibilities seriously and caring for the house with rare dedication. When she took over, the blinds were pulled down all over the house to safeguard the priceless textiles, and her standards of housekeeping ensured the perfect preservation of the treasures.

From 1915 Miss Alice lived the life of an invalid. She died in 1922, leaving Waddesdon to her great-nephew, James. Lord d'Abernon remarked, when he heard of this change in his friend's fortunes 'Waddesdon is not an inheritance, it is a career'.

Queen Mary

Queen Mary was never bored indoors, for, apart from the endless fascination of arranging the great royal collections and her own substantial additions to them, her thoroughness and her sense of history combined to make her wish to leave everything documented for prosperity. There is indeed hardly a piece of furniture, picture or print in the remotest bedroom or passage of the royal palaces and houses on which a label is not to be found in Queen Mary's handwriting describing its subject and origin.

(Lady Cynthia Colville, *Crowded Life*, 1963, p.124–25.)

Queen Mary was born Princess May of Teck on 26 May 1867, a cousin of her future husband, George V, and a great-grand-daughter of George III through his youngest son, Adolphus, Duke of Cambridge. She was brought up in Kensington Palace, London, where her parents, the Duke and Duchess of Teck had a suite of rooms, amidst the furniture of her predecessors. Queen Charlotte's sedan chairs belonged to her mother's family; they were in the hall and may have sparked her lifelong interest in the Queen. Princess May's most enthusiastic mentor for family historyand collecting of memorabilia was her Aunt Augusta, Grand Duchess of Mecklenburg Strelitz, Queen Charlotte's childhood home. Letters exchanged by aunt and niece are quoted extensively in James Pope-Hennessey's biography of Queen Mary, and they offer intimate insights into the strains of royal life.

Princess May shared childhood games with her Wales cousins and like them delighted in collecting diminutive objects such as china animals, shells, small photographs in frames, and miniature watercolours of Windsor, a taste she never really lost. She inherited her appreciation of furniture and *objets d'art* and her talent for decoration from her father, who had far too little to do and had to make a profession out of a pastime. H. Clifford Smith, long-time admirer and one of her most trusted professional advisers, extolled her 'special talent in the arrangement of works of art in the happiest relationship to their surroundings – a gift rarer than is commonly supposed and one requiring not only skill and taste but wide knowledge and judgement'.

Princess May's parents lived in a state of financial chaos because her father had no money of his own and her mother was famously extravagant. Some years were spent in Florence, economizing, so her education was unusually cosmopolitan for a British-born member of the royal family. But principally she remedied any deficiencies herself, by reading and by assiduous sight-seeing and museum visiting. Back in England in 1884 she now had to endure royal social obligations made hideous by her shyness and reserve. Her engagement in 1892 to the Duke of Clarence, eldest son of the Prince and Princess of Wales and heir presumptive, ended in bereavement only six weeks later. It was followed in just eighteen months by a second betrothal to his younger brother, George, an apparently cynical marriage of convenience that resulted in a lifetime's happiness and affection.

Following her husband's accession in 1910, Queen Mary moved into Buckingham Palace

Queen Mary, photographed by W. & D. Downey in 1902. National Portrait Gallery, London.

Queen Mary's Boudoir at Marlborough House, showing the installation of her collections.

and found a task that might have been invented to utilize all her knowledge and talents. As she wrote to her Aunt Augusta, 'everything at this moment seems to me to be chaos and with my methodical mind I suffer in proportion, no doubt some day all will be right again'. Although Edward VII had modernized and made good the horribly neglected building, it remained a virtually unexplored treasure house of historic royal art, furniture, decoration and memorabilia. 'I am trying to rehang the pictures in various rooms according to family, date, etc., not an easy task when one has miles of corridors to cover to find anything' she wrote a little later to Aunt Augusta. Store cupboards were crammed with surplus material, bought but never used, such as hand-painted Chinese wallpapers and embroidered hangings and rolls of damask and silks. Queen Mary found such quantities of Chinese work in the Buckingham Palace storerooms that she was able to decorate several rooms. Distant bedrooms had been equipped with butchered eighteenth-century furniture and there were drawers full of fans, parasols, trinkets and mourning jewellery. The redecoration and repairing of Buckingham Palace are recorded in the Royal Archives from 1911 to 1935 'under the personal supervision of Queen Mary'.

Queen Mary was far and away the most diligent of consort-collectors and certainly among the most acquisitive. As James Pope-Hennessy described in his biography:

She was for ever matching up, cataloguing, re-organising and adding to the historical parts of the Royal Collections. With her phenomenal memory there went a shrewd eye, and the staff of the various Royal residences found that it was impossible to remove for cleaning or repair the smallest coral object from some obscure vitrine without the Queen noticing its absence and sending to enquire whither it had been taken.

She was especially interested in objects relating to the royal family. The four-volume record of her collection was entitled *Catalogue of Bibelots, Miniatures and other Valuables, the Property of H.M. Queen Mary*; never was a publication more aptly named. Covering the period from her marriage in 1893 to 1946, when she was nearly 80 years old, it lists hundreds of small *objets d'art* accompanied by her own descriptions, the dates of acquisition and the source or donor. It enshrines her myriad interests – very much in the taste of her time – and her friendships. There are many Fabergé pieces, some gold and silver and a small amount of jewellery, mainly memorial pieces, but the greater part of the catalogue is made up of precious snuff boxes and étuis, workboxes and tea-caddies, Derbyshire spar vases (made of fluorspar, called Blue John, found only in Derbyshire), enamels from Canton (enamel painted on copper) and 'Battersea' made in England, jewelled watches, miniatures, Chinese and Moghul jades and carved crystals, bronzes, fans, silhouettes, ivories, lacquerwork and Chinese porcelains. Visits to India in 1905 and 1911 (for the great Coronation celebrations or Durbar) provided opportunities to add fine Moghul pieces, mainly crystal inlaid with gold and precious stones, and carved jades.

Queen Mary has been described as a museum curator manqué, and she was single minded in pursuit of historically significant items. A miniature version in marble of the sculptor Houdon's portrait of Voltaire has the following note: 'Queen Mary saw this statuette in Sir John Murray Scott's apartment in Paris in 1908, and always remembered it. She purchased it from the Mortimer Schiff sale at Christie's in 1938.' She was adept at conjuring objects out of the proprietors of the antique shops she frequented with such zeal, and from collectors whose possessions matched her own interests. She was particularly keen on recovering Queen Charlotte's possessions, and the first item in the catalogue is Queen Charlotte's pair of gold salvers from the Cambridge family, bought at the Cambridge sale in 1904. It is fascinating to come upon the Queen's 'Globe' worktable by Morgan & Saunders, acquired by Queen Mary in the 1930s andcatalogued as an 'exceptionally rare and interesting' example of Sheraton, about 1780. A tea-caddy of cedarwood veneered with ivory and ebony, set with ivory medallion portraits of George III and the Queen, was made in 1818 for the Bath Corporation as a presentation piece but the Queen died, and it was more than a century before it found its way into royal ownership. An embroidered satin pocketbook worked by Queen Charlotte in 1781, and given to Mrs Delany with a lock of her hair enclosed, entered the collection in the 1930s.

The royal family and the household knew royal memorabilia would be well received. Queen Victoria found these interests congenial and bequeathed to Princess May one of Queen

Charlotte's most intimate possessions, the four-strand pearl bracelet with George III's miniature set in diamonds sent to his prospective bride as a betrothal gift and mentioned in Queen Charlotte's jewel inventory. Queen Mary treasured a miniature of George IV in the original frame embossed with a royal crown and emblems, given by her husband in 1908. It had been bought at the Cambridge sale in 1904 and was one of many things he added to her collection.

The Museum of London was founded in 1912, and Queen Mary trawled through cupboards and drawers looking for intriguing items of royal association. When George V died in 1936, the new King Edward VIII decided to simplify the ponderous rituals of royal mourning, a move entirely supported by Queen Mary, and she poured countless pieces of now obsolete jet and hairwork jewellery into the Museum's coffers. She was a tireless supporter of the efforts to restore Brighton Pavilion, and she ransacked storerooms for furniture with the Pavilion mark, then persuaded first her husband then her son, George VI, to loan the pieces back where they belonged. So much that Queen Mary stood for is encompassed in her overriding interest in the annals of the British royal family; in her omnivorous collecting appetites and indifference to the monetary value of her prey; in her support of the V & A and its aims; and even in a childlike interest in childish things that found its perfect expression in the famous Queen's Dolls' House. Many of her cherished *objets d'art* were, in effect, toys. Glass cases and cupboards-full of miniature articles – tiny gold and silver tea-sets and services of 'Queen's Pattern' spoons and forks, tables and chairs, even a miniature grand piano, of polished hardstones and gold by Fabergé, and filigree trinkets and minuscule carriages – still line the corridors at Buckingham Palace and Sandringham.

Princess Marie Louise claimed credit for harnessing the love of minuscule things to a really worthwhile project. The Queen's Dolls' House was designed by the foremost architect Sir Edwin Lutyens, and almost everyone of any significance to the art and culture of the day contributed to its contents. It was given to her in 1920 and exhibited for the first time in 1926 at the Great Empire Exhibition at Wembley. It is Queen Charlotte's fruitful contemporary patronage mirrored in miniature, but the Dolls' House has raised very large sums for charity in the years since it was made.

In 1936, after the death of George V, the widowed Queen returned to Marlborough House, where she had lived when Princess of Wales. Never wasteful, she brought back the green silk wall-hangings, which she had taken with her to Buckingham Palace a quarter of a century earlier. Her collections were displayed around the reception rooms in standing glass-fronted cabinets and in hanging glass cases on the walls. The work of cataloguing continued for another ten years, the final volume taking the record up to 1946. She endured the Abdication crisis in 1937 and then the death of one of her sons, the Duke of Kent, in World War II. In 1952 the King, her second son, died prematurely aged only 56. Queen Mary herself died in the following year; considerate to the last, she had stipulated that there should be no mourning to mar the coronation of Elizabeth II.

The full flavour of Queen Mary's omnivorous collecting appetites is apparent from her catalogues and inventories.

Princess Marie Louise

Dear Queen Mary found my sister's and my home a positive treasure trove, and a little van from the Royal Mews used to draw up before 78, Pall Mall, and many of our treasures were packed and taken off to Frogmore.

(Her Highness Princess Marie-Louise, *My Memories of Six Reigns*, 1956, p.29)

Princess Marie Louise, Queen Mary's cousin and her junior by just five years, shared the family passion for collecting and many of the same interests as the Queen. She was ardently attracted to royal memorabilia, with the result that she became the Queen's prey – as indicated by the rather tart quotation above. She led a very different life from Queen Mary's, shuffled from pillar to post at the mercy of more fortunate members of the family, even at one time living in a rather sordid and uncomfortable bedsitting-room in a residential club. Condemned by birth to a supporting role in the royal pageant, she managed to hang on to sufficiently magnificent jewels to sustain her public royal appearances, although they would have alleviated many financial problems.

Princess Marie Louise was one of Queen Victoria's many grandchildren, the daughter of Princess Helena and Prince Christian of Schleswig-Holstein. She had married Prince Aribert of Anhalt for love when she was only nineteen and the marriage went disastrously wrong, ending in an annulment less than ten years later. However, she had benefited from the great cultural tradition fostered by the rulers of the independent German states, many of whom were enlightened and generous patrons of the arts. Marie Louise loved music, and her married life brought her in contact with the cultivated and musical German court of her parents-in-law, and through them she met Wagner and his second wife, Cosima von Bulow, at Bayreuth. One of the family possessions was the castle of Zerbst, childhood home of Catherine the Great. Princess Marie Louise's father-in-law still owned souvenirs of the Empress – her travelling clock and the dress that she had worn for entry into St Petersburg. The young couple lived for a while in Dessau, where the family still used a solid silver service from the time of Frederick the Great for picnics. Summer months were spent at Wurlitz Castle with its ravishing eighteenth-century English-style garden.

However, her married years were unquestionably a nightmare, partly on account of the almost medieval court etiquette that still prevailed – even in the last decade of the nineteenth century – throughout the small German principalities, which was to her an almost unbearable curtailment of liberty. Her husband terminated the marriage in a shower of the most outrageous and unmerited accusations, and it was immediately accepted that Marie Louise could never return to live with him. She was the only one of her parents' children to marry and when she returned to England she made her home with her family, living for many years with her sister Victoria (known as 'Thora') at Schomberg House in Pall Mall, which was once the home of Thomas Gainsborough.

With her marriage over and no prospect of a second marriage, since she still felt bound by her religious vows, Princess Marie Louise cast about for an absorbing occupation. On a visit to Gibraltar she became friends with the chief justice, Sir Stephen Gatty, an artistic dilettante who was experimenting with enamelling, and this inspired her new interest. It was Sir Stephen who recommended her teacher, William Soper, a member of an enamelling dynasty enjoying royal favour as enameller by appointment to Marie Louise's mother, Princess Christian. She copied Fabergé pieces, including a brooch belonging to her sister, which the owner mistook for the work of the master himself, but her great distinction was to be the first member of the royal family to exhibit at the Royal Academy.

Although an avid collector, Marie Louise's activities were bound to be overshadowed by the more powerful and financially better off members of the royal family, but she forged a distinct line for herself in her hobby. In her autobiography she wrote 'My hobby is Napoleon', claiming that 'I may say with all truth that I possess a most unique collection of bronzes, china, ivories and snuff boxes, of which even an experienced and learned collector of antiques of one special period would approve and might perhaps envy.' Presumably her Napoleonic memorabilia was safe from the plundering visits of Queen Mary's van. She wrote detailed accounts of her proudest discoveries, for example, the Sèvres porcelain coffee-set gilded with Napoleon's device of 'N' in a laurel wreath, which he gave to his marshal, Jourdan. This she found in a hotel in Orléans, surrendered for a small sum by an impoverished descendant, Mme la Baronne de Jourdan. Among other treasures, she owned a seal with the arms of the Empress Marie-Louise and Napoleon's head in ivory for a handle, a carved ivory figure of Napoleon, given to her by Mrs Maitland, a descendant of the commander of the *Bellerophon,* who conducted Napoleon into exile on St Helena, and who was presented with the ivory in gratitude for his thoughtful treatment of his prisoner. Delicate ivory plaques with portraits of the Emperor and his first wife, Josephine, drawn in sepia and worked in hair must have been among the choicest treasures, since the Princess included them as an illustration in her autobiography. She was able to visit St Helena and to see Napoleon's house, Longwood, for herself. She took a small cutting from a willow in the grounds growing next to the Emperor's now empty tomb, and this was nurtured in the garden of her Lady-in-Waiting until it developed into a fine tree.

Princess Marie Louise's lasting achievement was the Queen's Dolls' House. One Easter at Windsor Castle, Queen Mary had taken it into her head to furnish a dolls' house with some of the miniature *objets d'art* in which the royal collections abounded – all the royal collectors had apassion amounting to mania for tiny things – and when Marie Louise joined the party she found her mother and sister ransacking their own cupboards. At this point she was inspired to suggest that her close personal friend Sir Edwin Lutyens (1869–1944) be asked to design a doll's house for the Queen. Sir Edwin, who was at that time deeply immersed in the large task of building New Delhi in India, 'looked rather taken aback' but gave a considered response:

> Let us devise and design something which for all time will enable future generations to see how a King and Queen of England lived in the twentieth century, and what authors, artists, and craftsmen of note there were during their reign.

This set the seal of seriousness on a project that must have had other great men of the time looking 'rather taken aback'. The Queen was approached and asked whether she would accept the

Princess Marie-Louise in old age.

gift, and she, too, was 'extremely surprised at first' but she became fascinated by its progress and herself arranged some of the rooms including her own bedroom and boudoir.

The Princess devoted a long passage in her autobiography to a record of its inception and achievement, almost as if she feared that others might one day take the credit. Although she was deputed to take the responsibility for practicalities and to be the project's liaison officer, it was indeed snatched from her grasp when a committee of ladies was set up to deal with the plans and the future of the dolls' house. It was decided that the architectural style of the house should be Georgian, on four floors with a basement, and the surrounding garden was designed by the eminent gardener Gertrude Jekyll. The dining-room seats eighteen diners and is equipped with gold plate and a service of Royal Doulton china. In the library are 200 volumes the size of a postage stamp, each written by a well-known author in his own hand. Each one is bound in red leather with Queen Mary's cypher stamped in gold on the front. The portraits are replicas in miniature, all the paintings are by artists who were admired at the time, and portfolios bulge with 700 watercolours and drawings. Everything in the house is an exact replica in miniature of the original, and everything in it works; the books can be read, the baths fill with water, the lavatory pans flush, there is wine in the bottles, and the nursery gramophone plays 'God Save the King'. Some idea of the trouble that this involved can be understood from one anecdote related by the Princess. She borrowed a linen tablecloth from Buckingham Palace, and having insured it for £100, sent it to Belfast where an exact copy was made only two inches square. The bed-linen took 1,500 hours to weave. The garage houses expensive reproductions of the royal Daimlers. The whole enterprise was a test of ingenuity and, in a sense, an affirmation of contemporary patronage; most importantly, the Queen was pleased.

Princess Marie Louise lived to a great age, and became a valuable repository of royal anecdotes too trivial to find their way into history books. She lived to attend the coronation of Elizabeth II in 1953, which Queen Mary missed by a few short weeks, and was persuaded to write her reminiscences in 1956, when she was 84 – in her own words in order 'to show you a side of life of a member of the Royal Family which does not appear in the Press or the *Court Circular*' – and to give a more human aspect to Queen Victoria. Another of her declared intentions, to rehabilitate the reputation of the Kaiser, is even today probably pretty much of a lost cause. She died in the following year.

CHAPTER VI

The Spell of Fabergé

Queen Alexandra (1844–1925)
Empress Marie Feodorovna (1848–1929)
Marjorie Merriweather Post (1887–1976)

The precious miniature objects made by the imperial Russian goldsmith Peter Carl Fabergé (1846–1920) exercised a compulsive fascination for collectors. Queen Alexandra, her sister Dagmar (Empress Marie Feodorovna), her daughter-in-law Queen Mary and her niece-by-marriage Princess Marie Louise all owned collections and even now the list of lenders to a Fabergé exhibition will read like a rollcall from the Almanach de Gotha. Alexandra and Dagmar were princesses of Denmark who married respectively Edward, Prince of Wales (later King Edward VII), and Tsarevich Alexander of Russia (later Emperor Alexander III). These Fabergé collectors all had many other interests, particularly Queen Mary, whose collection of the decorative arts was justly famous, and features in Chapter V. The importance of Queen Alexandra and her younger sister lies in their having initiated Fabergé's popularity among the crowned heads of Europe. It is their possessions along with those of Nicholas and Alexandra, the last Tsar and Tsarina, that are the most sought after by modern collectors.

Princess Cantacuzène, the first American visitor recorded by the firm of Fabergé, was received by the Dowager Empress Marie Feodorovna at the Anichkov Palace in St Petersburg: 'Her Majesty asked me to sit down,' she wrote in her memoirs; 'There were several comfortable chairs, with little tables by them. The latter seemed covered with bits of old silver, tiny animals carved in precious stones by Fabergé, or various enamels of his making, a small clock among others – things such as anyone might have in a sitting-room.' This was an irresistible model for collectors seduced by the romance of pre-revolutionary Russia.

Marjorie Merriweather Post was both an heiress and a shrewd businesswoman who enormously increased her inheritance. The collection, now in Washington, she assembled of Russian works of art is reputed to be the largest outside Russia. Mrs Post was a collector of Fabergé, rather than a client, since she did not start buying until after the demise of the firm in the wake of Russian Revolution. This put her in the position of being able to acquire objects with the grandest associations, many of them to the imperial family, that were now antiques and memorabilia.

TWO DANISH SISTERS

Queen Alexandra and Empress Marie Feodorovna

The elder daughters of an impoverished Danish king, Christian IX (reigned 1867–1906), became respectively Queen of England (Alexandra, Consort of Edward VII, married 1863) and Empress of Russia (Dagmar, known as Marie Feodorovna, married Alexander III, 1867). Success in the lottery of European marriages was due in no small part to the princesses' exceptional beauty. The splendour of their individual destinies contrasted with their modest and unsophisticated upbringing in war-torn Denmark, a country in dire financial difficulties, whose royal family was relatively poor. There was no money available for precious, useless trifles and the princesses made their own clothes and trimmed their bonnets. When Alexandra and Dagmar married they left all thoughts of economy behind for ever, but Alexandra never let these accomplishments lapse, and she continued to design her own dresses and hats. When she was satisfied with an outfit she had no compunction about wearing it often, even into a second season, showing independence of character and a certain indifference to the *convenances* of royalty.

Like Queen Charlotte a century earlier, Alexandra was selected from among the European princesses of suitable religion and political affiliations. Her looks were an important consideration in the search for a wife who would fix the roving attention of the 21-year-old heir to the British throne. It was later apparent that her lack of intellectual attainments was a critical drawback, but for the moment her beauty was an unalloyed advantage. She had strong religious beliefs, was small and elegant but physically strong and always dressed with exquisite simplicity. She was dignified but with charmingly informal manners. She loved sports and dancing, was full of cheerful optimism and spontaneous gaiety but persevering and obstinate as well, and hopelessly and incurably unpunctual – a real fault in a royal person. She preferred family life and simple amusements, sharing the royal family's taste for practical jokes, and she was passionately fond of animals. She was hopeless with money and could never resist any plea for help, however undeserving the petitioner. Her great contribution was her hospital work and her efforts to improve the status of the nursing profession. Her talents included watercolour painting, needlework and music, conventional accomplishments of royalty but pursued with professional dedication and expanded into philanthropic schemes such as the 'Alexandra Technical School' to teach the local boys skills at Sandringham. As well as the piano and the harp she played on the zither and the dulcimer.

On her arrival Alexandra was greeted with almost hysterical enthusiasm. It was hoped that the gloom enveloping the court with the mourning of Queen Victoria would be lightened by the Prince and Princess of Wales. They were married in 1863 when she was barely eighteen, and quickly produced a family of six children; the birth of Princess Louise, her third child, was followed by a devastating illness which left her lame and seriously handicapped by deafness, an inherited trait which much worsened. Their last child, Prince John, who lived only a day, was born in 1871, after which they waited in the wings for thirty years, performing the visible functions of royalty and masking the much-criticized seclusion of Queen Victoria.

The Princess of Wales (later Queen Alexandra) with her sister Dagmar (Marie Feodorovna, wife of Alexander III of Russia), photographed in 1873 wearing matching polka-dot dresses. National Portrait Gallery, London. The beautiful sisters, dressed identically as here, caused a sensation when they drove out together in London.

In December 1864, the seventeen-year-old Dagmar was engaged to the Tzarevitch Nicholas, heir to the Russian throne, but he died the following spring, and she later married his younger brother, Alexander. The future Alexander III was a huge man of Herculean strength, and a strict disciplinarian. Queen Victoria remarked that he was 'a sovereign whom she does not look upon *as a gentlemen*'. Alexander was anti-reform, a committed Russophile, and the Romanov court took on the colourful and savage splendour of its mediaeval origins. Ceremonies were conducted with archaic formality, and the jewels were incomparable, the finest in the world. For her silver wedding Princess Alexandra asked for a copy of her sister's kokoshnik-style (traditional Russian headdress) diamond tiara as her present from 'the Ladies of Society'.

Louisa, Countess of Antrim, who lived as a girl at Windsor Castle and St James's Palace at the very centre of court life, remembered the impact the two sisters had in London in the early years of Alexandra's marriage:

> *The Tzarevna was sister to the Princess of Wales and they went everywhere together dressing exactly alike whether driving in the Park in blue and white foulard or blazing with diamonds and orders at balls and parties. ... The Tzarevna was not as beautiful as her sister, but she too was very attractive with fine eyes and colouring and the same perfect figure. It was said that as a matter of course all the Russian officials succumbed in turn to the charms of the Empress.*

Dagmar's life in Russia was far grander than her sister's London social round, but for all its savage magnificence the imperial lifestyle was probably less comfortable than that of the politically and financially secure British royal family. The Prince of Wales had debts, but he had plenty of generous supporters, and it was widely appreciated that he was bearing an unfairly heavy financial burden in carrying out the public duties that the widowed Queen refused.

Alexandra immediately took her place as the leader of society, and her popularity never faltered throughout the long wait for her husband's accession. Louisa Antrim observed:

> *It was the fashion to drive in Hyde Park in the afternoons, and there was always a crowd waiting to see the Princess of Wales. On most days she made one or two rounds of the Park in an imposing swinging barouche of a deep claret colour picked out with a narrow red line . . . The Princess of Wales looked lovely . . . Her charming smile which seemed personally to include everyone and her unfailing recognition of acquaintances gave universal pleasure.*

Due to her husband's many flirtations Alexandra contemplated flight, but was restrained by pleas from Queen Victoria; her brief nine-year reign as Queen-Consort was the culmination of a life spent enduring her husband's very public infidelities and putting on an unfailing parade for the populace.

Alexandra was domestic by nature and her energies were expended on her homes, Marlborough House in London, and the newly acquired country estate at Sandringham in

THE SPELL OF FABERGÉ

Norfolk. At Marlborough House one room was used simply for the unpacking and viewing of official gifts by the royal couple, who would then direct where they should go. The Indian Room, fitted up with display cases like a museum, contained a priceless collection of works of art given to the Prince at the time of his tour of the subcontinent in 1874. A fireproof plate room in the basement, with security to match the enormous value of the contents, was installed by the crown jewellers, Garrard's, in 1888 to take the valuables given as silver wedding presents.

Arthur Beavan wrote a detailed description of this and other aspects of Marlborough House in 1896:

> In the centre is a magnificent case matching the others, of the thickest plate-glass, around which one can walk, as at the Tower [of London] while inspecting the Crown Jewels . . . Here may be seen presentation services (breakfast, dinner and tea), elaborate centre-pieces, richly chased salvers, caskets, flagons, tankards, bowls, vases, racing-cups and yachting prizes . . . silver trowels, candelabra, keys inlaid in silver and gilt, candlesticks, beautiful models of buildings and animals, dainty specimens of Indian art-work in the white metal, statuettes, gold and silver cups, old silver spoons, silver-gilt salt-cellars, tea and coffee services, Christening gifts, birthday gifts, wedding presents . . . So extensive is the collection that it necessitates the employment of three or four men to clean it and keep it in order.

The finest items of plate were displayed in the dining-room at official banquets.

When Marlborough House was prepared for the Wales's occupancy in 1863, great care was taken to patronize native industries; the London firm of Holland & Sons acted as furnishers and upholsterers, the silk was ordered from Spitalfields, the damask from Manchester, the linen from Belfast, the Axminster carpets from the Wilton factory in Wiltshire. The pianos were supplied by Broadwood and Brimsmead. This echoes Queen Charlotte and her patronage of 'our own manu-factures', but the Princess of Wales did not make her collecting into an occasion for philanthropy, being more interested in precious trifles from Fabergé.

The floor of the saloon was covered with an enormous Axminster carpet given to the Prince as a wedding present, a perfect foil for Gobelins tapestries from the 'Don Quixote' series. The chairs and sofas were upholstered in tapestry panels of *Aesop's Fables*, a present from Napoleon III. Marlborough House acted as a showcase for French diplomatic offerings, just as Pavlovsk had half a century earlier. Tapestries after Goya in the dining-room at Sandringham were among the greatest artistic treasures. Like his predecessors, the Prince owned magnificent Sèvres porcelain, but new purchases were from Minton's of Stoke-on-Trent.

Royal social obligations dictated a degree of splendour in the public rooms, but in the private apartments Alexandra indulged her preferences. She had her own painting room, and her sketches hung in her boudoirs and private sitting-rooms. In London and at Sandringham her rooms were cluttered with screens hung with photographs and miniatures and tables laden with personal mementoes. At Marlborough House 300–400 vases of cut flowers were renewed every day; this was in addition to the magnificent Kentia palms in every room. The table decorations were superb, often most unusual, using autumn leaves or wild flowers as well as hothouse blooms. The Princess's favourites – particularly violets – were forced in hothouses at Sandringham. Among the sea of little tables and satin-upholstered chairs were cages of canaries, bullfinches and other songbirds and a tame pigeon flew about the rooms. Persian cats and pet dogs raced and romped unchecked, doing a great deal of damage to curtains and upholstery, so that the repairs constituted a considerable item in the royal accounts. Her Sandringham bedroom was crowded with family photographs, holy pictures, a small version of the sculptured figure of *Christ* by Bertel Thorwaldsen (1768-1844), crosses and a large crucifix. She loved lace of which she had an extensive and valuable collection.

One of the Princess's more unusual accomplishments was as a photographer, and she added significantly to the royal collection initiated by Queen Victoria. As soon as photographic technology became simple enough for the amateur, members of the royal family took it up, but Alexandra is acknowledged to have been one of the more gifted. She was presented with a camera by the Kodak Company in 1892, and all her negatives were developed by the company. She would allow no one else to handle them and pasted the prints into her albums herself, with titles or a commentary on a tour or cruise. She was taught by the Usher of the Servants' Hall at Sandringham, one Frederick Ralph, a Norfolk photographer. The hobby appealed to her in combining art with an intensely personal record of family activities and she collected pictures of her friends and views of places of family interest. Her own work is represented in the royal collection, including an unusual item, a tea-set decorated with photographic views, made by Brown-Westhead Moore & Co. of Hanley. She participated in exhibitions mounted by the Kodak Company at the turn of the century, and in 1908 a collection of her photographs entitled *Queen Alexandra's Christmas Gift Book* enjoyed a huge success.

Alexandra and Dagmar owned outstanding collections of the work of Fabergé. Fabergé took control of the family business in 1870, and in 1884 Alexander III appointed the House of Fabergé as goldsmiths and jewellers to the court. The appointment initiated the annual series of Imperial Easter Eggs on which the celebrity of the firm rests. After the death of his father in 1894, Nicholas II continued the gifts to his mother as well as giving an egg to his wife. The eggs were intensely personal and rarely seen outside the imperial family, except at the Paris Centennial Exposition in 1900, when the two empresses permitted Fabergé to show them, making him into a household name internationally. The first egg was ready for Easter 1885 and 56 had been made, of which 47 survive, by 1917; ten are still in the Kremlin in Moscow. Two of the eggs made for the Empress Marie were bought by Marjorie Merriweather Post and are now in Washington. Queen Mary acquired two, the 'Colonade Egg' and the 'Mosaic Egg', both made for the Empress Alexandra. When the Empress Marie gave her sister a frame with her portrait in it in about 1890, she hooked the collector who was to be Fabergé's 'great patroness in the West'.

Fabergé's distinctive use of materials – and notably the Russian hardstones from which more than 90 per cent of the carved pieces are made – singled his work out from the mass of precious trifles that were to be had in London and Paris. Hardest for Fabergé himself was the constant search for novelty; Edward VII wished to 'have no duplicates', and this was in a collection of many hundreds. In 1907 the King commissioned models from life of the domestic pets and farm animals at Sandringham. Artists were sent from St Petersburg, and an English sculptor was recruited. The Queen was enchanted with the tiny sculptures of the animals, which were carved in hardstones as close as possible in colour to nature. Among them was the King's favourite dog, Caesar, and his famous Derby winner, Persimmon, cast in silver. Because each animal was a faithful portrait, and as lively and natural as possible, these models are the finest in existence. The Queen's other love was for enamel and gold flowers in rock-crystal vases. Her celebrated skill as a photographer prompted a charming device, that of setting imitation photographs in sepia enamel into the lids of boxes. Her collection was the largest in the world, including some 300 animals, the finest of the flowers and masses of boxes, frames, bell-pushes and other elegant accessories. This was in spite of the fact that she gave many pieces back to the donors at the time of the King's death in 1910.

In 1909 Viscount Knutsford was invited to Sandringham for Queen Alexandra's birthday. He packed a small selection of gifts, but was transfixed by the splendour of the display revealed after breakfast on the day. Donors were evidently aware of the Queen's preferences, and had bought accordingly:

> *The Queen likes most agate animals, of which she has a magnificent collection in two large glass cabinets in the drawing-room, which every evening are lit up by electricity. There is a Russian in Dover Street who makes them, and a man in Paris makes flowers of the same stone. Some are cut out of jade. The King had given her an agate figure of a Chelsea Pensioner. The Prince of Wales a turkey with ruby eyes and a model of her favourite spaniel. Alfred Rothschild a lovely lace parasol, the stick made of what looked like amber, the handle and other end studded with diamonds and rubies, and each rib ending in a pearl.*

The 'Russian in Dover Street' was, of course, Fabergé, who must by this date have been quite pressed to find new models for the Queen's collection. 'Most of the presents were perfectly lovely. There were quite forty different animals, monkeys, penguins, dogs, birds, chinçillas, all exquisitely modelled by this Russian, and all made to order.' Happily Knutsford was writing detailed letters to his wife and not one gift escaped his notice:

> *A lady from Paris had sent a large hammered copper jar about 3 feet high, full of boxes of chocolates. The Sassoons gave her a little bag fitted up with gold fittings and a gold watch in it. What she will do with it, goodness only knows. Someone gave her George IV's watch, enamel back, set with diamonds. The Salisburys an old English red lacquer grandfather clock. There were jewelled paperweights, jewelled electric bells. Lord Rosebery gave an old clock with a lovely Battersea enamel plaque; paper cutters, magnifying glasses, splendidly bound books – in short, there were all the Bond Street jewellers and Asprey combined on those tables.*

Queen Alexandra expressed genuine pleasure even after 50 years of being showered with gifts, and this could not but charm the giver. Knutsford observed: 'What pleased her most, I think, was Howe's present of a little hippopotamus made of silver by this Russian, perfectly modelled, and when wound up, it walked by means of little clockwork wheels in the legs, and wagged its tail! . . .' The etiquette of giving was that the note should include as well as the donor's name 'any description of what the present is if it be anything curious, or old, needing an explanation'. That, in a nutshell, is the way royal collections grow.

Only a year later the King died aged 69, unrepentently smoking and drinking to the last. In spite of everything Alexandra was bereft. Her sister Dagmar had been widowed in 1894 when Alexander III died of Bright's disease at 45, and now the sisters spent more time together. Dagmar was estranged from her son and daughter-in-law over the unfortunate influence on them of Rasputin, and at the time of the Russian Revolution in 1917 she was at her palace in the Crimea, under the protection of the White Army. George V sent a British warship to fetch her in 1919, and, with an annual pension of £30,000 paid by him, she went to live at the expense of her Danish nephew, Christian X, at Amalienborg. Her nephews failed to persuade her to support herself and her daughters by selling the jewels that she had smuggled out of Russia, and it was only after her death in 1928 that they were discreetly slipped on to the market through the firm of Hennell's in London, with the intention of providing pensions for her daughter and grand-daughters. Largely due to misunderstandings that were never cleared up, a great scandal was to develop around the fate of the superb diamond-set jewels and pearls. Queen Mary bought many of them, including a diamond cluster brooch, two diamond and sapphire tiaras, a diamond choker and pearls galore, as well as the diamond and sapphire brooch with a pendant pearl, a wedding present to Dagmar from the Prince and Princess of Wales. The Dowager Empress's two grand-daughters believed that they had been swindled out of a large sum of money by their British royal relatives, and they never discovered that this was not true. Only very belatedly was proof of prompt payment, often above the valuations, discovered in Hennell's archive and published.

Queen Alexandra's final years were not happy; she feared the loss of her looks – a rare untouched photograph taken at the time of her coronation in 1902 shows that she had reason – and her deafness was now so profound that she was effectively cut off from most human contact. She lived on until 1925, still at Sandringham, while her son and daughter-in-law, now King George V and Queen Mary, were crammed into York Cottage, a short walk away in the grounds. The Fabergé collection was kept at Sandringham, and the drawing-room and Queen Alexandra's sitting-room were both stuffed with the other fruits of her collecting and her devotion to family souvenirs. However, she had an incomparable gift as a home-maker. Apart from the Goya tapestries there was little in the house of great artistic merit, though everything was of wonderful quality – and meticulously cared for – creating an atmosphere of comfort and luxury. Queen Mary was faced with the problem of making some practical order in her rooms after Queen Alexandra's death in 1925: 'All the rooms are more airey now and less full of those odds & ends which beloved Mama wld poke into every corner of the house which was a pity', she wrote in August, 1926. The dismantling of Alexandra's presence had begun.

Marjorie Merriweather Post,
miniature portrait in a gold and
enamelled frame by Fabergé.
Hillwood Museum, Washington DC.

Marjorie Merriweather Post

Much married and a stunningly attractive and spirited woman – as the many portraits of her show – Marjorie Merriweather Post was the sole heiress to an enormous breakfast-cereal fortune. Her father, Charles William Post, started life as a travelling salesman and only came upon the formula that made his fortune through searching for a cure for his persistent ill health. He taught his daughter early on to respect the obligations of great wealth, and she was to become one of the foremost American philanthropists of her day, giving enormous sums to educational and musical charities. She had a conventional upbringing in Battle Creek, Michigan, and at a finishing school in Washington DC, but Post introduced her to the business world and to board meetings at the Postum Cereal Company. She was devastated when, after another bout of ill health, he committed suicide in 1914.

In 1905 Marjorie had married into New York society. Edward Bennett Close was a lawyer with good connections, and the young couple lived with their two daughters in Greenwich, Connecticut. On her father's death she inherited millions and the Postum Company; her husband represented her on the board of the company, but they ran it from New York and to Marjorie's growing frustration left the world of Battle Creek and business matters to look after themselves. With the outbreak of World War I, Mrs Close proved her worthiness as a great heiress when she funded a Red Cross hospital with 2,000 beds at Savenay in France. She had changed from the shy mid-westerner, who had entered into married life as a naive and unsophisticated eighteen-year-old, and with her growing assurance the marriage to Close gradually fell apart.

If Close had found himself unequal to the challenge of maintaining and expanding a huge business empire, Marjorie's second husband, self-made stockbroker Edward Francis Hutton, was to prove the opposite. He was responsible for making the Postum Cereal empire into a major company, with an aggressive policy of expansion and flotation. In 1929 it became the General Foods Corporation and developed into the largest food business in the United States. One detail was to rankle with Hutton; it was his wife who had urged the crucial acquisition of the Birdseye Frosted Food business, which transformed the fortunes of the Postum Cereal Company. During the Depression Mrs Hutton was awarded the Cross of Honor of the United States Flag Association for her charitable activities. She was well-in with the Roosevelts, but her support for Franklin D. Roosevelt's New Deal and her charity work drove a wedge through her second marriage; in 1935 she was divorced again. It was while married to Hutton, however, that she embarked on the lifestyle that made her notorious among the big-spending millionaires of the 1920s.

With her huge inheritance and Hutton's successful nurturing of her fortune, she was now able to have everything in excess, homes, clothes – a lifelong passion – and precious possessions. Hutton was an admirer of eighteenth-century France and collected furniture, tapestries and Sèvres porcelain. For Marjorie this was a congenial change from the heavy neo-Renaissance furnishings of her first married home. She had already started buying French art and *objets de virtu* – gold boxes, *étuis* and the like – on her own account, and her preferred style of decorating was to be eighteenth century thereafter. Hutton embarked on a building spree, starting in 1920 with the famous 'Hillwood' estate on Long Island; this was an English Jacobean-style half-timbered mansion by Charles Hart, a Beaux-Arts-trained architect. A notable feature was the magnificent garden designed by Marion Cruger Coffin, a mixture of formality and naturalism inspired by Gertrude Jeckyll. An enormous shooting estate in South Carolina and a rugged – but supremely luxurious – 'camp' in the Adirondacks, catered for sporting pastimes. A masseuse and a hairdresser attended the guests, who were conveyed to Camp Topridge by private plane, chauffeur-driven limousine, a boat across the lake and, finally, a miniature funicular railway that went up from the lake to the house. Stuffed animals, chairs upholstered in leopard and bearskin and antler chandeliers formed the backdrop for a choice display of Native Americana.

Mrs Post shared a trait with other women collectors – she was a perfectionist. Her dining tables were laid with precision, as for a royal banquet, each solid gold place-setting conforming to set measurements with the aid of a ruler (she would check the final result for accuracy, the footmen being punished by a rap over the knuckles for any deviation). Most splendid of all was 'Mar-A-Lago', a Hispano-Moresque 'cottage' of enormous proportions at the resort of Palm Beach, designed by the Viennese Joseph Urban, whose main business was devising settings for the Zeigfield Follies. Urban was hopelessly impractical, and Hutton insisted that the project be a collaboration with a Beaux-Arts graduate, Marion Wyeth. It was fitted out at immense cost; Wyeth had secured an enormous collection of rare old Moorish and Spanish tiles from Mrs Horace Havermeyer and these were used for decorating the interior. The Roman dining-room (inspired by the Chigi Palace in Rome with frescoes imitating the originals) boasted a marble dining table inlaid with Florentine intarsia work said to be worth a million dollars (in the 1920s), but in fact designed by Urban at a cost of £4,000. Mrs Hutton's boudoir was compared by one visitor to Versailles. The scale of the entertaining at Mar-A-Lago was in keeping, with parties that have entered into the legends of between-wars society. One especially memorable event was a performance by the Ringling Brothers Circus. It is impossible not to be reminded of the Marx Brothers, and their succession of farcical society capers ridiculing this kind of entertaining.

Like Helena Rubinstein, Mrs Hutton was famous in American Society for the number and splendour of her jewels. She had a taste for fine precious stones, which she had set as jewellery by the Maison Cartier. Persian and Indian styles were still the fashion in the late 1920s, and the most important pieces form a suite of shoulder brooch and *sautoir*, incorporating very large carved Mughal emeralds in a setting of massed diamonds and black enamel. One of the emeralds has a carved inscription identifying it with a mid-seventeenth century Indian prince, a valuable antique in its own right. In 1929 she commissioned a ruby and diamond necklace, the rubies being taken from an old Indian ornament. This was the year when she was presented at court to George V and Queen Mary, and wore for the occasion a pair of diamond corsage pendants by Cartier. The same year she ordered a shoulder-brooch setting for fancy-cut diamonds – heart-shaped, navette (or pointed oval-shaped) and triangular stones – and the designer had to make several alternative arrangements before getting it to her satisfaction. At about this date an enamelled gold desk clock is recorded in her client account, and she commissioned from the New York branch enamelled frames for ivory miniature portraits in co-ordinated colours.

Meanwhile it is hardly surprising to find her attention turning towards Fabergé; in 1926 she bought – incidentally from Cartier – an amethyst quartz box by the workmaster Mikhail Perkhin (d.1903) from the Youssoupov family collection. Set in the lid in a circle of emeralds and large old diamonds is a ruby matrix cameo of a recumbent lion, possibly a carved Mughal piece. It seems legitimate to suppose that the connection with Mughal jewellery was the attraction, given Mrs Post's taste for Indian emeralds; it must surely have been the reason why Cartier earmarked this piece for her. Her next Fabergé acquisition was one of the most important. In 1931 her daughter Eleanor presented her with an Imperial Easter Egg, the Louis XV-style 'Grisaille' or 'Catherine the Great' Egg, made by workmaster Hendrik Wigström, and given by Nicholas II to his mother, Marie Feodorovna, in 1914. Reserved in the enamel are panels painted *en grisaille* by Vasily Zuiev with groups evoking the Arts and Sciences.

Marie Feodorovna wrote, in a letter to her sister Queen Alexandra:

Fabergé brought it to me himself. It is a true chef d'oeuvre, in pink enamel and inside a porte-chaise carried by two negroes with Empress Catherine in it wearing a little crown on her head. You wind it up and then the negroes walk – it is an unbelievably beautiful and superbly fine piece of work. Fabergé is the greatest genius of our time. I also told him Vous êtes un génie incomparable.

The piece was bought by Dr Armand Hammer in 1930, among a large number of precious objects from the post-revolutionary dispersals by the Soviet authorities.

Marjorie Merriweather Post might have settled for a life of conspicuous extravagance and entertaining, but she used her fortune to assemble the largest and most important collection of Russian works of art outside Russia, and to furnish a private museum, the Hillwood Collection, housed in a neo-Georgian mansion, elaborately refitted in the 1950s, at 4155 Linnean Avenue, Washington DC. As far as forming such a collection was concerned, she was in a particularly advantageous position, because she had remarried, just two months after her divorce from Hutton, to Joseph E. Davies, political friend and supporter of Roosevelt, who was named US Ambassador to the Soviet Union in 1936. It seems to have been Davies who initially fired her enthusiasm for Russian art. The Russian collection includes Fabergé, of course, but it has an enormous range, including paintings, porcelain, silver, icons and precious chalices. One of its greatest treasures is the diamond-set nuptial crown, worn at their weddings by all empresses and grand duchesses from the early nineteenth century. It left Russia in 1927 by order of a Bolshevik committee, to be auctioned at Christie's in London with other items from the Russian crown jewels, and was bought for £6,100.

Later she was to engage in a battle of wits with the eminent Fabergé dealer A. Kenneth Snowman, over another of her finest possessions. She wanted the magnificent gold chalice set with antique cameos and profusely enriched with diamonds, made on Catherine the Great's orders in 1793 for the Convent of St Alexander in St Petersburg, in memory of Prince Potemkin, but she was shocked by the enormous price Snowman was asking, at that time a record for an *objet d'art*. She offered a substantial reduction, which he refused, and so she withdrew. Snowman was convinced that he had forfeited this important deal and spent a sleepless night of regrets, but in the end it was he who had won, and she paid the full price.

The new Ambassador and his wife arrived in Leningrad in their yacht, the *Sea Cloud*, sailing up the River Neva like royalty. Mrs Merriweather Post was a collector – rather than a client – of Fabergé, since she did not start buying until after the demise of the firm in the wake of Russian Revolution. This put her in the position of being able to acquire objects with the grandest associations, many of them to the imperial family itself. At this period the prices of Fabergé pieces were relatively reasonable (as 'second-hand' merchandise, being resold barely a decade after they had been created) and it was religious artefacts, particularly icons set in silver and enamel, of which Mrs Post bought a great number, that were fetching really high prices. Using the palatial *Sea Cloud* as their base, Mr and Mrs Davies ventured farther into Russia. Later Mrs

Post would recall buying silver for the equivalent of 5 cents per gram weight, and of picking through piles of vestments from the outlawed Orthodox churches heaped on the floor of Soviet government commission shops. Her industrious pursuit of knowledge, which had included studying tapestries and textiles at the Metropolitan Museum, now stood her in good stead.

The Fabergé collection numbers approximately 90 pieces, including two Imperial Eggs, ultimate desiderata of the Fabergé aficionado. As well as the 'Grisaille' egg, Mrs Post owned the 'Twelve-Monogram' egg, composed of six panels in deep blue guilloché (engraved on metal) enamel inset with diamond 'A III' and 'MF' monograms, made in 1892 and presented by Alexander III to Marie Feodorovna as a silver wedding gift. This was bought in 1949 from Mrs G.V. Berchelli, an Italian collector. Other Fabergé pieces in the Hillwood Collection with imperial connections include, for example, a silver tea service made in the Moscow workshops in 1909, enamelled gold frames containing Romanov family photographs and diamond-set presentation boxes and miniature-set brooches from members of the imperial family. As well as the two imperial eggs, an unusual Rococo clock, copying an English eighteenth-century musical model by James Hagger in the manner of James Cox, also belonged to Marie Feodorovna (the clock itself, from the imperial collection, is now in the Walters Art Gallery, Baltimore). There is a strong bias in favour of pieces inspired by the French eighteenth-century, but Mrs Post also bought Moscow enamels in the 'Old Russian' taste (imitating seventeenth-century traditional work), as a link with the rest of her Russian collection. A miniature set into a fine enamelled silver-gilt *kvosh* (or traditional drinking vessel) shows a detail of the bridal couple taken from Konstantin Makovski's most popular painting, *The Boyar Wedding Feast*, which is itself in the Hillwood collection. She had a great liking for Fabergé's enamelled miniature and photograph frames, which were often filled with portraits of her own family. Two enamelled frames by Cartier with photographs of the Grand Duchess Olga and the Grand Duchess Tatjana complete the circle between client andcollector, complementing the Cartier frames commissioned by her in the 1920s.

Mrs Merriweather Post assumed her maiden name in 1964 after her divorce from her fourth husband, Herbert Arthur May, head of the Westinghouse Corporation. She was still collecting, encouraged by the distinguished curator at Hillwood, the Byzantinist Marvin C. Ross, whom she had poached from the Walters Art Gallery. She died nine years later, and her obituaries laid particular emphasis on her business acumen and her massive charitable disbursements, but her name is indelibly associated with Russian art and precious bibelots, those by Fabergé above all.

The Hillwood Museum (named for the now sold estate built with Hutton) was presented to the Smithsonian Institution by Mrs Post, but after her death it was returned to a Trust and it still has the atmosphere of private ownership. The visitor feels privileged, since security measures dictate very limited numbers. The jewel collection is so large that it has to be rotated, and the sensation of being admitted behind the scenes is enhanced by numerous family photographs, many of them showing Mrs Post's beautiful actress daughter Nedenia (Dina Merrill). In the grounds a *dacha*, the wooden chalet-type house occupied by city-dwelling Russians in the summer months, houses the more folksy of the Russian *objets d'art* such as the porcelain costume figures and traditional enamels, and – incongruously – the very fine collection of Native American art which was once at Camp Topridge in the Adirondacks. Mrs Post shared Queen Mary's taste for 'black' furniture, made of lacquered *papier maché* painted and gilt and inlaid with mother-of-pearl, which the Empress Eugénie had brought into fashion during the Second Empire in Paris. One of the Hillwood bedrooms is stuffed full of it.

CHAPTER VII

American Chatelaines

Isabella Stewart Gardner (1840–1924)
Mrs Potter (Berthe Honoré) Palmer (1849–1918)

I n his recent survey of American art, *American Visions*, Robert Hughes observed that in the second half of the nineteenth century 'the museum began to supplant the church as the focus of great American cities'. These cities needed a cultural framework to match their industrial might, and lacking either old royal collections or war booty to annexe, the responsibility fell on individuals to supply culture, in the form works of art and buildings to house them. In a field largely dominated by men, Boston and Chicago were unusual in seeing the creation of important art collections by formidable women. Possessed of great personal magnetism and individuality, both Mrs Gardner and Mrs Potter Palmer made their mark as prominent socialites before tackling the intellectually demanding role of art collector. If Mrs Gardner is the more obviously significant in international terms, Mrs Palmer has a particular interest in having an acknowledged feminist agenda in her cultural pursuits.

Isabella Stewart Gardner

The woman is standing, her feet side by side, her knees close together, in an almost hieratic pose. Her body, rendered supple by exercise, is sheathed – you might say moulded – in a tight-fitting black dress. Rubies, like drops of blood, sparkle on her shoes. Her slender waist is encircled by a girdle of enormous pearls, and from this dress, which makes an intensely dark background for the stony brilliance of the jewels, the arms and shoulders shine out with another brilliance, that of a flower-like flesh – fine, white flesh, through which flows blood perpetually invigorated by the air of the country and the ocean. The head, intellectual and daring, with a countenance as of one who has understood everything, has, for a sort of aureole, the vaguely gilded design of one of those Renascence stuffs which the Venetians call sopra-risso. The rounded arms, in

123

which the muscles can hardly be seen, are joined by clasped hands – firm hands, the thumb almost too long, which might guide four horses with the precision of an English coachman. It is the picture of an energy at once delicate and invincible, momentarily in repose, and all the Byzantine Madonna is in that face, with its wide-open eyes.

Visiting an exhibition of paintings by John Singer Sargent (1856–1925) in Boston in 1888, Paul Bourget wrote the above description of one of them in *Outre-Mer*, a book recording his impressions of America. It was a portrait of Isabella Stewart Gardner. Astonishingly, although he was a friend of Sargent, Paul Bourget did not know the identity of the woman in the portrait, whom he described so perceptively. Mrs Jack Gardner had known the artist for about two years and had heard of the scandalous and remarkable *Portrait of Mme X* (*Mme Gautreau*, Metropolitan Museum of Art), which had caused such a sensation in Paris in 1884; she was determined to have something equally sensational herself. The portrait was achieved with great anguish to the artist, Mrs Gardner having refused the first eight versions. It caused widespread comment, and it is said that Jack Gardner overheard men at the bar in his club discussing the sitter's daring *décolleté*. He immediately withdrew the picture from public view and instructed that it should not be shown again during his lifetime. Isabella, out of respect for his memory, did not show it even after she was widowed.

The iconic effect is enhanced by the background, a length of patterned silk still in the Gardner Museum's collection, with the design so placed as to form a halo behind the subject's head. The perfectly fitting dress was almost certainly from Worth in Paris, Mrs Gardner's preferred *modiste*. The pearls, which made such an impression on Bourget, were famous in Boston and something of a trademark of Mrs Jack's. The ropes were composed of necklaces purchased over a period from 1874, when the first was bought at Hancock's in London. Boucheron supplied five more from 1884 to 1892, and the resulting collection of 231 large pearls cost a small fortune. Sargent must have been allowed access to the portrait later to add the ruby pendants hanging from the pearls, since they were not purchased from Boucheron until 1892. Mrs Jack quickly learnt to use jewellery to make an effect and wore a diamond sun brooch on the back of her head so that it appeared to be setting. From her travels in the 1880s she acquired massive Mughal gold bracelets and an aigrette holder set with emeralds and other coloured gems, fashion accessories well calculated to startle Boston society. She was not beautiful but, in a way a far greater asset, she was full of spirit and sexually attractive, and her figure was quite remarkable for a woman approaching 50. One of her many portraits, by Anders Zorn (1860–1920), shows these qualities clearly.

When Sargent was painting her portrait Mrs Gardner had only just embarked on a serious collecting career. Contemplating the extraordinary riches of the Gardner Museum, it might seem that a lifetime had been spent in assembling them but, in fact, the core of the collection was established in hardly more than a decade of intensive activity. It is interesting to trace her arrival, after nearly 30 years of marriage, at the point of devoting her energies to the pursuit of world masterpieces in an extraordinarily wide field of art.

Isabella Stewart Gardner (detail) by John Singer Sargent. Isabella Stewart Gardner Museum, Boston.

Isabella Stewart was from a well-to-do New York family, and she used to emphasize the grandeur of her lineage by references to the Stuart royal dynasty. She married Bostonian Jack Gardner, the brother of a school friend, who was also well born and sufficiently wealthy, only days after her twentieth birthday in 1860. Her father built them a house in fashionable Beacon Street, and the young couple moved there in 1862. In the following year she had a son, and she was devastated when he died in 1865, not even two years old. At a stroke her life was irredeemably altered, since she already knew that she could not have another child. For two years she sunk into a profound melancholy, and with a great effort of will was persuaded at the end of 1867 to seek distraction in travel. Although she was still plagued by indifferent health and was to be for many more years, the distraction worked and the first seeds of her recovery were sown. Her latent aesthetic sense was reawakened in Copenhagen, where she was full of admiration for the sculptures of Bertel Thorwaldsen. The six months in Europe on that first trip were followed by travels in the East six years later. Her Egyptian diary is embellished with watercolours of the sights, and she kept, as usual, copious notes. Thereafter she spent weeks in Venice every year, renting the Palazzo Barbaro and entertaining friends there.

Meanwhile Mrs Gardner was making her presence felt in Boston with her unconventional clothes and her sensational style of entertaining. As a girl in Boston at the time, Mrs Winthrop (Daisy) Chanler remembered how 'Mrs Jack' was talked about for her 'unscrupulous flirtations, her lavish extravagance, and her seasons of repentant piety. On Ash Wednesday she would appear in penetential black with a rosary hanging from her belt . . . She stood out in vivid contrast to the people among whom she lived, and seemed to belong to another age and clime, where passions burned brighter, pleasures were more sumptuous, and repentances more dramatic than in sober Beacon Street.'

Many of the girls from Daisy Chanler's respectable Boston milieu were not allowed to attend her parties. In 1875 a Boston newspaper reported:

> *Mrs Jack Gardner is one of the seven wonders of Boston. There is nobody like her in any city in this country. She is a millionaire Bohemienne. She is eccentric, and has the courage of eccentricity. She is the leader of the smart set, but she often leads where none dare follow. She is 35, plain and wide-mouthed, but has the handsomest neck, shoulders and arms in all Boston. She imitates nobody; everything she does is novel and original. She is as brilliant as her own diamonds, and as attractive. All Boston is divided into two parts, of which one follows science, and the other Mrs Jack Gardner.*

She enjoyed the company of handsome men and was suspected of having affairs; she certainly lost her heart to the young novelist, F. Marion Crawford. They read Dante's *Divine Comedy* together, their two copies bound together by Tiffany to a design by Marion Crawford.

Stories of her escapades were legion, many of them untrue, but Morris Carter, her first biographer quoted her as saying 'Don't spoil a good story by telling the truth'. Having exhausted the pleasures of shocking Boston society with her eccentric behaviour, in 1878 she enrolled for a course of lectures given by Charles Eliot Norton (1827–1908) at Harvard University. Norton, friend of Ruskin, Dickens and Carlyle, was responsible for introducing the History of Art to the Harvard curriculum, and Mrs Gardner was to find his guidance invaluable in her early forays into buying art. It was through Norton that she began her book collecting, starting, naturally, with the works of Dante. In 1880 the Gardners bought the next door house in Beacon Street in order to give Mrs Jack a proper music room, and in keeping with the French character of the architecture the rooms were hung with French paintings of a slightly earlier period – by Delacroix and Corot and landscapes by painters of the Barbizon school, based in the Forest of Barbizon outside Paris. The Gardners' travels produced souvenirs and curiosities, stained glass, textiles and furniture, and these joined the French paintings in an ensemble typical of the taste of a fashionable American socialite. In 1888, the year of the Sargent portrait, Mrs Gardner also bought the ravishing *Lady in Yellow*, by Thomas Wilmer Dewing, one of a small group of Bostonian paintings acquired mostly on the recommendation of friends.

A trip to Europe in 1879 resulted in acquaintance with Whistler, who later made the first portrait of Mrs Gardner, a sensitive pastel entitled, typically, *The Little Note in Yellow and Gold*. Mrs Gardner's portraits were considerable works of art in their own right, the Sargent and the

Zorn being among the finest by either artist. Friends from the circle around Norton and Harvard now congregated in Beacon Street, among them Henry James and his brother William, Henry Adams, Oliver Wendell Holmes, all passionately committed to art. In his Boston novel *An American Politician*, Marion Crawford described the contrasting conversational themes on Dante and finance that dominated Mrs Gardner's drawing-room, where he himself spent much of his time.

Henry James paid her teasing compliments, and read her his dramatization of *Daisy Miller*, but he found her friendship oppressive and was not above complaining that 'the mere distant dim image of Mrs Jack 'going it' on the graves of the Caesars & the lifts of the Grand Hotels makes me huddle closer to my fireside'. He was her guest at the Palazzo Barbaro in Venice, where she had the imaginative notion of setting up his bed in the large and richly decorated library. He was a faithful visitor in her declining years when she was ill and neglected.

It was in 1886, also through Norton, that Mrs Gardner met Bernard Berenson, a momentous event in her life and his; any account of her collecting is bound also to be an account of Berenson's activities and his development as a world-renowned connoisseur. Their correspondence makes fascinating reading, from BB's early and self-consciously exquisite literary musings to the irritable screeds that followed Mrs Gardner's failure to find funds for his greatest discoveries. The tinge of sentiment in his early letters may indicate his wish to occupy the same niche as Marion Crawford, but Mrs Gardner seems to have discouraged this sharply, and there is a break of some years in the exchange between 1889 and 1894. The offering of his first book on art paved the way for the resumption of their correspondence, and from then on the subject matter is the pursuit of pictures for Mrs Gardner's burgeoning collection. Not long after he had started to counsel her in earnest he wrote: 'If you permit me to advise you in art-matters as you have for the year past, it will not be many years before you possess a collection almost unrivalled – of masterpieces, and masterpieces only.'

Berenson had set himself an impossible agenda, and with wonderful exceptions he unavoidably fell short of his own ambitious brief. It can hardly be coincidence that Mrs Gardner began her serious Old Master buying in 1891, soon after the death of her father had brought her $2,750,000. When the Gardners returned from Europe that year they carried with them five Old Master paintings, two Whistlers and a Rossetti. The Rossetti came from Frederick Leyland, an English collector who mixed contemporary art with Old Masters, and it may have been this ambience that appealed to Mrs Gardner, since she never bought another Pre-Raphaelite work. In the following year she made a tremendous coup, buying *The Concert* by Vermeer at the Thoré Bürger auction in Paris in December, encouraged by another artist friend, Paul Helleu. Her industrious sightseeing, backed by the annotated photo albums that she assembled, now paid off, and with the Vermeer to boost her confidence she moved inexorably forward towards the creation of the Gardner Museum.

Berenson's name is identified with the Renaissance, and it is the dominant theme of his writings, but his range in terms of connoisseurship was amazing. The first purchase that he negotiated successfully set the stakes high: Botticelli's *Tragedy of Lucretia* from the Earl of

Ashburnham was soon followed by works by Titian, Velasquez, Rembrandt, Rubens and Van Dyck. Mrs Gardner fought every inch of the way, complaining bitterly about the money, while trembling with anticipation as each new purchase made its slow way to Boston. The Gardners' still hazy notions of creating a museum crystallized with the purchase of the first of their four Rembrandts in 1896. This early self-portrait, bought at Berenson's recommendation from Colnaghi for £3,000, was to be joined within the space of five years by *A Lady and Gentleman in Black, The Storm at Sea* and *The Obelisk*. The Vermeer and Rembrandt's unique seascape were both stolen from the collection in 1990 and have not yet been recovered. *The Obelisk* is now re-attributed to Govaert Flinck (1615–60); inevitably a number of Berenson's 'masterpieces' have not stood up to subsequent scholarly scutiny, but Titian's *Rape of Europa* retains its title as the finest painting in the museum and possibly the best by him in the United States. It was bought in 1896, as a consolation after Berenson's failure to secure Gainsborough's *Blue Boy* from the Duke of Westminster, a chapter of disappointments that eventually turned Mrs Gardner against English eighteenth-century portraits. The *Blue Boy* is now in the Huntington Art Gallery in San Marino, California.

The following years are a headlong progress from one great work to the next: Van Dyck's beautiful *Lady with a Rose* in 1897; Rubens' impressive portrait of Thomas Howard, Earl of Arundel and Raphael's *Count Tommaso Inghirami,* both 1898; the Holbein portraits of Sir William and Lady Butts in 1899; Tiepolo's *Wedding of Barbarossa* in 1900, and so on.

This brief account details only a few of the triumphs and frustrations described in the lively exchange of letters between Berenson and Mrs Gardner. Itemizing the collection is not particularly helpful and is, in a way, beside the point; it is the ensemble that speaks for Mrs Gardner's achievement. Berenson began as early as 1896 to refer to 'your gallery', and the notion of buying for a collection that would eventually be open to the public added to the strong sense that pervades the letters throughout, that many of the opportunities might never occur again and should be seized, whatever financial constraints stood in the way. Although it seems to have been Jack Gardner's idea to create the museum, it is his restraining hand that limits his wife's huge borrowings as Berenson presents more and more compelling 'last chance' scenarios.

Jack Gardner chose the site, a hitherto undeveloped area of the Fenway, where it was possible to plan for natural light on all four sides of the building. When he died suddenly in 1898 Mrs Gardner was forced to soldier on alone with the vast project. She reduced her standard of living in order to assure the museum's finances for the future, and kept up a constant battle with the contractors to finish the work to her exacting standards. Boston was steeped in Italian culture, and the choice of the Renaissance style for Fenway Court was a foregone conclusion, but it may also have been a subliminal challenge to Boston's great cultural landmark, McKim, Mead & White's Renaissance Public Library. Mrs Gardner's Italian palazzo out in the fens even went one step further, by incorporating period elements from Venetian buildings and being filled with the spoils of real palazzos in Italy. The initial impression is of dazzling colour; a mosaic-floored courtyard, dripping with brightly coloured flowering plants from the museum's greenhouse, first decreed by Mrs Gardner and never altered, is the central focus of the building. The Venetian architectural fragments – window frames, balustrades, medallions and reliefs – decorate the four stories rising up to a glass roof. The central mosaic, Roman, dating from the 2nd century AD, is flanked by examples of antique sculpture and backed by a Venetian fountain in the manner of a Renaissance villa garden. The large window openings provide glimpses of the celebrated masterpieces within. The rooms retain a strong flavour of a private collection since the works are not arranged chronologically or by school, and the finest paintings are partnered by works presented to Mrs Gardner by artist friends or young protégés. The idea was to suggest the accumulations of a family over centuries, as would have been found in a great Venetian villa.

There was desperate competition for the 150 invitations to the opening on New Year's Day 1903. The novelist Edith Wharton was very curious to see the house, and confided to a friend that she was hoping to be asked, but rumour has it that she blotted her copy book by murmuring in French to her neighbour at the supper table that the meal reminded her of the fare offered at a provincial French railway station. When she took her leave Mrs Gardner is said to have assured her that she need not worry about being invited to eat again at the station restaurant.

Mrs Gardner continued to add to the collection. Degas, Manet and Matisse – a work by the latter, given as a present to Mrs Gardner, being the first to enter an American museum – modernized the collection, which was further enriched by the acquisition of Sargent's most successful Spanish subject, a painting of the dancer entitled *El Jaleo* (bought 1914). Mrs Gardner suffered a paralytic stroke in 1919, but with her iron will she continued to follow a routine of reading and drives in the city. Sargent did a magical watercolour portrait of her, entirely enveloped in white robes, and she acquired other works, among them the most intimate portrait of the notorious Mme Gautreau, which Sargent gave to the sitter's mother – as well as drawings and a sketchbook. Berenson had not given up urging desirable acquisitions, presenting Chinese sculpture and Han Dynasty bronze bears with as much eloquence as a Titian or a Rembrandt. In 1921 she bought her last Old Master painting, a *Madonna and Child* by Giovanni Bellini from the collection of Prince Hohenzollern-Sigmaringen.

In 1902, when Fenway Court was unveiled, Mrs Gardner's collection was, momentarily, the finest in private hands in the United States. She was buying at the last moment when such great works were either affordable or available to ordinary people, often in competition with the indefatigable German art critic Wilhelm von Bode, who was building up a museum for Berlin and who was, like Berenson, a connoisseur of worldwide repute. In spite of her relatively scanty resources in comparison with the great fortunes of men like Henry Clay Frick (1849–1919) and J. Pierpont Morgan (1837–1913), she had bought early and well. She seems not to have been unduly put out by an incident in 1909, which she reported to Berenson: 'We are rather amused by a newspaper account of the Great Collections of America. It eliminates Morgan's because much of it is in Europe and goes on to say the three great ones are Frick's, Widener's and Charles Taft's. No hope for me.'

In his study of American collectors published in 1938, René Brimo singled her out: 'C'est une femme, Mrs Isabella Stewart Gardner, qui disputa à Morgan la palme de la célébrité parmi les collectionneurs americains'. He had already highlighted the important contribution by women, citing among others Mrs Havermeyer, Miss Mary Cassatt, Mrs Florence Blumenthal, Miss Kate Buckingham and Miss Lillie Bliss. If these resonate less loudly than Mrs Gardner, it is because their benefactions are buried in huge institutions, with, at most, galleries in their own names. The last three benefited respectively the Metropolitan Museum in New York, the Chicago Art Institute (with the suberb Buckingham Collection of Japanese prints and European engravings) and the Museum of Modern Art in New York (with Miss Bliss's founding collection of important modern paintings).

Mrs Potter Palmer

The predominance of women in American collecting circles was no accident. Well-off young girls were much better educated than their European contemporaries, and much of the American upper class was drawn from the business and industrial world, ensuring that these girls were also rich. Curiously, René Brimo does not include a perfect exemplar, Mrs Potter Palmer of Chicago, in his round-up of important women collectors, though he mentions the Potter Palmer collection respectfully. She was almost ten years younger than Mrs Gardner, but their paths intersected in interesting ways even though their collecting tastes were so divergent, and it is impossible not to suspect some secret rivalry between them. Certainly Berenson was not above teasing his patroness with hints of dallying in Berthe Palmer's social circle and dancing attendance on her, and on one occasion he threatened to point a Velazquez her way if Mrs Gardner could not afford it.

Mrs Gardner's first mentor, Charles Eliot Norton, subscribed to the current belief that culture transcended the works of 'solitary individual artists' and must grow out of its roots in the past. Her collecting path was mapped even before she teamed up with Berenson. Berthe Palmer's way forward was into Impressionism. Advised by Sara Hallowell, respected oganizer of Chicago's international art shows and Paris representative for a number of American museums, and Paris-based American artist Mary Cassatt – significantly both women – the Palmers assembled a fine group of French Academic and Impressionist works, some of which eventually made their way into Chicago's Art Institute.

Berthe Honoré Potter Palmer was born in Kentucky, but raised in Chicago. At the age of 21 she married Potter Palmer, the successful property tycoon, who was more than twice her age. His wealth certainly did not weigh with her in her choice, since she came from a rich family. Potter Palmer installed her in Palmer House, his luxury hotel, and there she began her married life, only to have the whole edifice tumble overnight when the hotel was devastated by the great Chicago fire of 1871. Undaunted, Palmer rebuilt it bigger and better, but he had his sights set on something grander, a magnificent house of his own, fit to rival the millionaire mansions on New York's Fifth Avenue.

It is impossible to do justice to the richly carved, painted and gilded interiors of the Palmer Castle on Lake Shore Drive in a brief account. Carving, sculptures and stucco-work fought for supremacy from the marble mosaic floors to the coffered ceilings. Hardly surprisingly, the description of the grand entrances, the several art galleries, the reception rooms and the master bedrooms reads like the specification for a luxury hotel from this age of opulence. The crowning glory was a vast art gallery with red velvet walls above a marble wainscot, added in time for Berthe Palmer's social apotheosis at the 1893 World's Columbian Exposition, an event that marked Chicago's final step towards artistic and commercial pre-eminence in the Midwest. The gallery was built for the display of the Palmers' collection of French art, which had been inaugurated with the purchase of a Corot and some Gobelins tapestries in 1889 during their visit to the Paris World's Fair, an event that also inspired their determination to see a similar fair in Chicago. The next few years saw a frenzy of purchasing, mainly from Mary Cassatt's dealer, Durand Ruel in Paris – so many pictures that they could not all hang, and can be seen in a contemporary photograph leaning against the walls of the new gallery.

In 1891, with the Chicago Fair now assuming a concrete reality, Mrs Palmer was elected president of the Board of Lady Managers, Potter Palmer himself being vice-president of the overall Board. In order to drum up support in Europe she took houses in Paris and Rome, and through a relentless round of entertaining managed to engender greater enthusiasm for this distant enterprise than would otherwise have materialized. She was certainly more sophisticated than her fellow Lady Managers, and it is an indication of her social prominence, as well as her strength of purpose, that her avant-garde ideas were accepted. The Woman's Building employed only women on its design and decoration and showed art and craftwork by women from all over the United States. Its avowed purpose was 'the advancement of women'. Mary Cassatt was among the artists – largely lesser known – chosen to execute the vast murals and decorative panels. It was an important showcase for the American Arts and Crafts Movement, bringing the craftswomen respect and a wide audience. Not one to mince words, Griselda Pollock has described this venture as being 'the first to inscribe the Woman Question into the international script'. The managers went through many viscissitudes in bringing it to fruition – not least in tolerating much scepticism and criticism of the works, but it was finally judged to be a great success. Mary Cassatt said: 'I suppose it is Mrs Palmer's French blood which gives her organizing powers and her determination that women should be *someone* and not *something*.'

The Chicago World's Fair marked a change in the balance of power between Mrs Gardner and the younger woman. With Berthe Palmer's managerial role came vast social advantages; by being merely a lender to the exhibition of 'Foreign Masterpieces Owned By Americans' in the Fine Art pavilion Mrs Gardner inevitably played a lesser part. Here, too, Berthe Palmer made her mark; in a selection still dominated by French paintings of the 1830s and 1840s, the outstanding works were Impressionist pictures lent by the Palmers and Mary Cassatt's brother, Alexander.

As far as the sublimated rivalry between the two ladies was concerned, there was more than meets the eye to the episode of the Anders Zorn portraits. Mrs Gardner had been struck by a painting of his exhibited at the Fair, showing the interior of an omnibus. Zorn was at that moment wandering through the gallery where it was displayed, and by chance Mrs Gardner asked him if he knew anything about it. She bought the picture and commenced a lifelong friendship with the artist. In the following year in Venice he painted the vibrant portrait of her bursting through the French windows of the Palazzo Barbaro in Venice, a great contrast with the coldly perfect and stately image of Berthe Palmer, which he had painted in the year of the Chicago Fair.

Berthe Palmer's involvement with the 1893 World's Fair had brought her further official roles – most notably in Paris in 1900 – and an even wider international social circle. She took up many good causes and worked for them with characteristic fervour. In 1902 Palmer died and Berthe assumed control of the family finances, managing them with such brilliance that she doubled the value of her fortune before her own death in 1918.

Both the Boston Museum of Fine Arts and the Chicago Art Institute were developing rapidly at the same time as the Gardner and Potter Palmer collections. Often in their correspondence Mrs Gardner and Berenson referred with thinly veiled contempt to the purchasing activities of the Boston committee. In contrast, Mrs Palmer seems to have preferred to collaborate with the powers-that-be. Far from treating the burgeoning of Chicago's artistic reputation as an invasion of her personal territory, she bequeathed to the Art Institute a choice of pictures up to the value of $120,000 from her collection. This group of works was to become one of the ornaments of the Institute, and her son, Potter Palmer Jr, a sensitive and intelligent collector on his own account, became President of the Board. The paintings were received in 1922, and the cream, as the Board then perceived them, was illustrated in the Annual Report for that year: *Corn Husking*, by Eastman Johnson; *The Sacred Grove*, by Pierre Puvis de Chavannes; *The Little Shepherdess*, by J.-F. Millet; *Two Circus Girls*, by Renoir; *Ballet Girls on the Stage*, by Degas; *The Bridge of Trysts*, by Corot; *Argenteuil sur Seine*, by Monet; and *Dante and Virgil*, by Delacroix. The emphasis would be different today, with the Impressionists far more dominant.

Because of the long-established habit among mid-westerners of looking to France – and specifically Paris – for their cultural guidance, the Art Institute's French nineteenth-century paintings were for a long period the best in any public museum in the United States, not least on account of the Palmer bequest, which came at a moment when a number of important bequests were transforming its standing among American art galleries. Berthe Palmer had strong opinions and she bought pictures that appealed to her and, of course, sometimes her taste conformed to the fashions of the day. Everyone had Barbizon paintings in the 1880s and 1890s, and pictures by Corot (as well as having the misty and romantic landscape mentioned above, she also had a really strong figure piece, entitled *Interrupted Reading,* which had been in the Demidoff Collection); she bought two fine Delacroix paintings and several works by Charles Cazin (a specially American preference, this) and J.-F. Millet. It was clever of the Art Institute to select the Puvis de Chavannes, not a very obvious choice at the time, because the World's Fair murals were inspired by his vast decorative panel for Rouen Museum, and it showed recognition of *The Sacred Grove*'s particular relevance to Mrs Palmer. She came to appreciate the more daring approach of Degas, Pissarro, Renoir and Monet – he was a great favourite, and she was said to have owned enough of his work to form an unbroken frieze round her reception room. Mary Cassatt was probably responsible for turning her attention in this direction, but she would never have allowed anyone to dictate her taste without question. *Argenteuil sur Seine* of 1868 is an early Monet with wonderful contrasts of colour and light. Camille Pissarro's *Place du Havre, Paris*, was painted 25 years later but is a fine strong work bridging the gap between Impressionism and the newer Pointillist technique adopted by Seurat and Signac. With her *Two Circus Girls* and *The Rower's Lunch,* the Art Institute was riding high with Renoir even before these two undoubted masterpieces were joined by more supremely attractive examples from other Chicago collections. Delacroix's *Lion Hunt* rounded out a group that made a fitting rival for Mrs Gardner's early shopping in this fashionable area.

The Palmers also collected Chinese art, mainly porcelain, and Mr Palmer assembled a distinguished group of Chinese jade carvings. If the Palmer collections had survived intact, as Mrs Gardner's did, they too would have left a significant mark on the cultural map of the United States.

CHAPTER VIII
Collecting the Impressionists

THE AMERICANS
Louisine Elder Havemeyer (1855–1929)
Mary Cassatt (1844–1926)

THE DAVIES SISTERS OF WALES
Miss Gwendoline (1882–1951)
and Miss Margaret (1884–1963)

Two unusual aspects are pertinent to the unusually creative way in which several formidable women collectors amassed pioneering collections of French Impressionism. They were pioneering taste: a study of the Havemeyers, for example, simply bears the sub-title 'Impressionism Comes to America'. The fact that Mrs Havemeyer, with the advice of Mary Cassatt, bought so far in advance of American taste and that the Davies sisters in Wales, with the help of their advisers, bought so far ahead of their time not only for Wales but for the United Kingdom is difficult to explain.

These collectors took advice, studied the field, in some instances knew the artists, went to the ground-breaking art dealers and, perhaps above all, travelled in the continent of Europe, sharpening both eye and taste. It was a visit to an exhibition at Bernheim-Jeune in Paris in 1912 of Monet's Venetian views that persuaded the Davies sisters to ask their artist friend Hugh Blaker to look out for Impressionist pictures for them.

Moreover, several were extremely conscious of the public good, and deliberately determined to ensure that what they collected was eventually to present a public face. In the main women collectors had hitherto often concentrated on the applied and decorative arts. Here are a number of unusually firm-minded women not only collecting in the area of the fine arts (as well as the decorative arts – Mrs Havemeyer, for example, commissioned the leading decorators of the day to make special bespoke interiors for her New York City mansion) but collecting the absolute contemporary or the near contemporary.

What is unclear is how much the sense of the new and the fresh was appealing. Mrs Havemeyer's delightful memoirs do convey a sense of adventure, and a delight in travel; she is charmed as well as stimulated by her European journeys. For such a society lady, she was equally advanced in her espousal of the cause of the suffragettes and women's rights, albeit her own life of privilege was courtesy of her family and her husband. She was a beguiling mixture of the domestic – she was a devoted wife and mother, and passionately concerned to show art to the best advantage in her homes – and someone who found enormous satisfaction in learning about art, patronizing artists and exploring the unknown. The Havemeyer taste for Spanish painting and Mr Havemeyer's taste for Japanese art were again ahead of their (American) times.

Was there perhaps something thrilling about being involved with the here and now, the as-yet untried and untested by the peers of these original collectors? But that their advanced and adventurous taste has enriched ours there is no doubt.

Louisine Elder Havemeyer

It takes nerve as well as taste to be a collector.

Louisine Elder Havemeyer was married to the sugar-cane king of America, Henry Osborne Havemeyer (1847–1907) in 1883. H. O. Havemeyer was the head of the American Sugar Refining Company. Louisine came from a rich, well-connected New York family, and before her marriage had been entranced by contemporary art in particular during a visit to Paris where the Philadelphian Mary Cassatt, who was some years older, had not only taken the young enthusiast under her cultural wing but introduced her to the work of Degas. Louisine reacted to her first meeting with Mary Cassatt by saying:

> *She was very kind to me, showing me the splendid things in the great city, making them still more splendid by opening my eyes to see their beauty through her own knowledge and appreciation. I felt that Miss Cassatt was the most intelligent woman I had ever met . . . no one could see art more understandingly, feel it more deeply, or express themselves more clearly than she did.*

Herself a painter, Mary Cassatt, too, was discovering the art of Degas, and she persuaded Louisine to buy one of his scenes of a ballet rehearsal, a pastel and gouache over a monotype: 'It was so new and strange to me! . . . I believed it takes special brain cells to understand Degas . . .' It was 1877, Louisine was 22, and the die was cast for a lifetime of collecting. That same year she also bought a Monet in Paris, the first Monet to come to America.

Her taste for modern French painting informed that of her husband after they were married. Havemeyer had been a keen collector before their marriage, especially of Japanese work, and he gave generously to museums, most particularly to the Metropolitan Museum in New York. In 1888 he donated a portrait of George Washington by Gilbert Stuart (1755–1828) to the museum, in 1896 a big collection of Tiffany glass, which he and his wife had commissioned, and in the same year about 2,000 fragments of Japanese textiles that he had bought from the famous Art Nouveau dealer in Paris, Samuel Bing. His final gift to the Metropolitan embraced highly significant collections of Chinese and Japanese art in all media. The Havemeyer donation is the

A Woman seated by a vase of flowers by Edgar Degas (1834–1917); oil on canvas, 1865.
Havemeyer Collection, The Metropolitan Museum of Art, New York.

most important for the museum as a whole that it has ever received; moreover, a dozen other major museums in America have benefited from the family.

As a couple, the Havemeyers were devoted to each other; they were devoted travellers, devoted parents, devoted collectors and devoted to their remarkable town house with its magnificent, specially commissioned interiors by Tiffany. When the house was completed they turned back to collecting and became the world's greatest collectors of Impressionists; for a whole decade, from 1894 to 1904, the Paris dealers Durand-Ruel and Vollard gave them first choice of whatever was on the market. In this way they amassed at least 30 examples each of the work of Corot, Courbet, Manet, Degas and Monet.

The Havemeyers bought and bought. On their own, they were occasionally taken in, particularly by doubtful paintings with impeccable names attached – and sometimes seemingly

Louisine Havemeyer
(detail) by Mary
Cassatt. Shelburne
Museum, Vermont.

impeccable documentation, and certainly appearing to come from impeccable families and impeccable connections, in Italy. But changes of attribution for the works in their collection came later.

Impressionism came to America through the Havemeyers. They also bought remarkable examples of fine and decorative arts from other periods. They travelled incessantly throughout Western Europe. Their most glittering and popular collection was in European painting, but their gifts enriched the museum's holdings of arms and armour, including pieces from Egypt, the art of Islam and of Asia, Medieval, Greek and Roman art and American decorative and fine arts. Among the many remarkable purchases they made together were Courbet's *Woman with a Parrot*, Bronzino's *Portrait of a Young Man*, as well as paintings by Rembrandt. During their journey to Spain they fell in love with El Greco and purchased his only known pure landscape,

View of Toledo (1604–14). They bought Goyas too, including the *Majas on a Balcony* (1824-35).

They seem to have collected simply for pleasure and joy. They liked to live with their art, to share it and exhibit it – they opened their homes to visitors – and they liked to give it away. Unusually, their respect for and passionate interest in the past was combined with a commitment, in terms of both commissioning and purchasing, to the art of the present; they bought almost hot off the easel. Louisine and her mentor, Mary Cassatt, however, did not appreciate the new avant-garde, the art of Picasso and Matisse.

After her husband's death in 1907, Louisine continued not only to add to the collection, but to speak publicly on two topics – art and women's suffrage. Indeed, at the end of a demonstration in 1919 in favour of women's suffrage, as Congress was voting on an amendment to the constitution, she was jailed for a night in Washington DC. Three years later she published articles on her work for women's suffrage in *Scribner's Magazine*, entitled 'The Prison Special, Memories of a Militant' in May 1922 and 'The Suffrage Torch, Memories of a Militant', in June of that year. She was a grandmother at the time and certain members of her family opposed her suffragette activities and her son-in-law, Peter Frelinghuysen, refused to have a 'jailbird' in his house.

Boating by Edouard Manet (1832–83); oil on canvas, 1874.
Havemeyer Collection, The Metropolitan Museum of Art, New York.

In 1915 she started to write her own memoirs, explaining that while 'museums have histories of their own . . . little is known of the making of private collections'. Her charming descriptions of her travels and her purchases, *Sixteen to Sixty: Memoirs of a Collector*, was first published posthumously in 1930 and has been reprinted several times since.

In her Will she left everything to her three children, but she had also added three codicils: the first left 113 works of art to the Metropolitan Museum; the second left a further 29 paintings to the Metropolitan; and the third gave authority to her son Horace, also her executor, to give to the museum any work of art not mentioned specifically elsewhere in the Will. The generosity of the children was staggering; collectively they gave to the Metropolitan almost 2,000 works of art; they consulted the curators as to what would be acceptable; and they made no conditions other than that the art be identified as belonging to the H. O. Havemeyer Collection and be permanently accessible. At one fell stroke the Metropolitan was given one of the greatest collections in the world of French nineteenth-century painting: it has been said that the paintings of Courbet, Manet and Degas can be seen in better examples and to better advantage at the Metropolitan than anywhere else. But their collection was much more – not only paintings, but drawings, prints, sculpture, ceramics, glass, metalwork, lacquer-work and textiles, an enormous range of superb examples of the fine and decorative arts. The total number of gifts made to the Metropolitan Museum from the Havemeyers and their children came to something like 4,500 magnificent works of art, outstanding in scope as well as in quality. The Metropolitan's 1993 publication, on the occasion of an exhibition on the Havemeyer Gift, fully acknowledges their staggering generosity.

Mrs Havemeyer's three children were also collectors, and also made gifts of their art. Her daughter, Electra Havemeyer Webb (1888–1960), founded her own museum, the Shelburne Museum, on the shores of Lake Champlain in western Vermont. Mrs Webb inherited remarkable paintings from her mother, which can be seen at Shelburne. But her extraordinary interest was to collect whole buildings – for example, a two-storey lighthouse, a Methodist church of 1840, an inn, a blacksmith's shop, a barn and farmhouses, a sawmill and a general store. Perhaps most astonishing of all was a full-scale working steamboat, the 220-ft steam-driven, side-wheeler *SS Ticonderoga*, which had once plied Lake Champlain, a steam locomotive and one of the last covered bridges in North America. Americana in its widest sense is the subject of the Shelburne Museum, which is said to have some 180,000 items. Weather vanes, quilts, ship figureheads, carousel horses, rugs, costume, life-size carved wooden 'cigar store' Indians, cooking pots, furniture – all these are part of the Shelburne. The assembly of artefacts ranges from humble folk art to the finest American colonial furniture. On hearing that his mother was to have a recuperative holiday in Alaska, one of her sons, aware of her energy and ambition, begged her not to bring back Mt McKinley for the museum. She has been described as inheriting her father's ability to buy in bulk – he once told his daughter 'It takes nerve as well as taste to be a collector'. Electra followed her inclinations to collect American folk art, which was rather robustly referred to by Louisine as 'American trash'. Her fascination for Americana antedated the nationwide determination to embrace the artifacts of the American past.

Mary Cassatt

I felt that Miss Cassatt was the most intelligent woman I had ever met . . . no one could see art more understandingly.

(Mrs Havemeyer)

Mary Cassatt, the American 'aristocrat' from Philadelphia whom Louisine met in Paris, was a collector, as well as a painter and printmaker and one of the most important and significant American artists of her period whose work is being increasingly appreciated, but has always been loved. She was admitted to the circle of the Impressionists in Paris; Degas, notorious for his curmudgeonly attitude towards women, evidently rather grudgingly announced 'I will not admit that a woman can draw so well'. She was unmarried, which made it perhaps piquant that her characteristic and favourite subject was a mother and a child, or children. She did affecting portraits, including those of the Havemeyers.

Perhaps even more important than her achievements as an artist was her role as a catalyst who dramatically encouraged well-connected and wealthy Americans who came in a steady flow on the American version of the Grand Tour to Europe – friends, acquaintances, friends of friends – to collect art. She knew everybody in the art world: artists, collectors, dealers, scholars. Ambroise Vollard, the pioneering Paris dealer, described her energy on behalf of other artists as a 'frenzy' with which 'that generous Mary Cassatt laboured for the success of her comrades'. Cassatt scholars have suggested that the diminution of her own artistic powers meant that her role as an apologist and promoter for her artistic peers took on ever more importance, both for herself and for those she advised. She came from the same milieu – she was 'one of us', as the American aristocrats of wealth and class put it.

Mary Cassatt took it upon herself almost single-handedly to ensure that examples of the contemporary art that she so fervently admired, and the older art that she also considered to be among the finest achievements of Western art, found their way to America. In 1909 she wrote to a Boston collector, Frank Macomber, that it had 'been one of the chief pleasures of my life to help fine things across the Atlantic'. The impulse behind this was connected with her passion for making art and her memories of how little great art had been publicly available when she was young in Philadelphia. She shared with the collectors whose activities she encouraged a conviction that art was not only wonderful in itself but was a powerful educative force.

Buying from dealers and artists in Paris, she owned work by Courbet and Manet, as well as Berthe Morisot, Monet, Camille Pissarro, Cézanne, and Degas was probably the artist she admired most. Through her recommendations, the Havemeyers were eventually to own 30 Monets and over 40 Courbets; some of the Degas works she once owned were bought by the Havemeyers. She sold from her own collection if she felt that the purchasers – museums and other collectors – would further the cause. In her own collection there was a fine group of Japanese prints, just the kind of prints that had been so influential on the idioms and views of Impressionist painters.

Among the collectors and friends Mary Cassatt advised was another remarkable woman, an artist and photographer, Sarah Choate Sears, the widow of a successful Bostonian real estate entrepreneur, Joshua Montgomery Sears. Mrs Sears visited Paris regularly over more than two decades, and put together an adventurous collection of contemporary art. Sarah Choate Sears looked beyond Mary Cassatt, in fact, to the next generation, the artists admired by the Steins, especially Matisse. Mary Cassatt could never think of Modernist artists as anything but dreadful, and loathed both the paintings and the people that she witnessed during a visit to the salon held by Gertrude and Leo Stein. Be that as it may, it was left to others, including some notable women collectors, to move on into the twentieth century; but it was due to Mary Cassatt as mentor and advisor that so many 'fine things' made the journey west from Europe to the New World.

Miss Gwendoline and Miss Margaret

Collectors of 'advanced' taste

A small but perfectly formed collection of late nineteenth-century French painting and sculpture is one of the highlights of the fine art collections of the National Museum of Wales in Cardiff. It was created and then bequeathed to the museum by two sisters, Miss Gwendoline Davies and Miss Margaret Davies. While modern scholarship has questioned a number of attributions, a significant section of the art in the Davies Collection provides the most outstanding examples of the period in any British public collection. Moreover, the sisters were markedly ahead of their time in their choices.

Their grandfather, David Davies, started his working life as a carpenter and, self-made, rose to be a contractor, gathering together a substantial fortune in the mid-nineteenth century in the coal industry and in the new railways – especially the Great Western Railway – that were uniting the country. His son, Edward, carried on the family business and had three children, David, who became a Member of Parliament and subsequently the first Lord Davies, Gwendoline and Margaret.

The sisters shared their lives. They were brought up in Wales by their Canadian stepmother, and the younger sister, Margaret, went for a short while to the Slade School of Art in London. By their early 20s, both were buying paintings, on the advice of artist Hugh Blake (1873–1936), who was effectively also a dealer and whose sister Jane had first been the girls' governess and later their stepmother's companion. She also accompanied Gwendoline and Margaret on frequent trips to France.

They bought art almost compulsively from 1908 until 1924; in the course of their acquisitions they made what was then the largest collection in Britain of Impressionist and Post-Impressionist painting. Most of their purchases had as their subject landscapes and rural

Gwendoline Davies photographed in 1937.
National Museum of Wales, Cardiff.

Margaret Davies photographed in about 1930.
National Museum of Wales, Cardiff.

views. There are hardly any of the café scenes, the parties, the pastimes that so many associate with the artists of the period.

Why the Davies sisters, even with the encouragement of Hugh Blaker, decided to spend on art, and art of an 'advanced' kind, is not clear. When travelling, to London, to Paris, to Italy, they did visit galleries and exhibitions. But they did not mix in the art world, go regularly to exhibitions, know artists, visit studios. Rather, they looked at sale and exhibition catalogues and consulted with agents and dealers, often from their home in Wales. Works were sent to them for approval and decision.

They purchased the artists they admired with determined consistency; early on they bought six landscapes by Corot. Subsequently, including some spectacular highlights, they purchased three major paintings by Manet; nine late Monets, including scenes of Venice and Rouen Cathedral and of the famous waterlilies from his garden at Giverny, where form dissolves into rays of colour; fourteen paintings and five drawings by Daumier – more paintings by this artist than are in the French national collection – ten paintings by Jean-François Millet, the poet of the working people of French rural life; three magnificent oil paintings by Cézanne and three of his watercolours; and a vibrant landscape by Van Gogh, painted in July 1890, the month that he died. There is a surprising sensuality about several of the works they acquired. They bought Renoir's ravishing masterpiece, *La Parisienne*, the portrait of a young woman dressed in blue, and among the nine sculptures by Rodin was *The Kiss*, a once-controversial portrait of an embrace.

The Cardiff Exhibition, 1913, with the Davies Collection of French paintings and sculpture, showing Rodin's *The Kiss* in the foreground. National Museum of Wales, Cardiff. Although the thirty-eight paintings from their collection were lent anonymously to this exhibition the Davies sisters paid all the expenses, including the catalogue and the installation.

By 1924 there were about 200 works in the collection – a formidable number – about half of them by Impressionist, Realist, Symbolist and Post-Impressionist artists of the French School. All this was accomplished long before the majority of these artists became internationally renowned. In addition, by lending from their collection to a seminal exhibition of art in Bath, to exhibitions in London and to the Tate Gallery, the sisters also influenced the expansion of interest in modern art in Britain. A major Cézanne, *Montagnes, L'Estaque*, was lent by Gwendoline Davies to a 1922 exhibition of French painting in London devised by the artist, critic and champion of the school, Roger Fry (1866–1934); from that exhibition the Cézanne was lent to the Tate Gallery, the first Cézanne to appear in a national collection in Britain. Samuel Courtauld, textile magnate and supplier of funds to the Tate for purchases, who also compiled his own collection of Impressionist paintings, was, we are told, converted to the French School at that exhibition. Yet the Misses Davies perhaps remained unaware of and were certainly uninterested in the movements in art that came after the innovations of the Impressionists and Post-Impressionists. Moreover, they were the only collectors of these artists on such a scale in Britain who were

La Parisienne (Lady in a Blue Dress) by Pierre-Auguste Renoir (1841–1919); oil on canvas, 1874. Davies Collection, National Museum of Wales, Cardiff.

women. Other famous collections were being made and would be made by men, including Sir Hugh Lane of Dublin and London, Samuel Courtauld and the ship-owner Sir William Burrell of Glasgow.

Independently wealthy, in 1920 the sisters bought a remarkable house, Gregynog Hall in Wales, planning to use it as an arts centre and artists' retreat. Its private press, Gregynog Press, and its publications which appeared until 1939, became famous. Pottery and music were among the arts pursued at first. But in 1924, two years after their brother's marriage, the sisters went to live in Gregynog Hall, which was only a few miles from their family home. (It is now part of the University of Wales, a bequest from the sisters in 1960.) Gregynog became a centre for outstanding concerts, with some of the finest musicians of Britain performing there. The cost of living at

Gregynog and their other pursuits seems to have curtailed their acquisitions of art, although Margaret, the younger sister, started buying again later, but never on the scale and with the quality of the purchases before 1924.

That they were philanthropists is clear. Not only did they support the arts in various ways, but they were active in various other causes, such as welfare for girls and women, medical studies and intellectual pursuits through the University of Wales, the National Library of Wales and the National Museum of Wales. In their lifetimes they were generous in loaning their art for exhibition, and they gave works by Rodin and Augustus John to the National Museum in 1940. For most of their lives they lived with their art at Gregynog Hall. The 'advanced' taste that they exhibited in the majority of their purchases was not reflected in an outward exuberance or in any public presence, beyond their benefactions in Wales and a small section of the art world. They spent a life doing good, and they were obviously firm minded and clear headed. Their legacies have given lustre to the life of art in Wales.

CHAPTER IX
Stars in the Art World

THE STEINS IN PARIS
Gertrude (1874–1946), Leo (1872–1947),
Michael (1865–1938) and Sarah (1870–1953)

THE CONE SISTERS OF BALTIMORE
Dr Claribel (1864–1929)
and Miss Etta (1870–1949)

T he Steins – Gertrude, her brother Leo, and their sister-in-law Sarah – were extremely social beings. Their support and interest in art and artists during their years in Paris soon after the turn of the century had two focuses. They bought the work of artists in whom they were interested and, with formal regularity, held informal salons where the whole of the Paris art world visited as well as travelling Americans, who wanted to immerse themselves in contemporary culture. It was the elder brother, Michael Stein, who took charge of the family finances; and it was his vivacious and energetic wife, Sarah, who persuaded him to move his own family – wife and son – to Paris and to give up daily life in San Francisco. It was especially through Sarah that other Californians, for example Annette Rosenshine and Harriet Levy, were introduced to Paris and art in general and the work of Matisse in particular. They also went on to collect, although modestly in comparison to Sarah.

Leo was perhaps the most intellectually adventurous of the family, but he flitted from idea to idea, almost artist to artist, and indeed country to country, leaving Gertrude and France for Italy. Gertrude allied herself eventually to Picasso, but Sarah allied herself to Matisse. Although it was Gertrude and Leo who first bought his dazzlingly adventurous work from the Salon of 1905, it was Sarah who was the catalyst and inspiration behind the new taste. Brilliant recent investigative scholarship by Hilary Spurling, Matisse's biographer, has made clear the delightful details of Sarah Stein's involvement with Matisse's family and his art. Sarah with Matisse went on to start a small art school for interested friends and colleagues, and gave him the intelligent, insightful support that he so desperately needed, and he described her encouragement and judgement as crucial, referring to her 'exceptional sensibility'.

The Cone sisters, friends of Leo and Gertrude from both families' years in Baltimore, were introduced over several decades to the Parisian avant-garde by the Steins: they fell profoundly under the spell of Matisse's art, and Etta in particular was to become an unwavering patron of his work.

Gertrude Stein's writings claimed a central place for her promotion of the arts in Paris, and she tirelessly advocated her own work, while Sarah did not wish for the public persona that Gertrude enjoyed. Because the Stein family collections were eventually dispersed, there is no single place in which the extent of their patronage can be grasped and understood. However, a significant number of Matisse's masterpieces (including *Woman in a Hat*), purchased from the Steins by family friends, can be seen at the San Francisco Museum of Modern Art. The Cone sisters, richer and perhaps less distracted, have ensured that by their bequest to Baltimore, the Cone Collections, and their perspicacious judgement can be understood and enjoyed in one of America's most interesting public collections.

The Steins in Paris

Everybody who was anybody came to call.

From their apartments in Paris, the Steins were patrons, connoisseurs and self-proclaimed grandees of the intellect; or at least Leo and Gertrude were, while Michael, with family money made in San Francisco street cars, real estate and the stock exchange, tried to keep the expatriate show on the straight and narrow, and on the road. Gertrude Stein, a student of psychology at Radcliffe under William James – a medical student in Baltimore, and one of the most famous of all American expatriates – was to spend most of her life in France. She joined Leo in Paris in 1903 and by 1905 had met Picasso and Matisse.

According to Matisse, Sarah Stein had 'the most wonderful eye', and a remark he made about her has become legendary – 'she knows more about my paintings than I do'. It was Sarah who probably encouraged Leo Stein to purchase, from the Salon in Paris in 1905, the *Femme au Chapeau*, Matisse's portrait of Madame Matisse, which is now one of the jewels of the San Francisco Museum of Modern Art. In 1927 Michael and Sarah Stein commissioned the young Le Corbusier to build them a house, the Villa Stein (Les Terrasses) at Garches on the outskirts of Paris, in which they lived until they moved back to California in 1935.

Surrounded by contemporary painting at 27 rue de Fleurus, Gertrude was a catalyst for the expatriate American community, as both participant and observer of the avant-garde. She was as much ridiculed as admired and was a legend in her own time. Immensely social, even hearty, she evidently had a marvellously deep laugh, and Etta Cone, who knew her well, described her simply as 'great fun'. During Gertrude's life in Paris, where first she and her brother Leo had a Saturday night salon surrounded by paintings, 'everybody who was anybody' came to call. She and her household were visited, consulted and talked about, the heart of a literary and artistic gathering place. On the walls were paintings by Picasso (*Boy Leading a Horse, Two Nudes*), by Matisse until about 1907 (*Woman with the Hat, Olive Trees*), by Cézanne (*Portrait of Mme Cézanne, Bathers* and many more) and a multitude of others by such as Toulouse-Lautrec (*The*

Gertrude Stein in Hollywood in 1943.

Sofa), Daumier (*Head of an Old Woman*), Renoir (*Woman in a Fur Hat*) and Bonnard (*Siesta*). The Steins' support for painters was crucial. They were among the earliest to recognize the leaders of the artistic revolution in Paris; they bought when their recognition and encouragement mattered. Works from their collections – which represented the best of the period – were later often sold, partly because their enthusiasms fluctuated, particularly those of Leo, and partly because the their economic fortunes fluctuated.

Their first collections were divided when Leo and Gertrude Stein parted in 1913, Leo to live in Italy and to marry. He kept most of the Cézannes, and Picasso painted a little watercolour of an apple for Gertrude as a reminder of Cézanne's apples. Later, when Gertrude was joined by her life-long companion, Alice B. Toklas (1877–1967), a pianist from San Francisco who later became a famous cookery writer, they would both hold forth to their guests of literary and artistic distinction. Among the artists were Braque, Juan Gris and Derain and the American Marsden Hartley (1877–1943); the writers included Ernest Hemingway, Jean Cocteau, James Joyce and F. Scott Fitzgerald and Zelda. Mary Cassat visited, and loathed Matisse's paintings.

The Paris studio of Leo and Gertrude Stein, 27, rue de Fleurs, 1906.
The Baltimore Museum of Art (Cone Archives).

Gertrude Stein was photographed, sometimes with and sometimes without Alice, by the most famous photographers of the day from Cecil Beaton (1904–80) to Man Ray (1890–1977). Gertrude and other members of her family were painted and drawn by Picasso. She and Alice continued to collect – and to sell. Thus the Stein's collection is dispersed into private collections and the grandest public museums, with significant ex-Stein works in Baltimore, given by the Cone sisters, who faithfully bought from them. The Gertrude Stein papers are at Yale, supporting a continuous Stein industry. Gertrude herself is visually immortalized in her 1905–6 portrait by Picasso, which she bequeathed to the Metropolitan Museum of Art in New York. She sat for him some 80 times, but he finally completed it months later from memory, portraying her not as she then was but as the sacred monster she was to become.

Gertrude's prose style is hauntingly repetitive – perhaps her most famous phrase remains 'a rose is a rose is a rose'. She more than anticipated the stylistic revolutions embodied in the work of James Joyce – whom she detested – and in Dada, Surrealism and the Bloomsbury group. Her libretto (1934) for Virgil Thomson's opera *Four Saints in Three Acts* included the memorable phrase 'pigeons on the grass alas'. Her articles about both Picasso and Matisse were the first to be published in English; she later wrote a short and pithy book about Picasso (1938). *The Autobiography of Alice B. Toklas* (1933) is probably Gertrude's most straightforward work and was followed by an amazingly popular lecture tour of America; it was her first visit there for 30 years.

Gertrude herself was to see her writing as an equivalent in words of Picasso's visual genius: 'Well, Pablo is doing abstract portraits in painting. I am trying to do abstract portraits in my medium, *words*.'

The Cone Sisters of Baltimore

Hoping that 'the spirit of appreciation for modern art in Baltimore becomes improved'.

Dr Claribel Cone and her younger sister, Miss Etta Cone, were two very nicely brought-up German-Jewish sisters from a large and wealthy Baltimore family. They were two among thirteen children, Claribel was the fifth child and Etta the ninth, and they had one other sister and nine brothers.

Their father, Herman, had arrived from Germany in 1846 and with the help of relatives in Virginia became a storekeeper. Moving the family to Baltimore in 1870, Herman achieved a more-than-comfortable fortune in the wholesale grocery business. The children had a standard upbringing, the boys going into business, the girls anticipating marriage, and all were expected to play their part in their community. Herman was to sell the wholesale grocery business, and the two older brothers went on to found a financial empire based on southern cotton mills, the Cone Export and Commission Company; among its businesses was the world's largest denim manufacturer, White Oak Mills.

Yet from this conventional, solid and assured background these two sisters developed a strong interest in contemporary art, in particular the School of Paris and, even more particularly, in the work of Henri Matisse. Their joint collection was to comprise 42 paintings by Matisse, 18 sculptures, 113 drawings, 155 prints and most of Matisse's illustrated books and prints, one of the three or four most significant groups of his work in the world.

Dr Claribel and Etta never married. Etta delighted, however, in being an aunt and great aunt to many a nephew and niece and their progeny, nominating one after another to accompany her on what were almost annual shopping trips to western Europe – and between them the two sisters acquired assiduously for nearly 90 years. Without a domestic framework at home in America, Etta and Claribel often travelled together. They left a legacy of over 3,000 items – of the fine and decorative arts – which for quality and perhaps even breadth has hardly been surpassed in the history of twentieth-century collecting by women in America.

The domesticated Miss Etta at first managed the family home – the parent's house – in Eutaw Place in Baltimore, and she continued to act as a kind of domestic firefighter for the extended family. Dr Claribel was the elder, more dominating character, a large, flamboyant creature who was unusually self-sufficient and quite remarkably self-confident. Unlike most women of her class and time, she was totally uninterested in domestic life and indeed became one of the earliest women in America to pursue a medical education. Clinical work, however, was not her forte; for decades she was, intermittently, a research medical scientist and a pathologist; but her individuality and assured personality evidently did not necessarily work best with other members of a team. However, she was serious enough to work, teaching and doing research, for some time in Baltimore and in the Senckenberg Pathology Institute in Frankfurt, Germany.

The catalyst for the widening cultural experiences sought by the Cone sisters, and then their extraordinary foray into collecting, was their long-time acquaintance, not without its turmoil and vicissitudes, with the redoubtable Stein family. The orphaned brother and sister, Leo and Gertrude, had moved to Baltimore in 1892 to live with their maternal aunt, and had there met the young members of the Jewish *haute bourgeoisie*, including the Cone family. Claribel and Gertrude had shared journeys to medical school for several years in Baltimore, while Etta was perhaps especially under the influence of Leo. Together they lead an active cultural life of discussions, lectures, clubs and conversational gatherings. Etta was a highly accomplished pianist and continued to play and take lessons for almost her whole life. As a young adult, still living at home, Gertrude hosted on Saturday nights what was really considered at the time to be a salon.

The Cone sisters, like Gertrude, became very large ladies; and both were addicted to the pleasures and delights of colour: colour in jewels, in textiles and in painting. Dr Claribel, very plump indeed, was extremely interested in her own comfort. Idiosyncratically, when attending concerts or the theatre, she often bought two seats for herself, the one next to her to support all her endless clutter. Etta, the homebody, was granted funds in 1898 by her brother Moses to enhance the household, and enterprisingly she went to New York and bought a quintet of paintings from the estate of the pioneering American Impressionist Theodore Robinson (1852–96) for just $300: *Mother and Child, The Young Violinist, In the Grove, The Watering Place* and *A Lock*. Her family were astonished.

The sisters set themselves up independently in adjacent apartments in The Marlborough Apartments in Baltimore with their youngest unmarried brother, Frederic (b.1878); there the sisters' collections were installed in small rooms crowded with furniture and with paintings hung almost frame to frame. Dr Claribel opened her apartment as a museum by private appointment, a tradition followed after her death by Miss Etta. Dr Claribel, who died 20 years before her sister, bequeathed her own collection to Etta, with the direction that both collections should eventually be given to a public institution, indeed to Baltimore, if 'the spirit of appreciation for modern art in Baltimore becomes improved'.

Why did these two sisters become important patrons of Matisse, forming one of the best privately collected groups of his work to be made in his lifetime? Why were they obsessive collectors of textiles – Dr Claribel collected the more colourful fabrics, Etta was devoted to the

Etta and Claribel Cone
photographed in Paris
in about 1925.
The Baltimore Museum
of Art (Cone Archives).

finest examples of lace from northern Europe – of jewellery, furniture and a small but extra-ordinary hoard of primitive art, almost entirely African, as well as one or two outstanding antiquities, including Claribel's favourite, a bronze Egyptian cat?

The American version of the Grand Tour began in the late nineteenth century, and at times women travelled to Europe without benefit of male escort, perhaps a sign of a society

Dr Claribel Cone by Pablo
Picasso (1881–1973); drawing,
1922. Cone Collection,
Baltimore Museum of Art.

where women had greater economic freedoms although they were still supported by their families. When her sister Claribel was not available, and even in later life, Etta employed a nurse-companion to accompany her on her journeys.

It was Gertrude Stein who, after her days at Radcliffe College and her medical degree at Johns Hopkins in Baltimore, introduced the Cone sisters to her art world in Paris. Gertrude, whose reputation as a highly original writer parallels her role as the Muse of Modernism at her flat in Paris ('We hung all the pictures and we asked all the painters'), wrote a thinly disguised memoir, 'Two Women'; maddeningly perceptive, it is a curious, repetitive, disturbing, acute and fascinating faction of the two Cone sisters, in which it is apparent that she empathized far more with Dr Claribel, the colourful original, than with the timid Miss Etta. Before the advent of Alice B. Toklas, Etta typed for Gertrude; indeed at one point Gertrude offered to sell Etta the very typescript of the book – *Three Lives* (1909) – that she had worked on.

Etta made her first visit to Europe in 1901, when she was 30. She and two other female contemporaries, one her cousin, went to Italy for a three-week trip in the company of Leo Stein; it was Leo who first developed an eye for contemporary modern art, and Leo who contributed significantly to Etta's aesthetic education. While they were with the Steins, the Cones saw their first paintings by Matisse at the Paris Salon in 1905; and it was with Michael and Sarah that the Cone sisters first met Matisse.

The pattern of extended visits to Europe was set; Dr Claribel was indeed, through a sense of her own comfort, tempered by surprising inertia and then by circumstances, to spend the years from 1916 to 1921 in Germany. After her return from Germany, she and Etta travelled to Europe each year until Dr Claribel's death in 1929. The sisters bought separately and had separate although complementary interests.

Throughout the 1920s, the Cone sisters brought art shopping to a fine pitch, generally with Michael Stein acting as their private dealer. The collection expanded in particular to contain more paintings from the School of Paris, from Degas to Cézanne and Van Gogh to Gauguin. Much of the art the sisters bought during that decade was from dealers or at auction; the greatest single painting in the Cone Collection is perhaps Cézanne's *Mont Sainte-Victoire* (*c*.1897), acquired in Paris in 1925 for the highest price either sister was ever to pay for a single work of art. They also bought significantly from the Steins, as each Stein in turn offered items from their collections for sale, partly as a way of offering the Steins financial assistance. Among the works thus acquired was a lithograph of Cézanne's *Bathers*, purchased for 50 francs.

The Cone Collection is a core collection of Matisse's work and among the finest in the world. Several of the most ferociously colourful Matisses had at first been bought by others, notably the Fauve *Blue Nude* (1907), owned first by Leo Stein, who then sold it to the American lawyer and collector John Quinn. After Quinn's death, Dr Claribel purchased it at auction in 1926; *Blue Nude*, an intensely powerful painting, reminiscent of sculpture by Matisse, and his only painted nude to be set in an outdoor landscape, is the cornerstone of the Cone Collection. For two decades after Dr Claribel's death, Miss Etta continued to buy – and buy. Most touching perhaps was the visit of Matisse to see Miss Etta in December 1930, when he had come to the States to act as judge for the Carnegie International prize – which Picasso was to win – and to discuss with the idiosyncratic millionaire businessman Dr Barnes the commissioning of some specific decorative panels. Matisse took endless trouble over posthumous portrait drawings of Dr Clairbel, commissioned by Etta and portrait drawings of Etta herself.

The other holdings in the fine arts from the School of Paris are equally magnificent, including two outstanding works by Cézanne. These Cone holdings are perhaps smaller in quantity than many other twentieth-century collections of the fine arts, are perhaps unusually domestic in tone and also perhaps not 'advanced' in the terms defined by the now conventional wisdom concerning the art of the twentieth century. Miss Etta had no time for Cubism, and liked objects to look like something recognizable. The majority of the works bought by both the sisters not only had some form of easily identifiable subject matter but depicted people – portraits – or interiors. There are also landscapes, many of which, significantly, are peopled.

The Cone Collection thus forms several parts. There is a core holding of Matisse, a significant group, amplified by French School paintings and drawings, of important Cézannes and works by Van Gogh, Degas, Renoir and Picasso. They enjoyed, most heartily and fervently, the pleasures of shopping, and they also collected voluminous shawls, scraps of textiles and nineteenth-century Renaissance-style furniture,

Unlike a number of other collectors, both men and women whose fabulous and prescient collections were dispersed, the Cone sisters left a remarkable two-fold legacy. There is the art itself, helping to make Baltimore an appropriate goal for anyone interested in the heights of achievement in the arts of the twentieth century. And there are the Cone archives, the endless lists and accounts of Dr Claribel, the travel diaries of Miss Etta, filled with the aesthetic thrills of her observations on the art of Europe. The archives are themselves a record of the new kinds of Grand Tours initiated by Americans in Europe in general, and by these eccentric, charming, shambolic, enthusiastic sisters, who were simultaneously both touchingly naive and surprisingly shrewd.

CHAPTER X

Business Women

Helena Rubinstein (1871–1965)
Gabrielle (Coco) Chanel (1883–1971)

Rubinstein, the Polish-born American cosmetics magnate, and Chanel, internationally successful French couturier and inventor of the world-famous scent Chanel No. 5, used their huge fortunes to collect a variety of unusual objects with personal significance. They were using their collections to establish themselves, to emphasize their originality and to create a distinctive ambience in a world dominated by successful and powerful men. The parallels in their taste, and the omnivorous purchasing made possible by business empires built by their own hard work, give them a similarity that they might have been reluctant to recognize or to admit.

There seems to have been little rapport between them, although one curious incident observed by the New York style guru Diana Vreeland stands out. Chanel had agreed to dine with Vreeland and her husband Reed on the understanding that she wouldn't have to talk. Halfway through the meal, during which she had, according to Vreeland, talked incessantly, she suggested that Helena Rubinstein should be sent for. Astonishingly Madame came, in a wonderful floor-length coat of pink Chinese silk; the two women disappeared into another room and, as reported by Vreeland, they never sat down but talked standing face-to-face 'like men' for four hours about 'God knows what'.

Helena Rubinstein

'Quality's nice, but quantity makes a show!'

The beautician Helena Rubinstein ended her life as she had lived it, with a pugnacious resolve and bloody-minded courage that would have become an athlete of 19. At 93, standing less than 4ft 10in tall, she ejected three burglars from her antiques-filled New York apartment by yelling and bullying. The eventually terrified trio had tied up the maid, a secretary, a houseboy, and even Madame herself, who later emerged as the toast of Manhattan with her legendary collections intact.

That was in 1964. What preceded the incident, all the way from obscure origins in Poland in 1871, had made Madame Rubinstein the world's wealthiest self-made woman with a personal fortune of $100 million. One of her tyrannized associates described her as a hydra: 'of her nine heads', he said, 'eight are constructive, one is destructive'. She was tireless, relentlessly driven. Hard work was her duty, her reason for living, and from it sprang success. But success begot yet more hard work and in the process Madame Rubinstein, with a staff of 30,000, frequently drove employees to the very edge of their endurance. 'The business must come first!' she declared, pounding her fists on one of the gigantic desks in her scattered offices. And to the business for a period of 60 years she devoted almost her entire energies. Even the art collections she amassed with such zeal were vaguely justified in this way: 'I owe it to the business!' The same was true of her prodigious expenditure on jewellery, and upon the couturier clothes she loved from Chanel, Dior, Lanvin, Guy Laroche and Balenciaga. Dozens of closets in houses and apartments in three countries were crammed with them, some going back to purchases from Paul Poiret in Paris before World War I.

The Helena Rubinstein Foundation, which from its modest office on New York's Madison Avenue provides support for education, health, and community service projects that benefit women and children, is all that remains today of Madame's great enterprise, at least in a way that she would have recognized. By her own desire, her clothes were given away, many to museums, and the bulk of her art collections and jewellery were dispersed at auction. Her Will also stipulated that Helena Rubinstein Inc. was not to be sold. But with Madame's death profound changes occurred, and although the sale of Rubinstein's cosmetics was maintained in Europe, the brand was withdrawn in the United States. Now, after several changes of ownership, the last being to the French cosmetics giant L'Oréal in 1988, the name of Helena Rubinstein is to be reintroduced to North American shoppers.

Rubinstein's remark 'I was born to work!' was probably the naked truth, for although details of her upbringing in Cracow are hazy it is clear that her family was far from affluent. They were in the wholesale food trade, and Helena was the eldest of eight surviving children, all girls. Prone to selective amnesia about the past, the result of an enthusiastic interest in the present and the demands of business, her contradictory recollections effectively threw a veil over her early life. Patrick O'Higgins, who worked closely with her from 1950, who ghosted her autobiographical *My Life For Beauty* and who even published his own affectionate memoir of her, was not alone in his awe of her apparently abrupt entrance into the world of cosmetics.

Tiring of her native city, and refusing to marry a man of her father's choice, young Helena made her way upon a whim to visit an uncle in Australia. Her life, if anything, became even duller until the unexpected intervention of twelve pots of face cream that her mother had thoughtfully packed for the long journey. It transpired that Helena's fine European complexion attracted the admiration of her uncle's neighbours, a group of women whose skins had been toughened by exposure to sun and wind. At first she gave away the cream, made with the formula of a

Hungarian friend of the family, a Dr Lykusky, back in Crakow. But when the first pots had gone, Helena ordered fresh supplies, not this time intended as gifts. She had discovered a market and with it she established a business. The anonymous cream suddenly acquired a tempting name, Valaze Skin Food. With mounting profits she opened premises in Melbourne – the Maison de Beauté Valaze – and sent for help in the persons of Lykusky himself and two of her sisters, Manka and Ceska.

The usual accounts of this transformation of the beautiful young Helena from an inexperienced girl into a pragmatic businesswoman make the process appear miraculous. However attractive this version, it must largely have been fictional, nimbly fostered by the lady herself, a genius in publicity. First, she probably had a thorough grounding in business matters under her father's eye, and second her passage to Australia may not have been 'around 1900' but anything up to ten years before. So her triumph in Melbourne about 1903 was neither sudden nor was it easily achieved.

Helena Rubinstein's next move was from Australia to Europe to evade having to make a decision about a proposal of marriage from Edward Titus, a young American writer. To have fallen in love was a strange novelty, for until then her only passion had been the business. The latter now came to her rescue as she realized that Australia was no place to expand. Instead she settled upon London, hub of an empire and seat of one of the wealthiest societies on earth. It seemed a good choice. A new Maison de Beauté Valaze was opened in Grafton Street in the heart of Mayfair, to which Madame attracted a stream of affluent customers. In Australia she had recruited Nellie Melba, the celebrated international opera singer, to extol the virtues of the Valaze cream. Now in London she found a small army of velvet-complexioned stage beauties willing to support the product. The seductively named Lily Elsie was one, fresh from her success in *The Count of Luxembourg*.

Titus wooed and won Helena Rubinstein, joining her in London to make her his wife. Adoringly she bore him two sons, Roy and Horace, but whatever tryst she had with domesticity was short-lived. Back at work, ever eyeing the horizon for new opportunities, Madame discovered that Paris, rather than London, would be a more profitable centre for her operations. The city was already the heart of the fashion industry; furthermore it was home to a host of Romanians and Hungarians who were clever with skin: 'They taught me masses,' she recalled. So in 1908 Madame Rubinstein established a salon in Paris.

Here she met the wealthy, sociable Misia Sert and through her a network of acquaintances. As exiles they became close, sharing hazy memories of their old country. It was Misia's interest in antiques and the artistic world she inhabited that further attracted Helena. To the businesswoman these were hitherto unsuspected aspects of life, and the portraits of her new friend by Toulouse-Lautrec, Vuillard, Bonnard and Renoir set her fertile mind racing. 'It was she who gave me the idea of being painted', Madame Rubinstein remembered later. 'Good for publicity, good investment, good for all the empty walls! She also helped me collect things. She had an eye.' It was through Misia that Rubinstein commissioned from Paul Helleu a portrait of herself as early as 1908.

Helena Rubinstein in her New
York apartment in 1958.

Now Madame became addicted to collecting, particularly of portraits of herself. The
results of this latter preoccupation were shown in 1977 at the National Portrait Gallery, London,
in an exhibition of likenesses that were criticized as mostly exercises in flattery. But together they
formed a startling memorial to this woman who had practically invented the international
beauty movement and reigned over it for almost 60 years. The ageless features in many of these
pictures were persuasive endorsements both of her products and of her own durability. At 67 she
was tactfully painted by Christian Bérard for what became her favourite portrait. Another was
Salvador Dali's account of 1943, an example of 'Park Avenue Surrealism' and, according to Keith
Roberts in the *Burlington Magazine*, 'a piece of visual hyperbole the likes of which even an
Elizabethan portraitist might have thought twice about using'.

The least comfortable but ultimately the most successful of Rubinstein's portraits was also one of the last. This was the 1957 portrait of her (the second of two) by Graham Sutherland. The artist agonized over his composition, until the subject herself happened to mention that she'd just bought a new dress by Balenciaga. The designer's fierce colours and elaborately embroidered designs suited her love of the exotic, and on this occasion he had outdone himself with a rich, red evening gown glowing with appliqué. At first Madame was horrified by Sutherland's portraits; he had painted her with all the imperfections of her 86 years. 'I hate them . . . they'll be bad for business!' she complained. 'Look at me – so old! So savage – a witch!' Writer Roderick Cameron described Sutherland's view of her as 'a great middle-European peasant standing firmly in profile armoured by her own astuteness and hard work in a carapace of glitter, enamelled in beads and jewels, looking like some formidable Byzantine empress.' Nevertheless, she elected to purchase the seated version, recognizing that it was indeed a masterpiece. The picture, which shows Madame posed with all the majesty of an irresistible empress, powerfully captures her spirit of vigorous determination.

Once Helena Rubinstein's foot was on the first rung as a collector she was disinclined to ponder the problem too long. As a millionairess she could afford to buy anything and everything she wanted; as a busy businesswoman she could not afford to waste time. In this respect a collector like Elton John and Helena Rubinstein have much in common; like him, her taste was catholic and her purse deep. In between the meetings and the travelling, the negotiations in places as far apart as Brazil and Bangkok, her morning perusals of stock exchange reports and the late night advertising conferences, she was always alert to the siren song of dressmakers and jewellers, painters and antique dealers. This shrewd entrepreneur was also a shrewd purchaser, always bargain hunting, always, as befitted the manufacturing wholesaler that she was, preferring to buy works of art in bulk.

Her collection of African art, which comprised hundreds of pieces, was formed this way. She began it when first living in London, at the instigation of Jacob Epstein. In 1908 this was considered very advanced taste, but for the young sculptor, just then recovering from the outcry over his monumental nude figures in London's Strand, these African works were inspirational. A frequent visitor to France, Rubinstein offered to attend auctions in Paris for him, agreeing to buy any African pieces of his choice. His limit was £3 a piece. Madame was so intrigued by this new field that anything over that price she bought for herself. Later – some 25 years later – she was still interested when 'Hitler started being difficult', and she heard of a German Jew who had fled Berlin with little more than a lorry full of African art. 'I helped him out,' she recalled with satisfaction 'That's how to collect . . . by the wagonload'!

The declaration of war in 1914, so damaging to business, more or less obliged Rubinstein to leave Europe for America. No sooner was she there than she realized the potential of this huge new market and it was not long before her empire expanded even further, and in 1915 a New York salon was added to the London and Paris branches. After the war she started to sell her products wholesale, and she was on the way to her vast business empire. In 1941 she purchased a three storey apartment at the top of 625 Park Avenue, New York. Described as one of Manhattan's

Helena Rubinstein's Drawing Room hung with paintings by Modigliani, Matisse, Picasso, Dali and Dufy and furnished with her collection of American nineteenth-century furniture by John Henry Belter.

'largest, most lavish and most expensive', it became Madame's chief private residence. She shared it with her second husband, Prince Artchil Gourielli, whom she had married in 1938, and a veritable museum of paintings by Matisse, Renoir, Corot, Toulouse-Lautrec, Degas, Pissarro, Utrillo, Picasso, Braque, Modigliani, Chagall, Derain, Gris, Rouault, Dali, Mirò, Klee, Kandinsky, Roger de la Fresnaye, Léger, Tchelitchew, de Kooning and Laurencin, some of which had come direct from the artists. In 1934 the art dealer René Gimpel noted in his diary that Marie Laurencin had to forego an invitation to his wife's tea-party: 'She was so tired, she is working so much . . . preparing three canvases for Helena Rubinstein, the purveyor of beauty products, who will have reproductions done for her salons.' A critic sneered that Madame had 'unimportant' pictures 'by every important painter of the nineteenth and twentieth centuries'. But she was unconcerned, merely remarking, 'I may not have quality, but I have quantity. Quality's nice, but quantity makes a show'.

The 26 rooms of her New York apartment, those of flats in London and Paris, and in a house in the Parisian countryside and another in Greenwich, Connecticut, were stuffed with

Helena Rubinstein holding two African 'Mummy' masks from her collection, photographed on her arrival in New York in 1934.

pictures, furniture and every kind of art work. Jewellery, too, was one of Madame's many preoccupations and she loved to decorate her diminutive figure with bold, rope-like necklaces, bracelets, rings and brooches in nonchalant disregard for their intrinsic worth: typically big, gaudy *faux* pieces jostled the finest sapphires, emeralds and diamonds.

Sculpture was another of Madame's obsessions. She first encountered the Polish artist Elie Nadelman (1882-1946) in London in 1911, when she bought his entire show. Later she launched his American career. Many other contemporary sculptors were represented in her collection, perhaps chief of whom was Constantin Brancusi (1876–1959); his *Bird in Space* of about 1937 and the slightly earlier marble *Blond Negress* were among her best pieces. Rubinstein's taste was nothing if not eclectic, however, and beside these masterpieces was an odd assemblage of items, from Victorian pink opaline glass to American furniture of the same period, including richly padded mahogany sofas by John Henry Belter. The top floor of her Park Avenue triplex was dominated by the 68 by 17ft 'Recreation Room', but a smaller space adjoining, called the 'Doll House', contained one of Madame Rubinstein's greatest joys – her collection of miniature furniture and accessories. This was arranged in a series of 24 specially built rooms reflecting different periods of interior decoration. Madame gathered every imaginable item for the display, including silver and ivory, kitchen utensils, tables, chairs and chandeliers mostly dating from the eighteenth and nineteenth centuries. Fellow enthusiasts marvelled at the collection and at Madame's attention to the tiniest detail. But then, detail mattered to Helena Rubinstein.

The close of Rubinstein's long career coincided with her death at 94 on 1 April 1965. No one, least of all her business associates, could quite believe that the old tormentor had gone. As O'Higgins put it, 'Madame was a strange combination of paradoxes. She could exude sophistication and then be a child. She could be a calculating tycoon, a benevolent empress, a greedy peasant'. Her obiturist in *The Times* should have been more wary of the significance of her death on 'April Fool's Day': she had managed to clip eleven years from her real age and to manufacture a bourgeois upbringing for herself, all dutifully recorded for posterity. The true story was much more interesting.

Most of Helena Rubinstein's remarkable collections went to auction at Sotheby's in New York in April 1966. The overall quality, however uneven, reflected a collector's headlong enthusiasm, and few doubted the story that circulated about her having walked the streets of Paris with $30,000 in cash for impulse purchases. Friends said that many of her possessions 'were bizarre, rather than beautiful', and that she was born with the collector's instinct. Indeed so, but this instinct was driven by the same powerful forces that propelled her to succeed in business as few other women ever have. 'I am a merchant!' she was fond of saying, 'A merchant!'.

Gabrielle Chanel

At the time of her death, aged 87 and still hard at work to the last, Gabrielle 'Coco' Chanel, with her unforgettable gamine face and figure, and the products of her internationally successful fashion empire, were recognized the world over. She imposed her style on generations of fashionable women. The brilliant construction she made of her life in the public eye was the result of minute observation of the prejudices and latitudes of society allied with her sense – not always faultless – of how far she could flaunt convention. From her early 20s she mixed with people with little respect for conventional morality, rich men who chose the world of mistresses and secret hideaways before their traditional social obligations; Bohemians, avant-garde artists and writers, and theatre and ballet folk, notably Serge Diaghilev and Jean Cocteau. She possessed a highly developed and valuable talent for assimilation as well as innate stylishness. Her great innovation, sportswear, for example, came from the French and English sportsmen who were her early lovers, while the exotic patterns and embroideries of Slavic origin came from the Russian ballet and from her Russian lovers. The Duke of Westminster's passion for the sea produced the neat little sailor suits and jerseys, just as his extravagant gifts of jewellery resulted in the distinctive larger-than-life costume jewellery.

Chanel never married, though some of her liaisons hovered near the brink. From her first real prosperity during World War I, the balance of power was often weighted in her favour – some of her ex-lovers remained her pensioners for years – and she was even able to hold her own with the Duke. The inhuman bound which propelled her from the shadowy world of *irregulières* into the epicentre of the Parisian smart set gave her leave to remark of Cocteau's mother: '*Une brave femme, mais affrrreusement bourrrgeoise*'. Evidence of her blatant annexation comes from a 1960s American magazine article quoting her neat contrast between art and fashion: 'Fashion must be beautiful first, and ugly afterward. Art must be ugly first, then beautiful afterward.' This was lifted from Cocteau, who had expanded his favourite theme on the strangeness of beauty in modern art for a eulogy of Chanel herself in *Harper's Bazaar* in the 1950s.

Gabrielle Chanel was illegitimate, born in Saumur on 18 August 1883, to a family of humble peasant origins. Her parents were market traders, though her mother, who died when Gabrielle was twelve, had trained as a seamstress. Her early life was peripatetic, but she received a better education than these unpropitious circumstances would normally allow through being placed in a convent after her mother's death. By the time she was apprenticed in a draper's shop in Moulins, she had become strikingly attractive. Her looks were enhanced by the instinctive and stylish simplicity of her clothes. It was as an aspiring singer in a low-class music hall that she was given the nickname 'Coco', which was to remain with her for the rest of her life.

Meanwhile, at Moulins, a garrison town for a cavalry regiment, she had moved into the sporting military environment where she met her first protector, Etienne Balsan, with whom she went to live at his newly acquired sporting and racing estate, near Compiègne. At this point she seemed fated to follow the preordained route of the courtesan and significantly her great friend in later life, Misia Sert, compared her to Madame du Barry. But it was Balsan who set her on a different course, to an enormous business empire.

Etienne Balsan's family were prosperous, long-established cloth-manufacturers from Châteauroux, who lived in the manner typical of the French *petit-noblesse*, occupying the château and its dependencies in a vast extended family group. Balsan resisted the family pressure to marry and solved the problem of Coco Chanel's increasing restlessness and frustration with his harem-like ménage by setting her up in business as a milliner in his Paris apartment. He was relieved of any emotional obligation when Coco met and fell in love with one of his friends, an Englishman, Arthur Capel, commonly known as 'Boy'. Capel was a successful businessman with coal interests that were to enrich him enormously during World War I. He had a conventional upper-class upbringing, but his antecedents were mysterious, and he was reputed to be the illegitimate son of a Jewish French banker. It was probably the sense of being an outsider, much increased by his experience as a partly Jewish pupil at an English Catholic school, which drew him to Chanel.

Boy Capel was to be the love of her life, as well as the financial supporter who first set her business on a firm footing. It was her triumphant escape from indebtedness to Capel that gave her the sensation of true professional worth in her early business ventures. Her need to establish herself in the eyes of the world resulted in unexplained episodes of fainting, when confronted

Coco Chanel in 1936, photographed by Cecil Beaton.

with taxing social demands, which disappeared after she became a successful *couturière*. It was during the Capel affair that Chanel's attention first turned to her domestic ambience. She took over the task of decorating the apartment she shared with Boy in the Avenue Gabriel, and among her early buys were the striking lacquered Coromandel screens which later decorated her famous salon in the Rue Cambon. She bought not as a collector but as an interior decorator, another field in which she found she could excel effortlessly. Chanel chose a monochrome scheme, unbleached wool, natural colours and white, to set off the black and gold of the screens. She seems to have alighted quite spontaneously on the modern mix of old and new, traditional antiques with exotic artefacts, which remained the theme running through all her subsequent decorating ventures. The originality of her interiors masked the extent to which her collecting emulated the style of her artistic mentors.

The lure of the British aristocracy drew Boy away, and in 1918 he married a war widow, Diana Wyndham, the daughter of Lord Ribblesdale, though he could never bring himself to make a real break with Chanel. In 1919 he was killed in a motor accident, leaving her devastated. Towards the end of the war, Chanel met Misia Sert, who was to become her greatest woman friend, and it was she who strove to distract Chanel in her misery. Misia, confidant to both Helena Rubinstein and Chanel, was the perfect shopping companion, omnivorous and eclectic. And it was shopping, not art history or the pursuit of rarity, that drove Chanel's acquisitiveness. Collecting made Chanel and Rubinstein interesting and unconventional characters, and the proliferating objects acted as a smokescreen against inquisitive enquiries into their family origins and early beginnings.

Russian-born Misia had been the centre of the Parisian artistic world since early adulthood, and by this time she was married to the wealthy Spanish muralist and artist José Maria Sert. It was through Misia that Chanel encountered Diaghilev and the world of the Ballets Russes, Stravinsky, with whom she had an affair, Cocteau, whose plays she dressed, and Picasso, who was her collaborator on the ballet *Le Train Bleu*; these companions opened her eyes to art. The Serts whisked her off to Venice, travelling in a huge motor that gradually overflowed with the fruits of their bohemian collecting, including pictures and sculpture, Capo di Monte porcelain and rare books. Chanel watched, training her sharp acquisitive eye.

Growing success in her fashion business brought her to an elegant salon, 31 Rue Cambon, at the heart of the Parisian luxury quarter. Enormous riches followed the launch in 1922 of her perfume, Chanel No. 5, and in 1923 she acquired the ground-floor apartment in a magnificent town house at 29 Faubourg St-Honoré, stronghold of the Rothschilds, who at one time owned five of the Faubourg houses. The Serts were persuaded to transform the traditional green and gilded decor with eighteenth-century French chairs covered in beige-grey satin and walls decorated with pale *boiseries* or wood panelling. The Coromandel screens were imported into the grand salon with a fine piano, the first piece of furniture in the house. Diana Vreeland best conveyed the dramatic impact of the Faubourg apartment: 'It had an enormous garden with fountains, the most beautiful salons opening on to the garden, and something like fifty-four Coromandel screens shaping those rooms into the most extraordinary *allées* of charm'.

The Wertheimers, Chanel's partners in the perfume business, were collectors and patrons of the arts, Pierre Wertheimer being the Russian painter Chaim Soutine's first supporter. Chanel was therefore in a world that offered unrivalled opportunities to collect, but she possessed few works of art in the conventional sense. She had asked Marie Laurencin to paint her portrait when both were working on designs for Diaghilev's ballets but turned down the result, to Laurencin's disgust. 'Yet I pay her for my dresses,' she remarked, adding 'She's a good sort, but a peasant from the Auvergne. She wants me to try again, but she'll have to do without, I'm going to pretty up the one I did of her to sell it.' Harold Acton had seen the affinity between Chanel and Laurencin: he observed in his *Memoirs of an Aesthete*, 'Marie Laurencin expressed the mood of the moment in painting as Chanel did in dress'.

Nevertheless, Stravinsky gave her a Russian icon, which lived in her cell-like attic bedroom in the Ritz Hotel during World War II. A small painting of an ear of wheat by Salvador Dali provided a Surreal complement to the wheatsheaves standing in the salon that mockingly referred to her peasant origins. The sculptor Carl Lipchitz made her a pair of andirons.

Maurice Sachs, a young writer and protégé of Cocteau's, was hired on a large monthly retainer to find rare books and manuscripts but, as Cocteau had reason to know, he was not to be trusted and he served her ill. He bought incunabula, out-of-print books, first editions and other rarities, but they were less than first-class examples. The books, in their elegant black and beige bindings, became part of the backdrop. Mainly, she lived in a jungle of *objets d'art* and curiosities: articles of ivory, mother-of-pearl, gold and crystal, among them a dressing-table set of unimaginable grandeur. Magnificent Venetian blackamoor figures matched the splendour of the Coromandel screens. The monochrome simplicity of her early ventures in decorating gave way to mirrors and to crystal chandeliers.

Chanel was introduced in 1923 to Bendor, Duke of Westminster, who embarked immediately on an avid and obsessive pursuit of her. Nothing could have guaranteed his interest more completely than her independence. Chanel had no need of his wealth, and she made it quite clear that she was not tempted to add another admirer to her busy professional life. When the Duke gave her a book of blank signed cheques, she returned it unused. His gifts of jewellery were beyond the wildest extravagances of any of her previous lovers, but she used them simply to inspire the distinctive costume jewels for which she was to be famous. In the face of his persistence she finally succumbed – she was to say that the Duke had been 'sent by Boy', which in spite of the mystic overtones was, in a mundane sense, true. Percy Wyndham, the first husband of Diana, née Lister, whom Capel had married in 1918, was Westminster's half-brother. La Pausa, the house at Roquebrune they occupied together, was a symbol of Chanel's independence. It was assumed wrongly that the Duke had paid for it, but the whole cost was borne by Chanel from the proceeds of her fashion empire. Here, another opportunity to experiment with an unconventional decorating style presented itself.

With the help of Robert Streitz, a 28-year-old architect, she set about creating 'the ideal Mediterranean villa' of which he had long dreamed. The materials were to be of the very best and the furniture simple but appropriate. The garden was filled with lavender, mimosa and olive trees. Within the house she returned to her favourite monochrome, using beige and soft greys – like a painting by the seventeenth-century Spanish painter Zurburan, as Luchino Visconti, film and stage director, remarked on a visit in 1935. Chanel bought Provençal and Spanish furniture, which was then quite out of fashion. Her ornate iron bedhead was hung with amulets and flower garlands. La Pausa was descibed in *Vogue* as 'the essence of simplicity, without superfluous furniture. However, what there is, is the most perfect of its kind – old oak tables, chairs, and cupboards, and in the airy bedrooms old Italian beds'. However, the Westminster affair was doomed and did not long survive the completion of the villa. La Pausa was sold in 1953, the year of the Duke's death.

In 1932 the designer and illustrator Paul Iribe, a new lover, designed one of her most extraordinary ventures, an exhibition of diamond jewellery, transforming the Faubourg apartment with the jewels displayed on surreal Belle Epoque waxwork dummies in front of mirrored screens. None of the pieces was for sale, in keeping with Chanel's disdain for the intrinsic value of precious jewellery, and the entrance fee went to benefit children's charities. Iribe was then the proprietor of a design and decorating shop in the Faubourg specializing in unusual art objects. Just as he and Chanel seemed certain to marry, he died suddenly in 1935. The Faubourg apartment was given up, and her collection moved to the private hideaway above the Rue Cambon premises.

After World War II Chanel reopened her business, which she had shut down amidst great criticism in 1940, leaving only the sale of perfume to sustain the name. Because many of her wartime activities could not bear exposure, she had to wait until 1954 to restart. Now in her 70s her life was concentrated on her austerely furnished apartment in the Ritz Hotel and in the private quarters above her salon at 31 Rue Cambon, all paid for by the Wertheimers from the sale of Chanel No. 5. Chanel revelled in contrast; her glittering jewels were offset by the 'Chanel' suit or a little black dress, in her apartments the plainest designs existed side by side with the fabulous. From new friends and bewildered aspiring biographers, who were treated to a baffling flow of fantasy and obfuscation, a picture emerged of the rooms at the top of the mirrored staircase in the Rue Cambon. Against a wall of finely bound volumes flanking an enormous gilt-framed antique mirror, a vast beige suede sofa acted as a foil for eighteenth-century French gilt armchairs. A low table was covered in precious boxes and caskets. Her fifth-century BC torso of Venus shared the chimneypiece with a meteorite shaped like a praying monk. She owned a nearly life-size sculpture of a bronze deer, a wild boar and, because her astrological sign was Leo, lions of all sizes and materials. She had a troupe of carved hardstone animals including a Fabergé pig. The Coromandel screens, mirrors, chandeliers, Venetian blackamoors, Chinese jades and pottery horses and other precious *objets d'art*, all set off by black fur rugs, existed as a framework for Chanel herself, rather than a collection in the strictest sense of the term. There she spent her days, returning as late as possible to sleep at the Ritz. She died on 10 January 1971, but her distinctive style lives on still.

CHAPTER XI

Creators of Museums

THE LADIES OF MOMA

**Mrs Abby Aldrich Rockefeller (1874–1948),
Miss Lillie Bliss (1864–1931)
and Mrs Mary Quinn Sullivan (1877–1939)**

Katherine Dreier (1877–1952)

Gertrude Vanderbilt Whitney (1875–1942)

In the twentieth century, women have played a particularly notable role in the creation of public institutions. Perhaps the most alluring triumvirate was the three women – known as 'The Ladies' – who were the prime movers behind the creation and initiation of the enormously influential Museum of Modern Art in New York.

A common denominator in these ladies – Mrs John Rockefeller Jr, Miss Lillie Bliss and Mrs Mary Quinn Sullivan – was a belief in the power of art, in its importance, and a profound interest in the art of their own time. Their belief in the spiritual and high educational power of art led naturally to the idea that for art to function in this way it had to have a public face: and in order for public and art to meet as soon as possible institutional arrangements had to be made.

The great heiress Gertrude Vanderbilt Whitney was the prime mover behind the Whitney Museum of American Art in New York, which opened two years after the Museum of Modern Art. She was concerned as much by the need to support emerging American artists by buying and showing their art as by the necessity to have a publicly accessible institution in which to do so.

Katherine Dreier was involved in questions of social reform as well as being an adherent of the most advanced art of her time. Her museum was one beyond the walls, a museum of temporary travelling exhibitions, with an educational programme.

The redoubtable ladies of MOMA shared some of the concerns of Katherine Dreier: however, unlike Gertrude Vanderbilt Whitney and the more modestly financially endowed Miss Dreier, these ladies were not themselves artists, although they were the initiators of the greatest museum of twentieth-century art in the world. The ladies were not looking for social prestige, but art gave them a cause, and one that was increasingly acceptable, albeit that their taste was in the majority of instances well in advance of most of their peers. Their social confidence and financial resources gave them intellectual independence and the means to travel, to entertain and to persuade. They certainly needed the confidence that such special independence could give in order to set and lead taste, rather than to follow fashion.

Mrs Abby Rockefeller at Colonial Williamsburg. Abby Aldrich Rockefeller Folk Center.

Ladies of MOMA

Art makes all those who appreciate it 'more sane and sympathetic, more observant and understanding'.

(Abby Aldrich Rockefeller)

Mrs John Rockefeller Jr, Miss Lillie Bliss and Mrs Mary Quinn Sullivan were friends and yet three very disparate characters. Mrs Abby Aldrich Rockefeller was a firm personality and an organizer; she liked modern and contemporary art, although her billionaire husband, John Rockefeller Jr, didn't. She too came from a grand family; her father was US Senator Nelson Aldrich from Rhode Island and her brother Winthrop Aldrich of the Chase Manhattan Bank. Her sons were the five Rockefeller brothers, and almost all the family were art collectors on a grand scale. She and her husband collected Old Masters, but increasingly she was drawn to contemporary art.

Miss Lillie Bliss, photographed
in 1927. The Museum of
Modern Art, New York.

She believed, as did Katherine Dreier, that art had a spiritual dimension. She wrote to a
friend that art was 'one of the great resources of her life', offering spiritual enrichment and
making those who appreciated it 'more sane and sympathetic, more observant and understanding'. According to Nelson Rockefeller, his mother's purpose in her determination to found a
museum of modern art was specifically 'to reduce dramatically the time lag between the artist's
creation and the public's appreciation of great works of art'. In the mid-1930s Mrs Rockefeller
gave MOMA a very large collection of American Modernists and also funds specifically
designated for purchases.

Mrs Rockefeller and Lillie Bliss were serious collectors, who had met by accident when
wintering in Egypt, and Miss Bliss was already in her 60s when they started to collaborate. Miss
Bliss was shy but resolute, a gifted pianist, and a spinster. A decade older than Mrs Rockefeller,
she also came from a rich family – her politician father had made a fortune in textiles – and his
retiring daughter obviously received enormous satisfaction from her ability to indulge her very

Mary Quinn Sullivan. The Museum
of Modern Art, New York.

sophisticated and independent aesthetic sense. She was converted to the cause of modern art by
the famous Armory Show of 1913, from which she bought works by Degas, Renoir and Odilon
Redon. She left the best part of her collection to MOMA on condition that an endowment was
raised for its maintenance. Her bequest included some of the star artists of Impressionism, Post-
Impressionism and Modernism from Renoir, Cézanne and Gauguin to Matisse and Picasso. Both
Miss Bliss and Mrs Rockefeller did not regard their collections as inviolate, and MOMA was
allowed to sell and trade-in for better examples if the curators so wished.

Mary Quinn Sullivan had been an art teacher and travelled extensively in England and
France; she and Miss Bliss knew and admired the artist Arthur Davies and helped him to finance
the Armory Show, which he organized. It was Arthur Davies who, convinced himself of the
crucial need in America for a modern art museum, convinced the ladies of the importance of
such an institution. And it was 'The Ladies' who set about finding other like-minded men and
women to help inaugurate and fund such a museum, which started in 1929, opening in an office
building a week after the Great Crash, with a staff of five. MOMA gave the first dedicated
specialist platform in the USA to the permanent display of modern and contemporary art and,
later, added the works of architecture, design and photography.

Katherine Dreier

The art of Matisse was 'an aesthetic shock like a douche of cold water – it left one gasping'.

A second-generation American, Katherine Dreier was the daughter of wealthy German immigrants from Bremen. She was brought up in Brooklyn Heights, across the East River from Manhattan, and her family, liberals all, devoted much of their time, as did Katherine, to socially responsible good works. Both she and her sister Dorothea were artists.

In effect, Katherine Dreier invented the notion of a museum devoted to contemporary art some nine years before the Museum of Modern Art in New York was founded in 1929, one of the first in the world. She had an almost overpowering belief in the necessity for and redemptive power of education, and she came to believe in the redemptive power of art as well. She was daring, independent, well travelled, resolute, strong-willed and a feminist before her time. According to some, she was also domineering, moody, volatile and opinionated.

After both private art education and two years at the Brooklyn Art School, Katherine Dreier toured Europe in 1902–3 with her sister, Dorothea, studying the Old Masters. Later, she studied in Munich, then lived and worked at her art in Paris and London, where her artistic and literary friends included the American artist John Singer Sargent and the writer Henry James. She was 'married', briefly, to an expatriate American artist called Edward Trumbell, but he was found to be a bigamist and had children.

In Paris, she visited the apartments of Leo and Gertrude Stein and was astonished at what she saw. She was to write that seeing the art of Matisse at that time, 1907–8, was 'an aesthetic shock like a douche of cold water – it left one gasping'. Her passion for contemporary art was stimulated futher by her visit to the famous Sonderbund exhibition in Cologne in 1912 to see about 125 paintings by the Dutch Post-Impressionists. Indeed, soon after, she bought a portrait by the Dutch artist, Vincent Van Gogh.

The following year she translated into English and wrote a vivid introduction to the *Personal Recollections of Vincent Van Gogh*, by his sister, whom she had sought out in Europe after seeing the work of Van Gogh at the Sonderbund exhibition. She made clear then her newly minted allegiance to the innovatory in art.

Back in America, in 1913 her interest was again expanded by the enormous, infamous exhibition of avant-garde art at the New York Armory Show, which included her own work, and to which she also lent her Van Gogh, a 1890 portrait of a young woman, now identified as Mlle Ravaux. This International Exhibition of Modern Art was held in the 69th Regiment Armory, New York; exhibited were something like 1,300 works by 300 artists, and it was devised and chosen by American artists Walt Kuhn and Arthur Davies. It was the first major exposure in America of 'advanced' European art from the earlier nineteenth century to 1913; the Metropolitan Museum of Art purchased its first Cézanne from the Show, *The Poorhouse on the Hill* (c.1877) for $6,700. It was the first of Cézanne's paintings to enter an American public collection. The *success de scandale* was the work of the French Dadaist ironic iconoclast, Marcel Duchamp, in particular his Cubist-influenced *Nude Descending a Staircase No. 2* (1912), which was caricatured and ridiculed. The shock of the new at the Armory Show changed the course of American art and art history, and its impact was the first event that helped to turn Katherine Dreier – along with several other influential American collectors – into nothing less than an evangelist, a proselytizer for advanced, avant-garde, contemporary art.

In 1913 Dreier was still a representational painter. She exhibited two of her own oil paintings at the Armory (for sale at $300 each), one called *Blue Bowl*, the other *The Avenue, Holland*. She was captivated by the new and made her first major purchases at the Armory. Both were surprisingly cautious – two prints of the late nineteenth-century French School, one by Gauguin and the other by Odilon Redon, artists whose work she thought of as the precursors of the modern art of the twentieth century.

Katherine Dreier translated her interest in the art of others into practical action by founding the Society of Independent Artists in 1916. It was through the Society that she met the French artist and chess fanatic Marcel Duchamp (1887–1968), orchestrator of the ready-made, creator of installations, enigmatic ironist. He is now considered by many art historians to be the most influential artist of the twentieth century, a view that has gained ground since World War II, during which period the United States has increasingly been seen as dominant in contemporary art. In an interview he gave in 1946, the Surrealist catalyst, writer and poet André Breton (1896–1966) described Duchamp, who was adored by artists and patrons, as the 'great secret inspirer of the artistic movement in New York during the years 1941–45, as during 1918–23'.

Ironically, when Dreier was looking at submissions for the Society's very first exhibition in 1917 she voted against including *Fountain*, Duchamp's notorious sculpture of a urinal, signed and sent in by the artist under his assumed name, 'R Mutt'. Duchamp resigned from the board of directors of the Society in protest. The ensuing dialogue between them resulted in a friendship that lasted for 35 years, until her death. He became her mentor, a role he also adopted towards others, including Peggy Guggenheim, and his presence, personality, intelligence and eye guided Dreier to become one of the leading collectors of modern art in the world. She in turn had an almost maternal affection for him – some have seen it as an unconscious infatuation; she looked out for his welfare and exerted enormous energy to help him escape from occupied France during the war.

In 1918 she commissioned from him what was to be his last and largest painting on canvas, *Tu m'* (its title still enigmatic) for her library. Its long shape suited its installation above bookshelves. Later, it was reinstalled in her successive country homes, The Haven at West Redding, and then at her last country home, Laurel Manor, in Milford, both in Connecticut. She owned one of his greatest works, *The Large Glass*. As her executor after her death, Duchamp eventually arranged its transfer to the Philadelphia Museum of Art.

Two years later, in 1920, Katherine Dreier embarked on her life's work as patron and collector of and proselytizer for contemporary art. In collaboration with the American Dadaist photographer and Surrealist, Man Ray, and with Duchamp, she created the Societe Anonyme,

Katherine Dreier, photographed in 1941 at Yale University.

Inc. The name is a play on words: 'société anonyme' means 'limited company' in French, so, as she liked to say, the society was an 'incorporated corporation'.

The Societe, whose aims were to act as an 'International Organization for the Promotion of the Study in America of the Progressive in Art', opened galleries in New York and organized 84 travelling exhibitions between 1920 and 1940 as well as lectures, often given by Dreier herself. She wrote that the Societe was to ensure that there was 'on view a permanent exhibition of good examples of the so-called "Modern Expression of Art"'. As the Societe's president, Dreier travelled frequently to the art centres of Europe, to Italy, France and Germany; she made the acquaintance of the artists of the Bauhaus at Weimar (founded in 1919), that visual powerhouse that brought together artists from all visual disciplines, from design to photography. In 1926, she organized the Societe's most comprehensive and largest international exhibition at the Brooklyn Museum. The Societe was first to show the work of the Russian Wassily Kandinsky (1866–1944) in America. While it gathered a magnificent collection of modern art, it always remained more a concept than a museum; rather like a modern *kunsthalle*, it did not own premises with a permanent display. When the Museum of Modern Art was founded in New York, dedicated to displaying a permanent collection of modern art as well as initiating temporary exhibitions, it filled the place Dreier had once imagined would have been occupied by the Societe, which closed officially in 1949.

Katherine Dreier greatly admired Kandinsky's work and philosophy, and she introduced his paintings to America (*The Waterfall*, 1909, *Improvisation No. 7*, 1910, *Multicoloured Circle*, 1921). She shared with him a sense of the spiritual in art, and in particular aspects of theosophy. His philosophy and artistic attitudes were set out in the essay 'On the Spiritual in Art' (1912), and he explored the emotions that could be conveyed by an abstract vocabulary of form in his book *Point and Line to Plane* (1926). Dreier wrote that Kandinsky's art would speak to the eye as music spoke to the ear, and his painting was a strong influence on her own art, which became abstract after about 1918.

A paramount feature of her collecting had been to collect only the work of living artists, often near the beginning of their careers and reputations. Moreover, she regarded many of them as friends, some of whose work she admired greatly and others with whom she simply maintained close relationships without necessarily supporting their work. A significant number of the 'advanced' artists of her time – Mondrian, Naum Gabo (1890–1977), the German Dadaist Kurt Schwitters (1887–1948), Max Ernst and Paul Klee – were friends.

Duchamp was an executor of Dreier's Will, charged with distributing her holdings to public collections. He carried out this task with brilliance, sensitivity and vision. Some went to the Guggenheim, some to the Phillips, in Washington, and some to the Museum of Modern Art. Yale University received, from the collection of Dreier's Societe Anonyme and her own private collection, over 1,000 works by 180 artists. In 1941 she had already presented over 600 works herself to the Yale University Art Gallery.

Katherine Dreier collected the work of many artists who were more distinguished by association than in their own right. Perhaps she did this consciously, perhaps she was identifying herself with their endeavours (she was far too aware not to realize that she, too, was a minor artist). She was convinced that the *zeitgeist* had to be represented as fully as possible by all those who had participated in the creative milieu of their time and committed themselves to the making of art. She gave the public a profoundly helpful study collection, as well as scores of great works of twentieth-century art.

Gertrude Vanderbilt Whitney

Mrs Whitney said she had 'collected the work of American artists because I believe them worthwhile and because I believed in our national creative talent'.

Cornelius Vanderbilt – whose surname became synonymous with wealth itself – was perhaps the richest man in North America in his time, and Gertrude Vanderbilt Whitney was his daughter. The family fortunes were founded by Cornelius's grandfather, 'Commodore' Cornelius Vanderbilt, first on steamboat companies and then on the coming of the railroads.

Gertrude was herself multi-talented. She used her vast resources to help art and artists and almost single-handedly led the way for the fashionable intelligentsia, the rich, and the establishment, to appreciate American art. In a very real sense, she melded the worlds of the international ultra rich and bohemian society (she was a sculptor herself), and was among the first to do so. Her own preference was for realistic, representational and figurative art. Yet, directly and indirectly, she also supported 'advanced' and avant-garde art. Her financial and practical support for American art and artists was unwavering, and she rose above personal taste. In the first four decades of the twentieth century, she helped artists by showing their work, buying from them, helping in kind, offering them teaching contracts, assisting with studio costs and the expenses of materials, meeting personal bills, awarding bursaries and scholarships and initiating the organizing of exhibitions.

The lasting legacy to her work is the Whitney Museum of American Art in New York City. Today, the interest and allure of American art from the eighteenth century on is taken for granted, but it was, of course, not always so; the National Museum of American Art, Washington DC, was not recognized as a separate entity until 1980. Serious collectors, private and public, of the past of American art only really began to emerge in the early twentieth century, and slightly later for contemporary American art. In the early years of the century, the Metropolitan Museum, then as now a dominant institution in the visual culture of America, refused to show contemporary American art (now it has an American wing and departments devoted to contemporary art).

In 1896 Gertrude Vanderbilt married into another hugely rich family; her husband was Harry Payne Whitney, polo-player, race horse owner, all-round sportsman; they had three children. She was only 25 when her interest in art – she had drawn as a child – revived, and she determined to be a sculptor. She and her brother had been portrayed in carved relief by the most eminent American sculptor of the time, Augustus Saint-Gaudens (1848–1907), and her father was deeply involved with the Metropolitan and personally collected figurative, representational, academic art. Her vocation became a passion for art.

Although the family backgrounds of her husband and herself were markedly similar (Harry was the boy next door), their lives diverged; he was as obsessed with horses, horsemanship, polo, breeding, racing, as Gertrude was with art. The marriage became semi-detached; Gertrude had numerous crushes, affections, liaisons and *amitiés amoureuse.*

Portrait of Gertrude Vanderbilt Whitney
(detail) by Robert Henri. Whitney
Museum of American Art, New York.

Just after the turn of the century, she began to support American art and artists. In 1907 she helped to organize an exhibition of contemporary American Realist painters at the Colony Club. In 1908 she contributed financially to a show under the auspices of the National Sculpture Society at the Municipal Arts Society building in Baltimore and in 1913 to the enormously influential Armory Show in New York.

By 1917 she was both a director and the financial linchpin of the Society of Independent Artists, founded by Katherine Dreier, whose primary purpose was to hold exhibitions of contemporary art of both American and foreign artists, as well as to support a full programme of lectures and publications, thus anticipating by decades the enormous growth of the public education role of museums and galleries in the interwar period. Her support for the cause of art extended to backing a magazine called *The Arts* for much of the 1920s. Gertrude Vanderbilt Whitney also underwrote exhibitions and other public activities in her own studio in New York, the Whitney Studio, from 1914 to 1927, and its successors, the Whitney Studio Club, from 1918 to 1928 and the Whitney Studio Galleries, 1928 to 1930, until the founding of the Whitney Museum.

A celebrated individual cause she supported financially was the successful case brought by photographer Edward Steichen in 1927 concerning the import to America of a sculpture by

Bronze figure of Gertrude Vanderbilt Whitney by Jo Davidson with bronze of Jo Davidson by
Gertrude Vanderbilt Whitney, both *c*.1917. Whitney Museum of American Art, New York.

Romanian-born Constantin Brancusi (1876–1957), *Bird in Space*, which he owned: customs assessed the Brancusi under 'Kitchen Utensils and Hospital Supplies' and demanded duty of $600. Gertrude Vanderbilt Whitney paid the legal costs of this landmark case, which set legal precedents for the definition of modern art – for customs purposes at least.

During World War I, Gertrude crossed and re-crossed the Atlantic, donating a whole hospital unit to the allied effort which the French deployed in Belgium. In 1914, on board the *Lusitania* sailing to New York, she wrote in her war journal that she wanted to take up a place that up to the present she had ignored: 'I wish to have a certain power, and to have that power I must be someone, not only though my private or artistic life, but through the influence which by reason of my position I can exert.'

Gertrude Vanderbilt Whitney's most public activity was the foundation of the Whitney Museum of American Art in New York City in 1930 to show American art exclusively. It occurred a year after the foundation of MOMA and a year after she had offered her collection as a gift to the Metropolitan Museum in New York and had been turned down. The core of the Whitney was over 600 of the works she owned – paintings, drawings and sculptures – of American art, fundamentally by living artists. Among the artists represented were Charles Birchfield, George Bellows, Gaston Lachaise, Max Weber, Charles Demuth, Gaston Lachaise, Elsie Driggs, Thomas Hart Benton, Start Davis, Robert Henry and Edward Hopper. She also appointed the dynamic Juliana Force, who had kept a professional overview on her patronage for some years, as the Whitney's first director. At the opening of the first Whitney Museum of American Art in downtown New York in 1931, Gertrude said in her speech that during the past quarter of a century she had: 'collected the work of American artists because I believe them worthwhile and because I believed in our national creative talent. Now I am making this collection the nucleus of a museum devoted exclusively to American art'. Throughout the youth of the museum she had founded, Mrs Whitney continued to purchase and donate. By 1935 she had added another 350 works to the museum's holdings. It was not until 1949 that a work of art entered the collection of the Whitney that had neither been given directly by Mrs Whitney nor paid for out of funds she had supplied.

For her own studio on the Whitney family estate in Long Island, Gertrude commissioned murals from some of the leading artists of the day – exotic flora from Howard Cushing, an underwater scene by Robert Chanler and an extensive medieval scene by Maxfield Parrish. Thomas Hart Benton painted a series of murals called the 'Arts of Life in America' which were installed in a library of the first Whitney Museum.

In her own sculpture studio she began to study sculpture, as a practitioner, in 1900. She would also work in her studio in Paris, meeting Rodin when the great sculptor was in his 70s (around 1911) and not only buy from him but show him her own work and accept his constructive criticism. She was drawn almost exclusively to figurative work and to work with social significance.

As a highly successful academic figurative sculptor, Gertrude Vanderbilt Whitney won major commissions, including the monument to the sinking of the *Titanic* for Washington DC (1913). She created war memorials, for example the Washington Heights War Memorial in New

York City (1922), and portraits. The conservative, even with hindsight the academic, nature of her work has meant that by and large she has been excluded from the major dictionaries, anthologies and encyclopaedias of art by women, which have been such a feature of the past 30 years, a period which has also seen, in 1987, the foundation of the Museum for Women's Art in Washington DC.

The art of Gertrude Vanderbilt Whitney is now given scant attention; the patronage of Gertrude Vanderbilt Whitney transformed the course of American art and its public.

CHAPTER XII

The Ladies of Texas

Ima Hogg (1882–1975)
Dominique de Menil (1908–97)

T exas is a huge and characterful state, with fabulous wealth based on ranching and on oil. Its image has been brash, and boastful, but in fact at the end of the twentieth century it can indeed boast outstanding modern architecture, academically distinguished universities, and some of the finest museums and galleries in America, not to mention several US presidents.

Ima Hogg, the daughter of a governor of the state of Texas, had an inherited fortune and a highly developed sense of Texas patriotism. She wanted to do her very best, culturally, for her native state, and collected art deliberately to that end, not only because she enjoyed it, but because she believed such collections would enhance the life of the milieu to which she was devoted. Dominique de Menil, the sophisticated, elegant Frenchwoman who had been at home in Houston since the years of World War II, when her family's oil business relocated from war-torn Europe to Texas, was also fiercely loyal to her adopted home. She was wooed by France, and indeed a significant selection from the Menil collection was exhibited at the Grand Palais in Paris in 1984; the French made no secret of the fact that they hoped very much the collection would eventually find its way to France on a permanent basis. But Dominique de Menil, together with her husband Jean, who changed his name to John, contributed to Houston on a very broad basis, by funding and involving themselves in several higher educational institutions, cultural institutions, and also in political areas involving civil rights. And it was to Houston that Dominique de Menil gave an unusually beautiful and special museum, and a fascinating collection.

Like the Ladies of MOMA and Katherine Dreier, these ladies of Texas believed in the uplifting power of art; Ima Hogg believed in art's power to set an example and to educate; and Dominque de Menil believed, too, in the spiritual power of art, and both wished to endow their own city with whatever was in their power to give. The fact that Houston, Texas at the end of the twentieth century is an important city on the cultural map of America is due in no small part to the deliberately patriotic actions by affluent and dedicated women Houstonians.

182

Ima Hogg.
The Museum of Fine
Arts, Houston, Texas.

Ima Hogg

Ima Hogg dreamed of joining Texas 'to the heart of an American heritage which unites us'.

James Hogg, Ima's father, was the first Texan-born governor of Texas, a lawyer and a newspaper owner. She was a little girl of nine when he started his four-year term in the 1857 Governor's Mansion in Austin, the state capital of Texas. Even as a little girl, she was a Texas patriot, and she was to remember the 'thrill' of inhabiting the big colonial-style bed that had belonged to Sam Houston (1793–1863) himself, the patriarch of Texas independence. From a very early age, she was steeped in the Texan past, and indeed seemed to be living the nation's history; she travelled with her father to the East Coast, when only twelve, and to Hawaii accompanying a political delegation with him when Hawaii was annexed to the United States.

After returning to the practice of law, at the turn of the century, James Hogg became involved in the beginnings of the oil industry, participating in the founding of the oil company that was to become Texaco. Governor Hogg died in 1906, but not before buying a big property south of the city of Houston, which he was convinced had oil deposits. Oil and real estate development became the basis of a great family fortune.

Ima Hogg was an ardent musician. She moved to New York City to study the piano when she was nineteen and later went to Berlin (1907–10) to continue her musical education. The inception of her passion for Americana seems to have come from an episode in New York: in 1920, while sitting for her portrait by the American painter Wayman Adams, she noted in his studio a maple armchair and, after curiously enquiring about it, discovered it was a New England colonial chair. Ima was to tell people that she had heard collecting was a disease, and that she was sure she must have had that disease, incurably, from childhood. She seems to have begun her own collection by buying English antiques.

Her first purchase of Americana – the decorative and fine arts of America – was made shortly after that fateful encounter in Adams' studio. Bought from the New York antique dealers Collings & Collings, it was a colonial armchair similar to the one she had been so attracted to – simple and elegant, with turned legs and stretchers, a rush seat and slender wooden arms carved in reddish-brown American maple. From then on she started to build a collection, which she housed in her own enormous house, Bayou Bend. Ima's life passion became to create the best holding she possibly could of Americana for her native Texas, and in particular for the city of Houston.

She was devoted to her bachelor brother Will, a fellow collector. Will and Ima and their brother Mike had settled into Bayou Bend in 1928, but Will died in 1930. In the following few years after his death Ima turned her attention away from Americana, buying instead the Native American pottery of the American Southwest, then an 'advanced' interest, and contemporary European art, both of which specialist collections she gave to the Museum of Fine Arts, which Will had founded in 1924 and to which he gave specific donations.

Ima Hogg's interests broadened to encompass the range of media available in the decorative arts of textiles, metalwork, ceramics and glass – and fine art: also in paintings, sculpture and work on paper. Continuing to live in Texas, she was concerned that Houston's distance of several thousand miles from the great shops and collections along the Atlantic seaboard would perhaps prohibit her from finding the finest examples. Needless to say, aware of her interests and her resources, dealers found choice examples for her over the decades. And she herself studied the greatdecorative art collections on the East Coast, making friends with other major collectors in the field, who helped her to formulate the idea of the house museum.

Some of her finest items of Americana were acquired in the 1950s: a rare Massachusetts high chest, *c*.1750, decorated lavishly with oriental scenes in the most exquisite japanning (lacquer-work using gold and silver leaf and powders); a Massachusetts easy chair, *c*.1770, with original Irish stitch-work cover in cheerful folk yellows and reds and the monumental (more than 8ft tall) Newport desk/bookcase, *c*.1770, with its elaborate internal arrangement of sculptured drawers and cubby holes. Ima bought her first early American paintings in 1954, launching the collection in grand style with seven works (two oils, two pastels and five drawings) bycolonial America's dominant portraitist, John Singleton Copley (1738–1815).

Above all, the 1950s marked the expansion of Ima Hogg's collection of early American silverand pewter ware, notable for the wealth of simply-shaped, country-looking seventeenth- and eighteenth-century porringers, tankards, mugs, spout cups, tumblers, cream pots, plates and candlesticks.

Bayou Bend, complete with Ima's collection, is now part of the Museum of Fine Arts in Houston after her gift of its contents in 1957. Still known as the Bayou Bend Collection, her old home is now a Decorative Arts wing of the museum; it reflects decades of committed acquisition. She had both conceived a singular mission, and fulfilled it, through art: she wanted to join the state of Texas, by means of her all-encompassing collection of Americana 'to the heart of an American heritage which unites us'.

A chapel and a museum for a city: Art á deux

Dominique de Menil

> *Art is what lifts us above daily life. It makes us more open, more human, more refined, and even more intelligent.*

The story of Dominique de Menil is the exception that proves the rule. Singular woman after singular woman has appeared in these pages, each with an overtly strong character that determined the kind of collection she made. But Dominique de Menil evidently felt that men were superior to women, in intellect and talent. She always insisted her husband had taken the lead, yet study of the essays she left behind, the exhibitions she organized and the collection itself indicates how extremely important her own personality was. Not only are her daughters significant art collectors and animators, but it is her own character, her intuition and perception, and her flavour that infuses the collection. It was she who, several years after her husband's death, carried forward the idea of the museum and realized one of the most exquisite galleries anywhere in the world. Her daughter Adelaide said that the museum reflected her mother's 'modest style'. In her later years, Dominique gave even greater expression to her identification with the spiritual in modern art, while at the same time embarking on a voyage of discovery of Byzantine art.

For three decades, Dominique and her husband Jean de Menil (later anglicized to John) collected together, with imagination and seriousness. John was given, upon occasion, to the grand gesture, such as buying an entire exhibition by the Swiss sculptor Jean Tinguely and giving it to the Museum of Fine Arts in Houston. Together they envisioned the Rothko Chapel in Houston. Then, for nearly a quarter of a century after her husband's death in 1973, Dominique strove to realize her vision of the museum they had discussed and planned for together, providing the concept – an opulent austerity – and after it opened in 1987 remaining deeply involved.

Born Dominique Schlumberger in France, she remembered collecting things as a child: little objects, shells, seeds, 'tiny miniature things'. Her father was a brilliant academic physicist who invented an electromagnetic sounding device for locating underground oil deposits. He set up the Sclumberger oil company and fast accumulated a massive fortune. Dominique studied physics and mathematics at the Sorbonne. In 1931 she married Jean de Menil, who came from an aristocratic but impoverished family and worked as a banker in Paris. Jean joined the Schlumberger family firm in 1936. In 1941, with their young children, they escaped warring Europe and fled to the United States via different routes, reuniting in Houston, which had become the international base and headquarters of Schlumberger.

In their early years in Paris, the young couple had met a Dominican priest, Father Couturier, who later, with the passion of a crusader, attempted to interest the Church in art, especially by commissioning art for churches and religious art from contemporary artists. His legacy and inspiration lives on in the chapel at St Paul de Vence decorated by Henri Matisse, in Le Corbusier's Notre Dame-du-Haut, Ronchamp, and in the commissions for artists like Léger and Rouault for French churches. Jean de Menil met Father Couturier again in New York during the war, where the Dominican had been exiled during the occupation of France.

Dominique credited her husband with launching their collection with a watercolour by Cézanne, which he brought back to Houston in his briefcase after a visit to New York art galleries with Father Couturier in 1945. The couple began to acquire across a wide spectrum: twentieth-century art from the School of Paris (Braque, Rouault, Léger, for example), pre-Columbian art from Latin America and ethnographic art from Africa. Their antiquities were to include notable artefacts from throughout the ancient world, in particular Sumeria, Greece, Italy and Egypt, with an especially significant collection of Egyptian Fayum paintings – funerary portraits painted on wood in a delightfully naive and fresh style, dating from the first to the fourth centuries AD.

Their passion worried Dominique's family: Madame Schlumberger, Dominique's mother, told Father Couturier that if the couple continued to buy 'they will have to eat crumbs'; Father Couturier is said to have answered, 'Madame, let them eat crumbs but have good paintings on the wall'.

An earlier beginning in art had not seemed at all promising: in order to help a struggling artist, the de Menils had commissioned the Surrealist Max Ernst to paint a portrait of Dominique. Initially they did not like it at all, only realizing its quality when they recovered it from their Paris apartment after the war. Ernst was to become more than an artist they admired profoundly. Indeed, they attempted positively to promote his work: an exhibition they organized in 1952 at the Contemporary Art Association in Houston, as the artist was to recall, produced large crowds but no sales. The de Menil collection ended up containing nearly 130 works by Ernst – paintings, sculpture, works on paper.

There was music and old art in Houston, and wealth and more wealth; but the city, now the tenth largest in the United States, had not yet embraced the idea of the modern with anywhere near the kind of enthusiasm that had made New York the world leader. It was a provincial cousin of the great centres of art and music on the East Coast. However, the de Menils attempted to energize various institutions with varying degrees of success. They were involved from time to time with The Contemporary Arts Association and with the museums and art history departments at St Thomas University and at Rice. In both universities, Dominique took on a role in organizing exhibitions, many of national importance, and all predicated on her intuitive imagination.

Portrait of Dominique
(Dominique de Menil, detail)
by Max Ernst.
The Menil Collection,
Houston, Texas.

Their home, too, was avant-garde at that time for Houston. In 1949, they commissioned Philip Johnson, the famous American architect, to design a relatively austere single-storey home in the River Oaks suburb, where the massive mansions were reminiscent of the southern plantation style. It was among his very first commissions; Philip Johnson described Dominique de Menil as 'a mysterious woman yet her strength was so obvious'.

The Rothko Chapel for Houston was initiated in 1964 and opened seven years later; it is a small, exquisite octagonal brick building housing fourteen specially commissioned paintings, in blacks and maroons, by the American Abstract Expressionist Mark Rothko (1903–70). Although Rothko regarded this series of sombre canvasses as his masterpieces, he did not live long enough to see the chapel open, committing suicide a year after finishing them.

As the world's first eucumenical centre, the Rothko Chapel's inaugural ceremony and dedication was attended by Christians, Jews, Hindus and Muslims. It has since become a place of pilgrimage, host to sacred music of all kinds, to small conferences and to visits from Buddhist monks, Hindu priests and the Dalai Lama. In front of the chapel, designed by the Houston architect Howard Barnstone, there is a major sculpture by Rothko's contemporary, Barnett Newman, called 'Broken Obelisk', sited in a reflecting pool and dedicated by Dominique to Martin Luther King. The de Menils had wanted Houston to join with them in donating the sculpture to the city; but their commitment to the black community and the struggle for civil rights was still at the time too much for some of their fellow citizens. The Barnett Newman was therefore sited on de Menil property. The couple continued to be passionate champions of the struggle for civil rights, befriending Afro-Americans at a period when this was not done socially by white Americans. Marrying both interests, they financed a vast research project and the publication of *The Image of the Black in Western Art*.

The de Menils finally decided to build their own museum – or what they referred to as a 'storage center' – in a neighbourhood where they owned streets of unpretentious housing. The Menil Collection, Houston, which opened in 1987 in a building designed by the Italian architect Renzo Piano (of the Pompidou Centre, 1977, in Paris and the Beyeler Museum, 1997, in Basle) and the Houston architects Richard Fitzgerald and Partners, is one of the most individual and important collections put together in the post-World War II period. The building is strikingly unassuming: two storeys high with five working levels, steel-framed and clad in silvery cypress wood and glass. With natural daylight pouring through the roof and internal courtyard gardens, it is a place for meditation and reflection. Dominique's vision was that it would appear small on the outside, large inside: a place of 'beauty and enchantment . . . where things can be seen on multiple levels, with a relationship made between the objects and the way they are presented'.

'Like children, treasures of a collection are what they are', Dominique wrote about the major collection the 'family' had made. 'Complex sets of circumstances brought these treasures into the family; a chance encounter, a visit to an artist or a dealer, a glance at an auction catalogue, a successful bid and, of course, a favourable moment for spending.' In her museum she wanted to preserve some of the intimacy she had enjoyed with art.

Besides Father Couturier, the de Menils had two other unusual advisers who opened Dominique's eyes gradually. She described the Egyptian-Greek art dealer Alexandre Iolas, who was absorbed by Surrealism and helped 'convert' her, as 'so convinced of the importance of what he was showing. I remember my scepticism in front of our de Chirico . . . I was not taken in; I bought it on his word, on faith'.

Teacher and curator Dr Jermayne MacAgy, who died tragically at the age of 50, spent her last nine years in Houston, first as director of The Contemporary Arts Association, and then as head of the art department financed by the de Menils at the University of St Thomas. Dominique defined MacAgy's brimming talent as an infallible artistic judgement: 'She could bring together a few apparently unrelated objects and they started to live and express some mysterious relation.' Yet in time Dominique became 'more difficult to please; objects have to have something very special. It was very late before we would admit we were collectors'.

The result of this passionate pair's activities is astounding: some 10,000 paintings,

North Entrance Façade of The Menil Collection, Houston, Texas, designed by Renzo Piano
(opened 1987).

sculptures, prints, photographs, rare books and objects, encompassing antiquities from the palaeolithic to the Classical; Byzantine and medieval art; ethnography and twentieth-century art. Works from tribal cultures embrace Oceania, the Pacific Northwest of North America and African cultures. In twentieth-century art, the School of Paris, from Cubism (Cézanne, Georges Braque, Fernand Léger, Mondrian) to Surrealism and the New York School of Abstract Expressionism, followed by Pop Art and Minimal Art, are strongly featured. Of all these, Surrealism is considered to comprise the most celebrated body of work within the collection, with seminal pieces by René Magritte (notably his bronze sculpture *Madame Récamier* and the painting *Golconde,* with its rain of rain-coated businessmen). Of the New York School group the collection contains not only much of the strongest work of Abstract Expressionists Barnett Newman and Mark Rothko, but also highly significant representations from Jackson

189

Pollock, Clifford Still, Willem de Kooning, Robert Motherwell, Larry Rivers, Alexander Calder and Robert Rauschenberg.

About half the collection consists of prints from the sixteenth to the nineteenth centuries, grouped according to subject matter, from the fantastic to the grotesque. In much of the art of the past they collected there is an element of the absurd, the distorted, the fantastical, the surprising, a strain of Surrealism. After John's death, Dominique continued to collect, notably Byzantine art; her son was to design a Byzantine Chapel for a fragmented fresco on loan from the Cypriot Church to – and restored by – the Menil Collection.

Dominique de Menil was a perfectionist; a Houston nickname referred to her as 'the iron butterfly': her fragile, delicate appearance was but the outer shell for an indomitable determination and tenacity. Like others before and since, her spirit found in art something of the spirituality that characterizes religion. She wrote: 'Art is what lifts us above daily life. It makes us more open, more human, more refined, and even more intelligent.' The non-denominational Rothko Chapel, home to religious colloquia and seminars and conferences, inspired her to suggest that 'through art, God constantly clears a path to our hearts'.

CHAPTER XIII

Patrons and Collectors of Surrealism

Peggy Guggenheim (1898–1979)
Gabrielle Keiller (1908–95)

Unlike the Ladies of MOMA, Katherine Dreier and Gertrude Vanderbilt Whitney, Peggy Guggenheim felt responsibility for both the art and the artist. She started to collect in order not to disappoint the artists whose work she showed in her galleries – she set them up in London, New York and Venice. She was not only highly influential as a collector and patron but also as a dealer. In addition to setting up her own museum in Venice in the last decades of her life she contributed to public museums all over the United States – she distributed at least twenty paintings by Jackson Pollock, whose work she promoted in this way and whose life she nurtured. The breadth of her interests in twentieth-century art was vast, from Cubism to Abstraction, and, like Gabrielle Keiller, it was Dada and Surrealism that caught her attention.

Gabrielle Keiller's Irish grandfather acquired an enormous ranch in Texas, and it was this inheritance, through her American father, that financed her collecting activities. She knew Peggy Guggenheim and her Venice museum, and both collectors responded to the work and influence of Duchamp. In Gabrielle's case it was especially through the work of Eduardo Paolozzi, the Edinburgh-born sculptor. She commissioned sculptures and collected other works – prints, ceramics and drawings – that hinted at Surrealist origins. Gabrielle Keiller has been justly described as the last great British collector of Surrealism, and she bequeathed much of her collection to the National Gallery of Modern Art, Edinburgh.

Peggy Guggenheim

Serving the future instead of recording the past.

The Guggenheim family, who came from New York, was fabulously wealthy, the money coming from mining and processing metals. Peggy's father was heir to a copper mining fortune, and he died in the sinking of the *Titanic*.

Interior of the Modern Art gallery in Peggy Guggenheim's Venetian home, the Palazzo Venier dei Leoni, now home of the Peggy Guggenheim Collection.

Solomon Guggenheim (1861–1949), Peggy's uncle, was the first art patron in the family. He set up the Museum of Non-Objective Painting in New York in 1939, for which work restricted dogmatically to that area alone was systematically collected on his behalf, and paid for out of his fortune, by the ardent and influential enthusiast, the German artist Baroness Hilla Rebay (1890–1967). This, the first of the Guggenheim museums, was dedicated to twentieth-century art and its precursors, and among its benefactors were Katherine Dreier and the Baroness herself. Now there are Guggenheim museums in Venice – the Peggy Guggenheim Collection – Berlin and Bilbao, Spain. (Another uncle of Peggy's, John Simon Guggenheim, had his own Foundation, which since 1925, among other activities, has provided Guggenheim Fellowships, to finance research time for academics and creative artists for decades, and so has directly influenced American intellectual life.) The New York Guggenheim Museum, dedicated to 'the promotion and encouragement of art and education in art', was in the vanguard, focusing on abstract art, notably the work of the Russian artist Wassily Kandinsky. It eventually widened its remit to include the entire spectrum of significant visual art activity in the twentieth century.

Peggy Guggenheim had a self-confessed deeply unhappy childhood, during which she was exquisitely lonely and emotionally dependent on her elder sister, Bettina. She was the poor

Peggy Guggenheim photographed in Venice wearing enormous sun glasses, with a Kandinsky on the wall behind her.

little rich girl, sporadically educated, unable to concentrate for long and finding happiness elusive. She was badly affected by her father's death on the *Titanic*. His then mistress survived and was to declare that Peggy was always searching, among her numerous lovers, for a father.

By 1919 Peggy Guggenheim was in Europe, where – appropriately in Paris – she lost her virginity with cool deliberation to the American Laurence Vail, who subsequently became her first husband. She remained in Europe, settling in Paris where in the 1920s she met everybody who was anybody in the world of the arts. Several years before her death, she looked back and described her younger self, perhaps with the benefit of the glowing memories of old age, as 'totally free financially, emotionally, intellectually, sexually'. A biographer described her as a 'voracious consumer of men'.

Looking for something to do, after liaisons of varying success had been truncated by her impetuosity, by incompatibility and once by death, a friend suggested a gallery. She opened it in London in 1938, calling it Guggenheim Jeune, a playful variation on a well-known Parisian gallery, the Galerie Bernheim-Jeune, and almost a direct challenge to her uncle's enterprise in New York.

Although Peggy had come from a remarkably wealthy family, she herself was not seriously wealthy. She was very rich, however, compared to most of her acquaintances (and dazzlingly well off compared to most artists); her maverick father had left the family firm before its mega success, and had on his own lost rather than made money. Peggy was to be supported by a number of comparatively small family trusts set up for her benefit, which neatly tied up the capital, and by an inheritance from her mother, Florette, who came from a prominent Jewish banking family, the Seligmans. In millionaire terms, Peggy made one of the most outstanding collections in the world on a shoestring. As Alfred Barr of the Museum of Modern Art put it, she possessed hard-won 'courage and vision, generosity and humility, money and time, a strong sense of historical significance, as well as of aesthetic quality'. He described her as a patron, someone who was not only interested in what artisists were doing and where they were going, but as someone who possessed both 'the means and the will to act upon this feeling'.

Her ventures in gallery ownership and the promotion of artists were underlined by her commitment to collecting and her own collections; she practised what she preached. In London her mentors were several: the critic and writer Herbert Read (1893–1968), Nellie van Doesberg, the wife of Theo van Doesburg, a leading Constructivist artist, and Marcel Duchamp, who organized everything, including teaching Peggy about modern art, about Cubism, Surrealism and Abstraction, and indeed the distinctions between Surrealism and Abstract art. She gave Kandinsky and the French Surrealist Yves Tanguy (1900–55) their first ever shows in London. She began to collect; in order not to disappoint the artists, she bought at least one thing from every show mounted in her gallery.

The London gallery closed after about eighteen months, and, with the help of the Herbert Read, then editor of the *Burlington Magazine*, the leading periodical on the visual arts, Peggy attempted to set up a museum of modern art in London, appointing Read as its director-curator to be. It was a project sabotaged by the coming war, but Peggy nevertheless paid him an agreed half salary for a period of five years.

Peggy took her energy and enthusiasm to her beloved Paris, where she again tried to find a space to show contemporary art. Then, with the $40,000 she had set aside for the abortive museum project, she bought, deliberately, a painting a day from artists such as Brancusi, Giacometti, Max Ernst and Léger, in an atmosphere which, shadowed by looming conflict, was a buyer's market. Her shopping list was the same as that Herbert Read had devised for the aborted museum project. With the coming of war, Peggy and a seminal number of significant avant-garde artists were to all intents and purposes refugees, who would find refuge together in New York. She escaped from France practically at the last moment, along with her extraordinary art collection, which was shipped as household goods from Grenoble, where it had found sanctuary.

The Anti-Pope, 1941 by Max Ernst
(1891–1976).
Peggy Guggenheim Collection, Venice.
This was a wedding present from the artist to
Peggy Guggenheim on their marriage in 1941.

She set up a gallery in New York, which she calmly and accurately called Art of This
Century (1942–47), where she provided an open house for artists and others. It was a showcase
for her own collection, the nucleus of her museum-to-be, and was regarded in part as a museum,
incorporating a library, and which for a while charged for admission. Its purpose, however, was
two fold: it exposed the New York audience to a huge array of Surrealist and other 'advanced' art
and it was a place, in her own words, where 'people who are doing something really new can show
their work', in effect a 'research laboratory'. Its special monographic and thematic exhibitions
showed the best of the new. Art of This Century had an interior design by Frederick Kiesler
(1896–1965) and installation photographs taken by Berenice Abbott (b.1898). It mounted 50 exhibitions in five years, mingling the best – in Peggy's view – of the innovative European artists with
the then, as yet, unknown stars of the future of the New York School, notably the American
Abstract Expressionists, whose idioms were profoundly influenced by Surrealism.

To show the range of her own interests, she wore to the opening of Art of This Century
one earring designed by Yves Tanguy and one designed by the American inventor of the mobile,
Alexander Calder (1898–1976). Her passions were Surrealist art and Abstract art, and some 'isms'
in between. Peggy titled the British edition of her autobiography *Confessions of an Art Addict*
(1960); an earlier publication of her autobiography had been called *Out of this Century*, a reflection of the name of her New York quasi-commercial gallery. The more conservative branch of her

vast Guggenheim family had referred to Peggy's book as 'Out of My Mind'. She seemed indeed to herself and to others to be an addictive personality, filled with extraordinary energy, and pursuing her goals with imagination and spirit.

Peggy's goals included men: she had numerous affairs, liaisons and attachments, although only two marriages and two children. For all her wildness and emotional extravagance, her autobiography is vivid as to her needs, inadequacies and energies. She described various of her aunts and uncles and other relatives as mad or demented; to her almost unbearable sorrow her daughter committed suicide.

For Peggy only the best in art would do. Most of those who contributed to the public effort for contemporary art that this private woman made are now among the best-known artists of the twentieth century. They include the German Surrealist Max Ernst (with whom Peggy had a long romantic liaison, a brief marriage and rapid divorce – he called her 'impetuous and clumsy'), Robert Motherwell, Hans Hoffmann, Mark Rothko, William Baziotes, Adolph Gottlieb, as well as Jackson Pollock. The base was Surrealism: André Breton, the Surrealist theorist, poet and general promoter of the movement, wrote the catalogue of Peggy's collection which was to form the basis for Art of This Century during its life in New York. In the 1940s, Baroness Rebay regarded her art activities as dangerous threats to the New York Guggenheim Museum.

Peggy considered her most honourable achievement to be her enlightened support for the artist who is increasingly seen as the giant of the period, the disturbed and disturbing Jackson Pollock. She discovered him working as a carpenter-technician at her uncle's Museum of Non-objective Art. She gave him four solo shows in her New York gallery, declared him 'the greatest painter since Picasso' and, uniquely, put him under contract for the work he showed in Art of This Century. Pollock created a 23f-long mural for her New York apartment, a mural that Peggy later gave to the University of Iowa. One little-known aspect of her extraordinary self-imposed mission to promote modern art is the fact that she donated works of art to museums around the United States.

Peggy Guggenheim had a fine sense of posterity. She had attempted – although she failed – to persuade the establishment in London to found a proper modern art museum with her collection as its seed corn; she had attempted – and failed – to found a co-operative society of artists in France. But finally she found a metier, for the last 30 years of her life. After World War II, Peggy returned to Europe and stayed for the rest of her life. She went to live in Venice and, after exhibiting her collection at the Venice Biennale, she settled in her own delightful palazzo, the eighteenth-century Palazzo Venier dei Leoni on the Grand Canal. The Palazzo was open annually from the spring to the autumn to display to the public its incredibly choice and highly personal collection of twentieth-century masterpieces.

Initially, when first opened to the public it was a house-museum; after Peggy's death visitors could even see her bedroom (including the silver headboard designed for her by Alexander Calder) and some personal mementos. Now it is indeed a museum; a careful expansion has brought Peggy's collection into the orbit of all the Guggenheim museums, but the personal flavour is still strong.

Peggy Guggenheim never attempted to make a comprehensive and representative collection of the best art of the twentieth century; rather she collected, as she lived – among the artists – their work that most appealed to her own original sensibility. Intellectually she was at first drawn to the work of the Old Masters, and almost religiously studied the writings of the American expatriate art historian Bernard Berenson (1865–1959), the connoisseur who had educated and inspired scores of art historians, scholars, collectors – and dealers. She took herself round the great collections in Italy with his precepts in mind. Yet she was eventually, through the accident of personal acquaintance and the determination of temperament, to commit herself, in a phrase set out in a press release from Art of This Century, to 'serving the future instead of recording the past'.

The 300 works of art and objects, of which about 200 are superlative, in the Peggy Guggenheim Collection, now an integral part of the Guggenheim museums, are not only a permanent legacy of one woman's determination, energy, imagination and commitment, but are among the classics of Modernism. By committing to the future in her own time, Peggy Guggenheim has left to the public some of the finest art of the past.

Gabrielle Keiller

'The Magic Mirror'

Gabrielle Keiller's life was divided between golf and art at the midway point. Tall and graceful, she was a highly gifted amateur golfer, playing for various international teams in the 1930s, and after the war she won several European championships. But in her 40s she became a serious student of archaeology and art, as well as making an outstanding and highly original collection of twentieth-century art. Gabrielle Keiller's selection of Surrealism, Dada and contemporary British art, now part of the Scottish National Gallery of Modern Art in Edinburgh, is of international importance. Her father's stepfather, John Adair, built a castle in Ireland and acquired a million-acre ranch in Texas, the JA ranch. Gabrielle's share, when it was sold in the 1940s, financed her collecting activities.

After two unsuccessful marriages, in 1947 Gabrielle met Alexander Keiller and married him in 1951. As well as being heir to a Scots marmalade and jam-making firm, he was a dedicated archaeologist involved with leading scholars, and in the 1920s started to excavate near Avebury in Wiltshire, later buying the land on which the mysterious Avebury Stone Circle is sited. In 1938 he opened the old stables of his agreeable stone sixteenth-century manor house, Avebury Manor, as an archaeological museum. In the 1940s the National Trust acquired the Wiltshire sites of Avebury and Windmill Hill. Alexander Keiller died of cancer in 1955. After his death, Gabrielle remained devoted to his archaeological activities and spent some years as a highly valued volunteer working on major British archaeological projects at the British Museum.

Gabrielle Keiller photographed in 1950. Scottish National Gallery of Modern Art, Edinburgh.

Gabrielle had already made a variety of unusual collections – a huge assembly of china creamers all in the shape of a cow, to which her husband and she devoted an entire room in their London flat; a parallel and smaller holding of silver cow creamers; and seventeenth- and eighteenth-century furniture. Her collection of Dada and Surrealist art comprised major works of art and a complementary, specialist collection and archive of ephemera – thousands of catalogues, letters, manuscripts, photographs, publications, periodicals, journals and artists' books. Gabrielle bequeathed both the artworks and the ephemera to the National Gallery of Modern Art, Edinburgh, where they form an integral part, with a specialist library, of the new Dean Gallery, a magnificent converted building of 1833. Here her collection has taken its place as an essential component of a wider twentieth-century collection that embraces works of art by the British sculptor, printmaker and archivist Eduardo Paolozzi and the collection of Surrealist art and its accompanying archive amassed by painter and collector Sir Roland Penrose.

In the 1960s, when she was in her early 50s, Gabrielle Keiller seriously began collecting twentieth-century, and she collected in an unusual and complementary way. Drawn to the anarchic wit and unexpectedness of Dada and Surrealism, she was also to commission and patronize some of the leading contemporary artists working in Britain, and in particular to furnish with major works of art her great garden at Telegraph Cottage, in Kingston upon Thames on the outskirts of London, which she and Alexander had bought the year before he died. As well as acquiring works by the young British sculptor Richard Long, she commissioned him to do a magical circle of slates. She had made a magical garden in over four acres of glades and lawns and groves, and she also sited with care and wit a number of major Paolozzi bronzes on her lawns. After a distressing fire in 1986, she moved from Telegraph Cottage back to central London.

Part of her contemporary collection was dispersed; a number of the sculptures she had sited in her garden were sold to public collections. The Keiller Collection in Edinburgh contains magnificent work by Eduardo Paolozzi, and work also by other British artists, John Davies, Bruce McLean and Barry Flanagan, all of whom could be described as being touched by the spirit of Surrealism.

The Surrealist part of the Keiller collection was exhibited anonymously in Edinburgh in 1988 under the title 'The Magic Mirror'. At the time of the first exhibition of the entire collection at the Scottish National Gallery of Modern Art in 1997, the art historian Elizabeth Cowling suggested that, as in the building of the collections of Katherine Dreier and Peggy Guggenheim, Duchamp was a formative influence, directly and indirectly, on Gabrielle Keiller. In 1983 Mrs

Richard Long (b.1945), *Six Stone Circles*, 1981, in the garden at Gabrielle Keiller's Telegraph Cottage.
Photograph, Anthony D'Offay Gallery, London.
Gabrielle Keiller Collection, Scottish National Gallery of Modern Art, Edinburgh.

Portrait of Maurice, Gabrielle
Keiller's dog, 1978 by Andy
Warhol (1928–87).
The Keiller Collection, Scottish
National Museum of Modern
Art, Edinburgh.

Keiller bought one of Duchamp's exclusive limited-edition *Boites-en-valise*, the 'box in a suitcase', in effect a portable museum that contained an original work and 69 reproductions of Duchamp's works; she gave it to Edinburgh in 1989. Duchamp, Elizabeth Cowling suggests, was the animator of Dada, intervened in Surrealism, and was a profound influence on Paolozzi. There are other links between him and Keiller; in 1960 Gabrielle visited Venice, where she not only saw Paolozzi's work in the British Pavilion at the Venice Biennale but became acquainted with Peggy Guggenheim and her collection, which was so strong in the works of the major Surrealist artists and which had at times also been animated by Duchamp.

Gabrielle Keiller was charming and much loved by close friends, who also were involved in art and its collecting; she took her study of modern and contemporary art seriously and for a decade was a volunteer guide at the Tate Gallery in London, which involved special training and study on a huge number of works – eighteenth- and nineteenth-century British art, and twentieth-century modern international art. She did original research, and in her early 70s studied art history. She refined and changed her collection, continually searching for better examples: she bought and acquired by quality. She did everything with elegance, wit and generosity.

In perhaps just a quarter of a century of serious collecting, Gabrielle Keiller's patronage and involvement made her a significant figure in the British and international art world: she was modest, yet determined, and a perfectionist. She certainly had style: in 1976 she commissioned Andy Warhol to do a portrait of Maurice, her dachshund; Warhol visited Telegraph Cottage, took photographs of Maurice for the painting, which he did in New York, and evidently he was one of the very few strangers with whom Maurice was on friendly terms.

Bibliography

John Alexander, *Catherine the Great,* Life and Legend, Oxford, 1989

Brian Allen and Larissa Dukelskaya, *British Art Treasures from Russian Imperial Collections in the Hermitage,* Newhaven and London, 1997

Cleveland Amory, *The Last Resorts,* New York, 1948

Elizabeth and Florence Anson, *Mary Hamilton, later Mrs John Dickenson at Court and at Home, from letters and diaries, 1756–1816,* London, 1925.

Louisa, Lady Antrim, *Recollections of Louisa, Countess of Antrim,* Shipston-on-Stour, 1927

Apollo, special number, 'French patrons and collectors', January, 1973

Apollo, special number, 'the Hermitage collections', June, 1975

Apollo, special number, 'Waddesdon Manor: Aspects of the Collection', June, 1976

Apollo, special number, 'the Empress Josephine', July, 1977

Nietta Aprà, *Il Mobile Impero,* Novarra, 1970

Clive Aslet, *The American Country House,* Newhaven and London, 1990

H. C. Bainbridge, *Peter Carl Fabergé,* London, 1949

Susan J Barnes, *The Rothko Chapel: An Act of Faith,* Houston, 1989

Judith A. Barter, (ed.), *Mary Cassatt: Modern Woman,* New York, 1973

Georgina Battiscombe, *Queen Alexandra,* London, 1969

Arthur Beavan, *Marlborough House and its Occupants,* London, 1896

Marie-Louise Biver, *Pierre Fontaine, Premier Architecte de L'Empereur,* Paris, 1964

Anthony Blunt, 'Destailleur at Waddesdon' in *Apollo,* June, 1977

Museum Boston, 1977

Paul Bourget, *Outre-Mer: Impressions of America,* London, 1895

René Brimo, *L'Evolution du goût aux Etats-Unis d'apres l'histoire des collections,* Paris 1938

Mrs Kernon Delves Broughton (ed.), *Court and Private Life in the Time of Queen Charlotte, being the Journals of Mrs Papendeik, Assistant Keeper of the Wardrobe and Reader to Her Majesty,* London, 1887

Van Wyck Brooks, *New England Indian Summer, 1865-1915,* Boston, 1940

Richard Calvocoressi and Elizabeth Cowling, *Surrealism and After:* The Gabrielle Keiller Collection, Edinburgh, 1997

Antonio Canova exhibition, Correr Museum, Venice, 1992

Carlton House, The Past Glories of George IV's Palace exhibition, The Queen's Gallery, Buckingham Palace, 1991–2

Morris Carter, *Isabella Stewart Gardner and Fenway Court,* London, 1925

Julian Cavalier, *American Castles,* New York, 1973

D. Chanler, *Roman spring: Memoirs by Mrs Winthrop Chanler,* London, 1935

Edmonde Charles-Roux, *Chanel: her work and the woman behind the legend she herself created,* London, 1976

William Clarke, *The Lost Fortune of the Tsars,* revised edition, London, 1996

H. Clifford Smith and Christopher Hussey, *Buckingham Palace*, London, 1931

H. Clifford Smith, 'Queen Mary as a Connoisseur and Collector', *Country Life*, 17 April, 1937

Emily J. Climenson (ed.) *Mrs. Lybbe Powys, Diaries*, London, 1899

Emily J. Climenson (ed.) *Elizabeth Montagu, Queen of the Blue-stockings, her correspondence*, 2 vols, London, 1906

Lucy Cohen, *Louisa de Rothschild and her daughters*, London, 1935

Lady Cynthia Colville, *Crowded Life*, London, 1963

Alice Cooney Frelinghuysen, Gary Tinterow and others, *Splendid Legacy: The Havemeyer Collection*, New York, 1993

Douglas Cooper (ed.) *Great Family Collections*, New York, 1965

Douglas Cooper (ed.) *Great Private Collections*, London, 1963

J. Cordey, *Inventaire des biens de Madame de Pompadour*, Paris, 1939

Louis Courajod (ed.), *Livre-journal de Lazare Duvaux, marchand-bijoutier ordinaire du roy, 1748-1758*, 2 vols, Paris, 1873

Vincent Cronin, *Catherine, Empress of All the Russias*, London, 1978

Anthony Cross, 'Russian Gardens, British Gardeners', *the journal of Baroness Dimsdale, Garden History*, 1991, vol.19, no.1

A. G. Cross (ed.), *An English Lady at the Court of Catherine the Great*, Cambridge, 1989

Mme D'Arblay, *Diary and Correspondence of Fanny Burney*, 6 vols, London, 1904

Edmond et Jules de Goncourt, *Madame de Pompadour*, Paris, 1888

Edmond et Jules de Goncourt, *Madame du Barry*, London, 1914

Dominique de Menil, Walter Hopps and others, *The Menil Collection*, New York, 1987

Baronne Henriette-Louise d'Oberkirch, *Memoires de la Baronne d'Oberkirch sur la cour de Louis XVI et la société française avant 1789*, Paris, 1970

Mrs James de Rothschild, *The Rothschilds at Waddesdon Manor*, London, 1979

Frances Dimond and Roger Taylor, *Crown and Camera, The Royal Family and Photography, 1842-1910*, London, 1987

Anne Distel, *Impressionism: The First Collectors*, New York, 1990

Emmanuel Duchamp (ed.), *Pavlovsk: the Palace and the Park*, 2 vols, Paris, 1993

Anne Eatwell, 'Private pleasure, public beneficence' in *Women in the Victorian Art World*, Clarissa Campbell Orr (ed.), Manchester, 1995

Nina Epton, *Josephine, the Empress and her Children*, London, 1977

Svend Eriksen and Geoffrey de Bellaigue, *Sèvres Porcelain. Vincennes and Sèvres 1740-1800*, London, 1987

Lesley Field, *Bendor, the golden Duke of Westminster*, London, 1983

Martha Gandy Fales, *Jewelry in America*, Woodbridge, 1995

Edward Fowles, *Memories of the Duveen Brothers*, London, 1976

John Gascoigne, *Joseph Banks and the English Enlightenment*, Cambridge, 1994

George III as a Collector, 'The Queen's Gallery exhibition', Buckingham Palace, 1974

René Gimpel, *Diary of an Art Dealer*, Paris, 1963, English edition 1986

Arthur Gold, *Misia: the life of Misia Sert*, London, 1980

Serge Grandjean, *Inventaire après décès de L'Imperatrice Joséphine à Malmaison*, Paris, 1964

Serge Grandjean, *Empire Furniture, 1800-1825*, London, 1926

John Greig (ed.) *The Diaries of a Duchess, extracts from the diaries of the 1st Duchess of Northumberland (1716-1776)*, London, 1926

Montague J. Guest (ed.), *Lady Charlotte Schreiber's Journals*, 2 vols, London, 1911

Revel Guest and Angela V. John, *Lady Charlotte: a biography of the Nineteenth Century*, London, 1989

Peggy Guggenheim, *Out of This Century: Confessions of an Art Addict*, London, 1960

Rollin Van N. Hadley (ed.), *The Letters of Bernard Berenson and Isabella Stewart Gardner, 1887-1924*, Boston, 1987.

Geza von Hapsburg, *Fabergé*, London, 1988

Geza von Hapsburg, *Fabergé in America*, exhibition, New York, 1996

Geza von Hapsburg and Marina Lopato, *Fabergé, Imperial Jeweller*, London, 1993

Charles E. Hardy, *John Bowes and the Bowes Museum*, privately printed, 1970

John Harris, Geoffrey de Bellaigue, Oliver Millar, *Buckingham Palace*, London, 1968

Francis Haskell, 'The Old Masters in Nineteenth-Century French Painting' in *Past and Present in Art and Taste*, New Haven, 1987

Louisine W. Havemeyer, *Sixteen to Sixty: Memoirs of a Collector*, New York, 1993

Peter Hayden, 'Pavlovsk', in *The Garden: Journal of the Royal Horticultural Society*, 1982, vol. 107, pp.219-24

Peter Hayden, 'Imperial culture at Pavlovsk', in *Country Life*, 11 June, 1987

Ruth Hayden, *Mrs Delany, her life and her flowers*, London, 1980

Edna Healey, *The Queen's House, a Social History of Buckingham Palace*, London, 1997

Olwen Hedley, *Queen Charlotte*, London, 1975

Francis Henry Taylor, *The Taste of Angels: A History of Art Collecting from Rameses to Napoleon*, Boston, 1948

Robert L. Herbert, Eleanor S. Aprter and Elise K. Kenney, *The Societé Anonyme and the Dreier Bequest at Yale University*, New Haven, 1984

Frank Herrman, *The English as Collectors*, London, 1972

Mark Alan Hewitt, *The Architect and the American Country House*, Newhaven and London, 1990

Howard Hibbard, *The Metropolitan Museum of Art*, London, 1980

John Hightower and others, *Four Americans in Paris: The Collections of Gertrude Stein and her Family*, New York, 1970

Bevis Hillier, *Pottery and Porcelain, 1700-1914, the Social History of the Decorative Arts*, London, 1968

Patricia Hills and Robert K. Tarbell, *The Figurative Tradition: Whitney Museum of American Art*, New Jersey, 1980

Wallace and Wilhemina Holladay and others, *The National Museum of Women in the Arts*, New York, 1995

Ann Holmes, 'The Menil Opens', in *Houston Chronicle*, 7 June, 1987

Simon Houfe, 'Cult of the Curious (Lady Dorothy Nevill as a collector)', in *Country Life*, 20 April, 1989

Georgina Howell, *In Vogue, 75 Years of Style*, London 1991

Gérard Hubert, in Napoleon and Josephine at Malmaison, *Connoisseur*, December, 1976, pp.259-70

Robert Hughes, *American Visions*, London, 1998

Sam Hunter and others, *The Museum of Modern Art, New York*, New York, 1984

John Ingamells, *The Davies Collection of French Art*, Cardiff, 1967

Gervase Jackson-Stops, 'The Palace of Pavlovsk, Leningrad, part I', *Country Life*, 30 October 1975, p.1142; part II, November 1975

T.F. James, 'Princess of the Beauty Business', (Mme Helena Rubinstein), in *Cosmpolitan*, New York, June 1959, pp.38-44

Madeleine Jarry, 'Napoleon and the Redecoration of the Imperial Residences', in *Apollo*, September, 1964, pp.212-8

Ian Jenkins and Kim Sloane, *Vases and Volcanoes, Sir William Hamilton and his collection*, exhibition, British Museum, London, 1996

Fred Kaplan, *Henry James, the Imagination of Genius*, London, 1992

Victor and Audrey Kennett, *The Palaces of Leningrad*, London, 1973

Rose Kerr, 'The Chinese Porcelain at Spring Grove Dairy', in *Apollo*, January, 1989

Ernest John Knapton, *Empress Josephine*, London, 1964

Viscount Knutsford, *In Black and White*, London, 1921

Nina Kosareva, 'Masterpieces of Eighteenth Century French Sculpture', in *Apollo* , June, 1975

Thomas Krens and others, *Art of this Century: the Guggenheim Museum and its collection*, New York, 1993

M. Kuchumov, *Pavlovsk, Palace and Park*, Leningrad, 1975

Michael Levey, *Painting and Sculpture in France in the Eighteen Century, 1700-1789*, Newhaven and London, 1993

Gail Levin and Marianne Lorenz, *Theme and Improvisation: Kandinsky & the American Avant-Garde 1912-1950*, Boston, 1992

R. W. B. Lewis, *Edith Wharton, A Biography*, London, 1975

Wilmarth S. Lewis, *The Yale Edition of the Correspondence of Horace Walpole*, Newhaven and London, 1937-83

Lady Llanover (ed.), *Autobiography and Correspondence of Mary Granville, Mrs Delany*, 6 vols, London, 1862

Christopher Lloyd, *The Queen's Pictures*, exhibition catalogue, The National Gallery, London 1991

Russell Lynes, *Good Old Modern: An Intimate Portrait of the Museum of Modern Art*, New York, 1973

Axel Madsen, *Coco Chanel, a biography*, London, 1990

Marya Mannes, 'African Art in the Rubenstein Collection', in *International Studio*, New York, May 1929, pp.55-56

Her Highness Princess Marie Louise, *My Memories of Six Reigns*, London, 1956

Suzanne Massie, *Pavlovsk, the life of a Russian Palace*, London, 1990

James R. Mellow, *Charmed Circle: Gertrude Stein and Company*, London, 1974

Karl Ernest Meyer, *The Art Museum: Power, Money, Ethics*, New York, 1979

Karl Ernest Meyer, *The Plundered Past*, New York, 1973

Oliver Millar, *Zoffany and his Tribuna*, Paul Mellon Foundation, 1966

Nancy Mitford, *Madame de Pompadour*, London, 1954

Bernard Morel, *The French Crown Jewels*, Antwerp, 1988

Nancy Mowll Mathews, *Mary Cassatt: A Life*, New York, 1994

Steven Naifeh and Gregory Hite Smith, *Jackson Pollock*, London, 1989

Francis M. Naumann, *New York Dada 1915-23*, New York, 1994

Nina Nemilova, 'Contemporary French Art in Eighteenth-Century Russia' in *Apollo*, 1975

Lady Dorothy Nevill, *Reminiscences*, London, 1905

Lady Dorothy Nevill, 'My Collection' in *Connoisseur*, March 1902, p.151

Guy Nevill, Exotic Groves, *A Portrait of Lady Dorothy Nevill*, Salisbury, 1984

Ralph Nevill, *The Life and Letters of Lady Dorothy Nevill*, London, 1916

Geraldine Norman, *The Hermitage: the biography of a great museum*, London, 1997

Patrick O'Higgins, *Madame (Helena Rubenstein)*, The Viking Press, New York, 1971

J. H. Plumb, *Royal Heritage*, London, 1977

Griselda Pollock, *Mary Cassatt, Painter of Modern Women*, London, 1998

Barbara Pollack, *The Collectors: Dr Claribel and Miss Etta Cone*, Indianapolis, 1962

Krzystof Pomian, *Collectors & Curiosities*, Cambridge UK, 1990

James Pope-Hennessy, *Queen Mary 1867-1953*, London, 1959

Polovstoff, *Les Trésors d'Art en Russie sous le régime Bolsheviste*, Paris, 1919

Clifford Pugh, 'The Magnificent Obsession', in *The Houston Post*, 3 May, 1987

Queen Mary's Art Treasures, exhibition, Victoria & Albert Museum, 1954

Bernard Rackham, *The Schreiber Collection*, catalogue, 2 vols, Victoria & Albert Museum, 1928–30

Herbert Read and others, *The Peggy Guggenheim Collection*, London, 1964

John Rewald, *Cezanne, the Steins and Their Circle*, London, 1986

Brenda Richardson & others, *Dr Claribel and Miss Etta*: The Cone Collection, Baltimore, 1992

John Richardson, *A Life of Picasso*, vols 1 and 2, London, 1991, 1996

Antonia Ridge, *The Man Who Painted Roses, The Story of Pierre-Joseph Redouté*, London, 1974

Jane Roberts, *Royal Artists*, London, 1987

John Martin Robinson, *The Royal Palaces, Buckingham Palace*, London, 1995

Pierre Rosenberg and Marion C. Stewart, *French Paintings 1500-1825*, The Fine Arts Museum of San Francisco, San Francisco, 1987

Marvin C. Ross, *The Art of Karl Fabergé and His Contemporaries*, Oklahoma, 1965

Miriam Rothschild, *The Rothschild Gardens*, London, 1996

Nancy Rubin, *American Empress (Marjorie Merriweather Post)*, New York, 1995

Helena Rubenstein, *My Life for Beauty*, Simon & Shuster, New York, 1966

Judy Rudoe, *Cartier, 1900-1939*, British Museum, 1997

John Malcom Russell, *From Nineveh to New York: the Strange Story of the Assyrian Reliefs in the Metropolitan Museum*, Newhaven and London, 1997

Sir W. H. Russell, *A Memorial of the marriage of HRH Albert Edward Prince of Wales and HRH Alexandra Princess of Denmark*, London, 1864

Lady St Helier, *Memories of Fifty years*, London, 1909

Aline Saarinen, *The Proud Possessors: The Lives, Times and Tastes of Some Adventurous American Art Collectors*, New York, 1958

Rosalind Savill, *The Wallace Collection, Catalogue of the Sèvres Porcelain*, London, 1988

Bernice Scharlach, *Big Alma: San Francisco's Alma Spreckels*, San Francisco, 1995

Barbara Scott, 'The Marquis de Marigny, A Dispenser of Royal Patronage' and 'Mme du Barry, A Royal Favourite with Taste' in *Apollo*, January, 1973, pp.25–35

Douglas Shand-Tucci, *The Art of Scandal: the life and times of Isabella Stewart Gardner*, New York, 1997

Ann B. Shteir, *Cultivating Women, Cultivating Science: Flora's daughters and botany in England, 1760-1860*, Baltimore and London, 1996

Mark Simpson, *The Rockefeller Collection of American Arts at the Fine Arts Museums of San Francisco*, New York, 1994

Osbert Sitwell, *Queen Mary and Others*, London, 1996

Kenneth Snowman, *The Art of Carl Fabergé*, London, 1974

Hilary Spurling, *The Unknown Matisse*, London, 1998

The State Hermitage: Masterpieces from the Collections, 2 vols, London, 1994

William Stearn, 'Pierre-Joseph Redouté: Royal Flower Painter' in Martyn Rix, *Redouté's Fairest Flowers*, London, 1988

Francis Steegmuller, *Cocteau, a Biography,* London, 1970

Renate Stendhal, *Gertrude Stein in Words and Pictures*, London, 1995

Denys Sutton, 'A Palace for a Paragon, the Hôtel de Beauharnais', in *Apollo*, June 1976, pp.502–7

Denys Sutton, 'The Incomparable Josephine, the Empress Josephine and her taste', in *Apollo*, July, 1977

Frederick A. Sweet, *Miss Mary Cassatt: Impressionist from Pennsylvania*, Oklahoma, 1966

Henry Swinburne, *The Courts of Europe at the close of the last Century*, London, 1895

Dickran Tashjian, *A Boatload of Madmen Surrealism and the American Avant-Garde 1920-1950*, New York, 1995

Calvin Tomkins, 'The Benefactor', in *The New Yorker*, pp.52–67, 8 June, 1998

Calvin Tomkins, *Merchants and Masterpieces: The Story of the Metropolitan Museum of Art*, London and New York, 1970

Paget Toynbee (ed.), *Horace Walpole's Journals of Visits to Country Seats*, Walpole Society (1927–8), vol.16, p.68

Karole P. B. Vail and Thomas Messer, *Peggy Guggenheim: A Celebration*, New York, 1998

Various authors, *La rime et la raison: Les collections Menil*, Paris, 1984

Diana Vreeland, *D. V.*, New York, 1984

Clive Wainwright, *The Romantic Interior, The British Collector at Home*, Newhaven and London, 1989

Diane Waldman, *Mark Rothko: A Retrospective*, New York, 1978

John Walker, *Self Portrait with Donors: Confessions of an Art Collector*, Boston, 1974

Marion Ward, *The Du Barry Inheritance*, London, 1967

David B. Warren and others, *American Decorative Arts and Paintings in the Bayou Bend Collection*, Houston, 1998

Peter Watson, *From Manet to Manhattan: The Rise of the Modern Art Market*, New York, 1992

Steven Watson, *Strange Bedfellows: The First American Avant-Garde*, New York, 1991

Frances Weitzenhoffer, *The Havemeyer's Impressionism Comes to America*, New York, 1986

John Whitehead, *The French Interior in the Eighteenth Century*, London, 1992

William Wilson, *The Los Angeles Times Book of California Museums*, New York, 1984

Brenda Wineapple, *Sister, Brother: Gertrude and Leo Stein*, London, 1996

Arthur Young, *Travels in France and Italy*, London (Everyman edition), 1915

Angelica Zander Rudenstine, *Peggy Guggenheim Collection*, Venice, New York, 1985

Index